The Guide to Gethsemane

John D. Caputo, *series editor*

EMMANUEL FALQUE

The Guide to Gethsemane
Anxiety, Suffering, and Death

TRANSLATED BY GEORGE HUGHES

FORDHAM UNIVERSITY PRESS
New York ■ 2019

This book was first published in French as *Le passeur de Gethsémani: Angoisse, souffrance et mort; Lecture existentielle et phénoménologique*, by Emmanuel Falque © Les Éditions du Cerf, 1999.

Fordham University Press has no responsibility for the persistence or accuracy of URLs for external or third-party Internet websites referred to in this publication and does not guarantee that any content on such websites is, or will remain, accurate or appropriate.

Fordham University Press also publishes its books in a variety of electronic formats. Some content that appears in print may not be available in electronic books.

Visit us online at www.fordhampress.com.

Library of Congress Cataloging-in-Publication Data available online at https://catalog .loc.gov.

Printed in the United States of America

21 20 19   5 4 3 2 1

First edition

To Jean-Claude and Laurent,
  too early gone to the Father

And in fond memory of Helen Tartar
  (1951–2014)

Contents

Translator's Note   *xiii*

Preface to the English-Language Edition   *xv*

Opening: The Isenheim Altarpiece or
"The Taking on Board of Suffering"   *xvii*

Introduction: Shifting Understandings of Anxiety   *1*

PART I: THE FACE-TO-FACE OF FINITUDE

1   **From the Burden of Death to Flight before Death**   7
    §1 The Burden of Death, 7 ▪ §2 Fleeing from Death, 8

2   **The Face of Death or Anxiety over Finitude**   10
    §3 Death "for Us" Humans, 10 ▪ §4 Genesis and Its
    Symbolism, 11 ▪ §5 The Mask of Perfection, 12 ▪ §6 The Image
    of Finitude in Man, 13 ▪ §7 Finitude: Finite and Infinite, 16 ▪
    §8 Finitude and Anxiety, 16 ▪ §9 The Eclipse of Finitude, 17 ▪
    §10 The Face of Death, 18 ▪ §11 To Die "with," 19

3   **The Temptation of Despair or Anxiety over Sin**   22
    §13 Inevitable Death, 22 ▪ §14 The Conquest of Sin, 22 ▪
    §15 Sin and Anxiety, 23 ▪ §16 The Temptation of Despair, 24

4 **From the Affirmation of Meaninglessness to the Suspension of Meaning**   *26*
§17 The Life Sentence, 26 ▪ §18 The Christian Witness, 27 ▪
§19 Meaninglessness and the Suspension of Meaning, 27

PART II: CHRIST FACED WITH ANXIETY OVER DEATH
§20 Two Meditations on Death, 29 ▪ §21 Alarm and
Anxiety, 31

5 **The Fear of Dying and Christ's "Alarm"**   *33*
§22 Taking on Fear and Abandonment, 33 ▪ §23 The Cup,
Sadness, and Sleep, 34 ▪ §24 Resignation, Waiting, and
Heroism, 35 ▪ §25 The Silence at the End, 36 ▪
§26 The Scenarios of Death, 37 ▪ §27 The Triple Failure
of the Staging, 38 ▪ §28 From Alarm to Anxiety, 39

6 **God's Vigil**   *41*
§29 Remaining Always Awake, 41 ▪ §30 The Passage of Death,
the Present of the Passion, the Future of the Resurrection, 42 ▪
§31 Theological Actuality and Phenomenological Possibility, 43

7 **The Narrow Road of Anxiety**   *45*
§32 Indefiniteness, Reduction to Nothing, and Isolation, 45 ▪
§33 The Strait Gate, 46 ▪ §34 Anxiety over "Simply Death," 47 ▪
§35 Indefiniteness (Putting off the Cup) and the Powerless Power
of God, 47 ▪ §36 Reduction to Nothing and Kenosis, 52 ▪
§37 The Isolation of Humankind and Communion with the
Father, 54 ▪ §38 Of Anxiety Endured on the Horizon
of Death, 55

8 **Death and Its Possibilities**   *57*
§39 Manner of Living, Possibility of the Impossibility, and Death
as "Mineness," 57 ▪ §40 Being Vigilant at Gethsemane, 59 ▪
§41 From the Actuality of the Corpse to Possibilities for
the Living, 60 ▪ §42 The Death That Is Always His: Suffering in
God; The Gift of His Life and Refusal of Mastery, 63 ▪
§43 The Flesh Forgotten, 66

PART III: THE BODY-TO-BODY OF SUFFERING
AND DEATH
§44 Disappropriation and Incarnation, 69 ▪ §45 Embedding in
the Flesh and Burial in the Earth, 70

9   From Self-Relinquishment to the Entry into the Flesh   *73*
§46 Suffering the World, 73 ▪ §47 Living in the
World, 74 ▪ §48 Otherness and Corruptibility, 74 ▪
§49 Self-Relinquishment, 75 ▪ §50 Passing to the Father, 76 ▪
§51 Oneself as an Other, 77 ▪ §52 Destitution and
Auto-Affection, 78 ▪ §53 Alterity and Fraternity, 79 ▪
§54 Entry into the Flesh, 80 ▪ §55 The Anxiety "in"
the Flesh, 81 ▪ §56 Toward Dumb Experience, 82

10   Suffering Occluded   *84*
§57 An Opportunity Thwarted, 84 ▪ §58 Called into
Question, 86 ▪ §59 Toward a Phenomenology of Suffering, 86

11   Suffering Incarnate   *88*
§60 Perceiving, or the Challenge of the Toucher-Touching, 88 ▪
§61 The Modes of the Incarnate Being, 91 ▪ §62 The Excess of the
Suffering Body, 94

12   The Revealing Sword   *97*
§63 Sobbing and Tears, 97 ▪ §64 Fleshly Exodus, 99 ▪
§65 The Vulnerable Flesh, 100 ▪ §66 The Non-Substitutable
Substitution, 101 ▪ §67 The Act of Surrendering Oneself, 103 ▪
§68 Toward a Revelation, 104 ▪ §69 Useless Suffering, 104

Conclusion: The *In-Fans* [without-Speech] or the Silent Flesh   *107*

Epilogue: From One Triptych to Another   *111*

Notes   *115*

Index   *157*

Translator's Note

The Guide to Gethsemane is the first volume in what Emmanuel Falque calls a "philosophical triduum." An important starting point of this volume was quite simply a deeply personal experience: namely, the shock of the untimely deaths of two close friends. Writing it was an attempt on Falque's part to make sense of these deaths and the implication of death for him in Christian and philosophical terms. Falque rejects the view that Christianity provides an escape from realities into a comfort zone of piety. He wants to use philosophy along with Christian theology as a way of facing up to the world in which we live. An important aspect of the book is thus the constant reference to the death of Christ and its possible meaning for us, as well as an examination of how we can continue to read Christ's progress through Gethsemane in a modern way.

The title of the book in French is *Le Passeur de Gethsémani*, which has been translated here as *The Guide to Gethsemane*. The French word *passeur*, in its simplest usage, means a ferryman (reminding us perhaps of Charon, who ferried dead souls across the river Styx in Greek mythology, in Virgil and in Dante's *Divine Comedy*). As used in contemporary French *passeur* can have other positive connotations: for example, to refer to the guides who smuggled Jewish refugees to safety during the period of the Occupation in the Second World War. It has also been much used recently to refer to people-traffickers and drug smugglers, obviously this time with negative connotations—usually in the plural form, *les passeurs*. Falque's usage is in the singular, *le passeur*, and refers specifically to Christ in Gethsemane, who undergoes his ordeal there for us. It has seemed most appropriate to translate *passeur* in this book as "guide," but, taking into account its connotations, it is worth emphasizing how in French the term strongly suggests not just guiding but *passer* (to pass), in the sense of a passing over or across with people or things, and "passage." For Falque *passeur* suggests the passage through Gethsemane to Golgotha and beyond, and in this context it is echoed in the word *pâtir*, to suffer from, take on board suffering, or suffer passively.

A further significant term for Falque in his discussion of death is the French word *angoisse*, here translated as "anxiety." (See, for example, the subtitle, *Anxiety, Suffering, and Death*.) To native English speakers *angoisse* may sound very like "anguish," and in philosophical texts it is sometimes close to what English calls "anguish" or (following Scandinavian or German usage) "angst." *Angoisse* certainly implies a serious form of anxiety and is generally taken to imply feelings of danger or panic that can lead to disturbing psychic or physical symptoms.

Christina Gschwandtner, in her essay on Emmanuel Falque, shifts between "anguish" and "anxiety" to translate Falque's term.[1] This translation sticks, on the whole, to using "anxiety" as the clearest way of showing the development of the argument of the book. "Anxiety" is particularly significant when Falque's project involves argument with philosophers such as Heidegger and Kierkegaard and theologians such as Hans Urs von Balthasar, who have developed their own theories of anxiety. Nonetheless, readers should be aware that the word as used by Falque always implies a deep anxiety, a troubling psychological state that might have physical implications. There is no fully satisfactory translation of *angoisse* into English, and it would be appropriate to recall that there are times, in Falque's version of Gethsemane, when it is often quite close to "anguish."

Preface to the English-Language Edition

The present volume completes what I have called a *Philosophical Triduum*: *The Guide to Gethsemane* (anxiety, suffering, and death); *The Metamorphosis of Finitude* (birth and resurrection); and *The Wedding Feast of the Lamb* (eros, the body, and the Eucharist).[1] My aim, following the three days of the Passion (Good Friday, Easter Sunday, Holy Thursday) in an inverse movement, has been first of all philosophical, proposing to start off from humankind and leading toward God, for we are eventually converted in him.

The reader will not find in this volume, or in the pages that follow in the rest of the triptych, an apologetic, at least in the current sense of the term as a defense and example of faith. I would justify my procedure here rather as the exposition of a *credible* Christianity ("expounded through the methods of research and the literary forms of modern thought"),[2] and not simply as *Christianity for believers* (aimed at those who have faith and are committed to it). As Maurice Blondel puts it, "The important thing is not to address believers but to say something which counts in the eyes of unbelievers."[3]

My triptych is completed in its English version with the translation of this third part of the philosophical triduum, *The Guide to Gethsemane*. And at the same time I have started work on another triduum concerned with the depths of Evil and with Holy Saturday (*The Mystery of Iniquity* in the framework of *Theological Recapitulation*).[4] I would like to express my thanks here to my translator, George Hughes, who in this long passage— or perhaps we might say this long canter—has undertaken so much to accomplish the task of translating the triduum. It is rare that a text has been so well understood and its sense so well conveyed, in an experience that has been, to say the least, shared by author and translator. Professor of English literature by profession, philosopher by election, and theologian by inclination, George Hughes is also an enthusiastic runner. Some readers may have suspected this, but with the final volume of the triptych it becomes readily apparent. One does not after all scale the "heights of the philosophy of religion" with impunity without finally providing evidence that one has achieved one's end, passed over the line, and carried off the prize. I hope my translator can now say, like St. Paul in his Letter to the Philippians, "I have not run in vain, neither labored in vain" (Phil 2:16 AV).

I would also like to express here my sincere gratitude to my editors at Fordham University Press, who have shown such confidence in my triptych, even when it was still in progress. It can now be read in English in all three volumes, along with my volume *Crossing the Rubicon*, which is its "discourse on method," outlining the possibility for philosophy itself to treat the objects of theology differently, thus avoiding either dressing itself up (in renouncing the key subject of finitude) or self-consciously protecting itself (by defining its own corner too narrowly in advance).[5]

Finally, I wish to dedicate the whole of this philosophical triduum, with the deepest respect, to Helen Tartar of Fordham University Press, who was killed in a tragic road accident in March 2014. It was through Helen that this journey first began. She saw the original manuscript and was also able to see the possibilities of my work in progress and estimate what it might go on to accomplish. I would hope that her memory is honored in what follows, particularly in the section in this volume on suffering and death. Certainly there would be nothing here without the linkage, so strongly forged, of a deep and deeply valued friendship with Helen.

Boston
Monday, November 7, 2016

Opening: The Isenheim Altarpiece or "The Taking on Board of Suffering"

Perhaps one has never suffered, or at least never understood what it is to suffer, unless one has confronted the Christ of the Isenheim altarpiece (1512–16), now in the Unterlinden Museum, Colmar, Alsace (Figure 1). Not that this polyptych altarpiece—or for that matter *The Guide to Gethsemane*—aims to justify suffering. Rather, it is that Christ the man is held there on the cross in a "suffering," or in a "pure suffering taken on board" [*pâtir pur*], to which we shall all be exposed at some time, and from which none of us can fully draw back.[1] The ordeal of suffering, from sickness to death, grips humankind, as Emmanuel Levinas says, in an "impossibility of retreat."[2] There are no exemptions; and if we try to claim exemption we risk lying to ourselves about the burden of what is purely and simply our humanity. There are agonies that challenge us to the very limits, that make us see the seriousness of our own decease, even if we share a belief that only God can give us, that we are subsequently to be raised from the dead. *agonies in the face of the promise of another life*

A book or a body of work, like life itself, always has to start with some "suffering," or in any event one has to take on board "suffering" it. Christianity, which was falsely satisfied with the illusion of purification through suffering, now nourishes itself with a respectable attempt at conciliation (irenicism). In general, it prefers the wonder of the newly born to the convulsions of someone about to depart this life or the rapture of revelation to the numb stupor caused by a death. *Thaumazein* ["wonder" in ancient Greek] can certainly knock us back in astonishment as a form of awe; but *the thing is endured, suffered* it can be coupled also with stupor as a form of terror or alarm. Thus, we might suggest a double reading of the altarpiece at Isenheim, according to which one can hold to the light of what is hoped for and, on the other hand, see the darkness of what is coming to all of us. The sick people who suffered in the Antonine hospice for which the altarpiece was commissioned would have known this double reading. Ordinarily the panels of the polyptych are closed, and it displays the Crucifixion. It can be opened first to a layer of panels showing the Annunciation and the Resurrection, but this is done only for the great liturgical feasts—Christmas, Epiphany, Easter, Ascension (Figure 2). When the panels are opened, however, there is a halo for the Resurrected One emerging from the tomb in his twisted shroud (the metamorphosis), and this seems like a response to the deep darkness around the Crucifixion that is ordinarily seen, an image whose dramatic intensity has never been equaled.

Nobody has expressed better than Matthias Grünewald (c.1470–1528), the artist of the altarpiece,[3] what I have made the subject of my research in *The Guide to Gethsemane*. That is: (a) The body as "exposed" rather than "purified" by suffering; (b) Agony as the usual burden of death before it becomes the way of salvation; (c) Anxiety as an interrogation of meaning, not simply the complaint of the wicked; (d) Life as a "taking on board of suffering [*pâtir*]" rather than life as *passage*.

It would be a bad mistake to see the *Crucifixion* by Grünewald (or for that matter my book) as an apology for suffering—or as an inescapable passage from a century that nurtured fear and a doctrine of the utility of pain that we have today left behind us. Rather, it is a question here, quite straightforwardly, of "humankind *tout court*," of humankind in pure and simple humanity, where God takes on and transforms *all* of ourselves that need salvation: our souls certainly, but also our bodies; our sins indeed, and also our ills.

In 1516, when Grünewald left the hospice of the Antonines at Isenheim, he had just finished this altarpiece now exhibited at Colmar. It was a work that aimed to hold the attention, to comfort, but also to "stupefy," the souls and bodies of the bedridden sick at the hour when they departed this life. In the same period, Martin Luther was preparing to denounce the sale of indulgences, or the aberrations of a Catholicism involved in the commerce of salvation, sending his ninety-five theses to the archbishop of Mainz on October 31, 1517, the eve of All Saints' Day, and posting them on the door of All Saints' Church at Wittenberg. And it was in the same period that the "Great Peasants' War" broke out in Germany, leading to at least a hundred thousand deaths (1524–25). Grünewald, who was prob-

we who happen – or perhaps must in our nature – to suffer, even if a fact, even a "necessary" one

Figure 1. Matthias Grünewald, Isenheim Altarpiece (closed view). Musée d'Unterlinden, Colmar, France. Erich Lessing / Art Resource, NY.

Figure 2. Matthias Grünewald, Isenheim Altarpiece (open view). Musée d'Unterlinden, Colmar, France. Scala / Art Resource, NY.

ably involved in the war, suffered exile and was then to die alone, forgotten by those who had suffered too much to continue the struggle.

It was also, above all, at this time that ergot poisoning, known as "ergotism," "St. Anthony's fire," or *mal des ardents*, decimated the population. The poisoning was a true "plague of the epoch" that ate into people's bodies and destroyed their hearts. The sickness, as we know today, derived from alkaloids in a parasitic fungus that grew on rye and that proliferates when there is too much rain. The alkaloids found their way into rye flour and would particularly be consumed by a poor and wretched population: "During centuries the nature of this sickness that seems to strip the skin off the bones, freezes the entrails, burns the flesh, blackens the arms, separates the feet from the legs, remained inexplicable."[4]

But it is this sickness that is depicted in the *Crucifixion* (Figure 3), as well as in the panel showing the *Temptation of St. Anthony* (Figure 4), where there are bodies whose repulsive appearance demands simply that we see, or dare look at, what a mutilated body really is, when it is riddled with the disease so far as to be disemboweled. It would be wrong to categorize such depictions simply as that of past evils, as if the present with its

Figure 3. Matthias Grünewald, Isenheim Altarpiece (closed view, detail from central panel showing the Crucifixion). Musée d'Unterlinden, Colmar, France. Erich Lessing / Art Resource, NY.

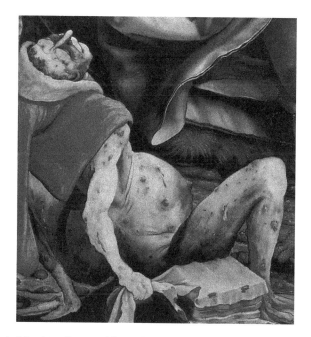

Figure 4. Matthias Grünewald, Isenheim Altarpiece (detail from interior panel showing the Temptation of St. Anthony). Musée d'Unterlinden, Colmar, France. © Musée d'Unterlinden, Dist. RMN–Grand Palais / Art Resource, NY.

development of medicine could make us forget what a mutilated corpse is actually like. One has only to visit our hospices or hospitals today (where there is end-of-life care, for example) to be confronted by the evidence. Camouflaged under carefully adjusted dressings, and despite the care taken to help us bear them, there are still open wounds, along with infected pustules, cracked and swollen skin, broken limbs, and horribly distorted faces. Our "contemporary cancers" can compete with the "ergotism" of the past, and the vision of the Crucifixion could certainly still say a great deal to those who know how to look at it and do not recoil before what it shows of our common humanity.[5]

(a) The "spread-out body" on the cross takes then, and takes on itself, the burden of our sins, but also and above all, astonishingly here takes on the *scourge* of our sicknesses. Christ's body shows us "exposure" rather than "purification," visibility of the flesh and not simply catharsis for our transgressions. We have only to compare, or perhaps we should say identify, the Christ on the Cross of the Isenheim altarpiece—his face swollen, neck broken, skin distended, muscles wasted, articulations dislocated, and skin cracked open—with the sick and forsaken man at the left corner of the panel showing the *Temptation of St. Anthony* (on the right when a second inner layer of the altarpiece is opened out). In Grünewald's *Crucifixion* the Word made flesh takes upon himself "ergotism," just as today he takes on our "cancers," our "tumors," and all of our "sicknesses." His body is exposed, and exposes to us, our own putrefaction, there on the cross. If it is not for us to see ourselves in the Crucifixion, the very least that could be said is that it helps us know ourselves better. *The Guide to Gethsemane* attempts to bring to the fore what is evident here in this altarpiece. There is a finitude for humankind—of age, sickness, or death—that does not depend solely upon sin (even though it might come to be connected to it) in the way in which we live through these things and the possibility, or what we may feel to be the impossibility, of letting others dwell in them. Corruption as deviation (anxiety over sin) becomes *grafted* onto corruption as wasting away (anxiety over death). Here, where we are afflicted by sickness, is also where we must cope with how to live through death agonies.

(b) Death agony is then the common burden of death before it becomes the way of salvation. There is nothing to indicate, at least at first sight, that the altarpiece can be opened up, that behind the Crucifixion there might lie a Resurrection. And what goes for the altarpiece in the Unterlinden Museum of Colmar goes also for the steep route from Gethsemane to Calvary, or for the road to Emmaus crowded with disciples who are crushed by news of the implementation of a death sentence using a method that nobody has ever survived. There is no follow-up, it seems, to the agony, other than the expected end of a life whose term has remained always predictable. "De-ceasing" one falls from oneself (*cadere*): one falls with all one's body. Pascal reminds us that "they throw earth over your head and it is finished for ever."[6] Martin Heidegger cites the statement of a medieval Bohemian peasant: "As soon as man comes to life, he is at once old enough to die."[7] For Christ also, it is enough to be born at Bethlehem to indicate that he will die at Golgotha or in some other place. All deaths are first of all in finitude, the consequence of being alive and incarnate. But does not every death bring us back squarely to the Word made flesh, which transforms the meaning of flesh through redemption of our sins?

The Crucified Christ on the Isenheim altarpiece does not simply take upon himself our transgressions, he also allows himself to go as far as taking on our own sicknesses, even if these were considered at the time a kind of punitive expiation rather than the law of the living. The framework of his tortured body is given to us to see, threaded onto the wood of the cross that stands in Golgotha, the "Place of a Skull," just as the bed-ridden sick and dying could be said to have been nailed to their beds in the Isenheim hospice of St. Anthony. Christ is still in his right mind: he has to find his own way, like any sufferer on the point of death. His mouth wide open, he suffocates to the extent that he can no longer draw air to breathe. His feet are swollen, limbs dislocated, skin gangrened, pustules multiplied. He is overcome by ergotism, the "burning sickness." He fixes and metamorphoses, or nails down, we might say, humankind's own sick bodies to the wood of the cross.

The Son of God takes on himself the scourges of all forsaken people, certainly those in the *Temptation of St. Anthony*, but also those of the poor and sick of the hospice. Mary and John shown in the altarpiece at the feet of Christ on the cross know this: they are not simply contemplating the way his heart has been pierced through; they see the whole of his helpless body. Sick, weak, as well as dying in agony, the Word made flesh has here almost a natural death (or at least the consequence of his own pathologi-cal condition), so that the function of the cross is to make us face up to, and to save us from, the brutality of our own sins. Every death in reality has its violent side, whether supposedly natural or not, because for those who are left, as for those who die, dying itself remains always against-nature. And thus, properly speaking, we are confronted by the insupportable (*un-bearable*) nature of our finitude that our humanity, as such, exemplifies.

"It is accomplished" (John 19:30 JB) certainly, for Christ, on the cross.[8] The message, however, does not really make sense: meaning too much, it takes us away from the absurdity of what is actually happening. Far from signing off his life heroically with his death, the Greek verb *tetelestai* used in St. John's Gospel acknowledges an unfailing avowal that "it is over," or "I've reached the end of the rope" (the sense of the same word used in Aeschylus's *Libation Bearers* [line 875]). It implies, "I can't take it any-more" and "I can't go on." What is true of all physical suffering, and sometimes of moral suffering, is even more true for this Christ of the Is-enheim altarpiece, joining what he suffers in his flesh with human tor-tures, there in the hospice, where life is sometimes, almost literally, a "Calvary." Alphonse Daudet, sick with syphilis in Paris in the 1890s, was afflicted by pain like the patients of the Antonines hospice suffering from ergotism. "Pain," he wrote, "blocks out the horizon, fills everything." Daudet describes his own situation as "Crucifixion." He says, "That's what it was like the other night. The torment of the Cross: violent wrench-ing of the hands, feet, knees; nerves stretched and pulled to breaking point . . . the spear prodding at the ribs. The skin peeling from my hot, parched, fever-crusted lips; to slake my thirst I took a spoonful of iodized bromide, salty and bitter. It was the sponge soaked in vinegar and gall."[9]

(c) Anxiety becomes a "questioning of meaning," not simply the complaint of the wicked. There is a passage from fear to extreme anxiety, including at Gethsemane—from a withdrawal to the self, to a total abandonment in the self, where friends are lost, together with any form of moral support. There is a nothingness here, not so much engulfing as questioning, holding one onto the question of meaning rather than deciding in favor of meaninglessness. *no decision can be made here, nothing affirmed but that nothing can be affirmed (so even this nothingness is called into question)*

For many people, in Nietzsche's phrase, "any meaning is better than none at all."[10] Because nothing is worse than not knowing, or worse than not to know that one does not know, and that one never will know. The Crucified One does not know, or in his humanity he at least remains in not-knowing, where all knowing is still suspended. A certitude remains for him, as for us: that of his "ending." And his filiation will also return to him as something proffered, rather than confining him here on earth.

When we look carefully at the Isenheim altarpiece, the "play of hands" in the panels communicates some of the meaning to us, as does the "body-to-body of suffering and death" that I have tried to analyze in *The Guide to Gethsemane* (Part III). Everything depends in reality not just upon suffering, but on our manner of living—where we have the possibility of sin as well as the gift of grace by which eventually we shall be saved. The famous hands of Grünewald's Christ are massive and nailed to the transept of the cross (Figure 5); his fingers are contracted and strained to a degree that we might think they could never withdraw from their own pain; but they do not only show the paroxysm of a kind of overwhelming suffering. It seems that these stiffened fingers, as it were immobilized in action, launch an appeal not to be definitively closed, not to be contracted upon themselves. Maybe they represent an attempt to remain open to a possible hereafter ("My God, my God, why have you forsaken me?" [Mark 15:34]), before accepting the strict law of this world ("Then Jesus gave a loud cry and breathed his last" [Mark 15:37]).

In support of this reading of the altarpiece, and this time looking at what is around Christ on the cross, we could point to a comparison between the hands of the kneeling Mary Magdalene, definitively encapsulated in her suffering, her palms pressed together and fingers bent to the point where they might never be straightened, and those of Mary, held up in the arms of John, her hands intertwining with a slight opening, as though closure would not be definitive, even in this pain of Calvary that is already such a trial for a mother (Figure 6). Another token of an opening is seen also in the index finger of John the Baptist, extended toward

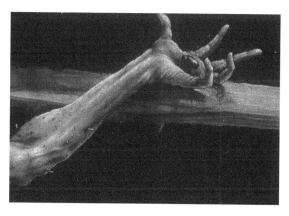

Figure 5. Matthias Grünewald, Isenheim Altarpiece (closed view, detail from central panel, showing Christ's hand). Musée d'Unterlinden, Colmar, France. Erich Lessing / Art Resource, NY.

Christ on the cross (Figure 7). John is making a sign toward the spectacle on the cross from which nobody can turn away, so that for himself he becomes part of the background. Just behind his arm is written in red letters *"Illum oportet crescere, me autem minui"* [He must increase, but I must decrease] (John 3:30). And, finally, we can cite the hand poised in benediction by the angel in the Annunciation scene, offering a certain hope to the spectator and shown on one of the panels of the altarpiece opened up on the Feast of the Annunciation (Figure 2). These hands seem to prefigure the proffered and stigmatized hands of the Resurrected Christ on another panel of the opened altarpiece, the openness of his hands cutting through all the tensions of the pain he has been through. And this "play of hands" on the altarpiece is not just a scene acted out; it is a kind of conversation, presenting to us the challenge of an ordeal that we shall all be called upon to traverse at some time.

Anxiety, "definitive for humankind," is not so for God. But we cannot assume from this what Heidegger suggests, in a concise and, as I see it, mistaken comment in *Being and Time*, that "the anthropology developed in Christian theology . . . has always already viewed death together with its interpretation of 'life.'"[11] For the Christian, death remains death of all the world, simply death of the human being as such. Charles Péguy speaks of "ordinary death, the death that we have in common . . . the death of all men, the death of all the world . . . the death of which your father died, my child, and the father of your father."[12] Christ was concerned with us orienting ourselves in another way, or living death differently, that brings

Figure 6. Matthias Grünewald, Isenheim Altarpiece (closed view, detail from central panel, showing Mary, Mary Magdalene, and John). Musée d'Unterlinden, Colmar, France. Erich Lessing / Art Resource, NY.

him back to the Father to "transform" it and to the power of the Holy Spirit to "carry this out." Christ, as the guide to Gethsemane, was to bear fully, and as far as Golgotha, the burden of suffering and death (*pâtir*), even if he was subsequently to serve as guide to those who could recognize him, in the four corners of the earth, in the form of the Resurrected One (*passage*).

Figure 7. Matthias Grünewald, Isenheim Altarpiece (closed view,
detail from central panel, showing John the Baptist). Musée d'Unterlinden,
Colmar, France. Erich Lessing / Art Resource, NY.

(d) Thus, we can say that *life* itself contains taking on board *suffering* that leads to *passage*: at first sight it is finitude, before it is eventually metamorphosis. Being-toward-death does not perhaps give us the last word about existence, though in any event it is the first. The sufferers in the hospice of the Antonines at Isenheim knew this: they could not turn toward the divine without first holding on to the human. They could not believe in a world beyond without remaining inextricably rooted in the here and now. Sickness nailed them down to their beds, as the Word made flesh was nailed to the cross. It is important, however, to consider what the artist shows us in the image of the Virgin Mary revealed on a central panel when the altarpiece is opened (Figure 2). Behind the Madonna, who carries the child here, there is a patient's bed, as well as a chamberpot and a bucket for washing the child.[13] The Word, who incarnates the flesh, has around him already all its uncertainties—its sin certainly, but also its cancers, all the scourges and sicknesses, and the possibility, if not of curing them, at least of bearing them, and along with humankind of dwelling in them.

Moreover, in the *Crucifixion* panel, an animal, the lamb, stands at the feet of John the Baptist. As Agnus Dei, Lamb of God, sacrificed for the forgiveness of sin, the Lamb represents here our own animality, and the blood shed on its fleece sends us directly back to Christ's wound on his side. What is at stake in taking on board "suffering" is not simply making divine, but also making human: the nodal point and place of synthesis of all filiation. I have found it necessary to write another book to show this in detail (*The Wedding Feast of the Lamb*), but the Isenheim altarpiece already indicates the possible conversion of our "animality" into "humanity" (salvation through solidarity), albeit in taking charge of our sins and thus our "bestiality" (salvation through redemption).

A tremendous force breaks out when the Isenheim polyptych is opened up precisely on the great liturgical feast days. The *ordeal of the Crucifixion* shifts suddenly to the *triumph of the Resurrection* (Figure 8): the open sepulcher, the stone rolled away from the tomb broken open, the God of all suffering standing now as a figure of hope. Shown springing from the tomb, along with his shroud, his face bathed in light, the Resurrected Christ strikes down Roman soldiers—who seem like toys or bodies that have tumbled over, while the limbs of their armor are dismembered. The "power of the metamorphosis" does not destroy the "burden of finitude." As the patients in the Isenheim hospice knew, it was not enough simply to open up the altarpiece to cure these sick bodies. But now the taking on board of "suffering" (*pâtir*) enters into the promise of a *passage*. And if such a process is not sufficient on its own to ensure that we do not despair, at

Is the "here and now" a sick bed? a cross?

Figure 8. Matthias Grünewald, Isenheim Altarpiece (open view, panel showing
the Resurrection). Musée d'Unterlinden, Colmar, France. © Musée d'Unterlinden,
Dist. RMN–Grand Palais / Art Resource, NY.

least it ensures that we do not make the ultimate term of our lives at the hour of death the word "finish." One of the sermons of Pope Leo the Great on the Passion tells us that "true reverence of the Lord's Passion means fixing the eyes of our heart on Jesus crucified and recognising in him our own humanity. No one however weak is denied a share in the victory of the cross, nor is anyone beyond the help of the prayer of Christ."[14]

Granges d'Ans July 15, 2016
(The Feast of St. Bonaventure)

Is contemporary philosophy (and in particular existentialism and phenomenology) capable of shedding light on Christ's ordeal in his anxiety and anguish, his suffering and his death, from Gethsemane to Golgotha? What follows in this book is a testing out of this ground, a kind of "essay." As an essay it may have certain shortcomings, but the book represents a transformation of the author (of the present work), especially as he remains also a reader (of the Gospel narrative). It might be called a meditation that is "metaphysical," in the sense that Christ, and Christ only, traverses from end to end (*meta*) what we are given in our nature (*phusis*). But what lay behind my reading of the Gospels here was something that was all the more crucial in that it happened so suddenly: the unbearable coincidence of the accidental death of one friend, and the suicide of another. Even beyond psychological affect this led me to a kind of metaphysical rebellion. Wasn't it true, in the words of Corneille's Polyeucte, that "The Christ once feared to die"?[15]

Introduction
Shifting Understandings of Anxiety

Should we give special priority to questions concerning anxiety, to questions of death and bodily suffering? Such topics, which once belonged exclusively to the domain of Christian experience, have, by a paradoxical reversal, recently been caught up in the nets of philosophy. In particular, meditation upon anxiety, as well as upon lack of suffering, once considered typically Christian and opposed to the impassive ideal of philosophy, has emerged as a key topic in modern and contemporary philosophy, from Hegel and Kierkegaard to Heidegger, Sartre, and Camus.[1] But having usurped the privileging of anxiety, as well as the assumption of suffering, from Christianity—which might be considered only a lesser evil—philosophy now also sometimes obscures the origin of these topics, going so far as to deny the Christian access to this privileged area. In the eyes of the philosopher, the ultimate truth concerning suffering and anxiety cannot be told other than in the inescapable finitude of the human condition and thus in death. Any interpretation seeing it in terms of life, or rather in terms of another life, is relegated to the sphere of false illusions or talk of other worlds. Heidegger emphasizes in a succinct note in *Being and Time* that "the anthropology worked out in Christian theology—from Paul to Calvin's *meditatio futurae vitae*—has always already viewed death together with its interpretation of 'life.'"[2]

Anxiety concerning death and the suffering of the flesh, themes that were traditionally seen as privileged territory for the Christian and that were opposed to the serene confidence of the philosopher, have become, in a kind of backlash, one of the bastions of contemporary philosophy. And this is despite all attempts to recover the ground in theology. Do we really have to stick with this trivial quarrel, where in reality if one side gains, the other side can only lose? Isn't the *gravity* accorded by the philosopher to suffering and anxiety, as well as to death, given its full weight in the value attributed by the Christian to the Resurrection? And on the other hand, doesn't the hope that the Christian finds in the Resurrection open up the supposedly unsurpassable threshold of despair of the philosopher?

To speak of anxiety about death and of incarnate suffering as a "metaphysical experience of God," if not in an act of *passage* at least as a form of taking on board suffering (*pâtir*), leads us first of all to affirm that all human beings on the threshold of their own deaths are faced in some way with experience of the divine in their anxiety and suffering as such. That experience is at the heart of a finitude that cannot be explained away as the result of sin, and it exists despite our irresistible tendency to give it meaning in order to suppress a silence that we find unbearable (Part I). Speaking in this way is to recognize that the Son himself, without ever ceasing to be a son, and insofar as he shares his humanity with us, receives from Gethsemane to Golgotha the uncompromising and unsurpassable ("not to be outstripped") experience of anxiety in the face of death (Part II).[3] We come then to understand, through the person of the suffering Christ, the cry born from a feeling of being totally abandoned, a feeling that goes so far as a "rupture of the flesh," so that the Other in him (his Father), who is also with him, takes upon himself the burden of insurmountable corruptibility and makes it pass into the incorruptible transforming glory of the Resurrection (Part III). The *metaphysical* meaning of the phrase "an experience *of* God," that of humankind facing or experiencing God (objective genitive), as well as God's experiment in becoming man (subjective genitive), is not that we have to transcend nature in order to discover its meaning (*metaphusis*). It is rather that only by posing questions about the impossible overcoming of nature can we open up and force ourselves to live anew our irreducible finitude—a finitude that proffers, through the gift of the Son to the Father, its evident meaninglessness.

We can then talk of a *meta-physical* experience of God at Gethsemane in the sense that it is there at least that God transcends nature, crossing it from part to part (*meta-phusis*)—that is to say, at the peak of his immanence. "Even for the spiritual man the experience of existence is *close to the earth and the world of the senses*," Hans Urs von Balthasar says—though Balthasar also tells us that after Irenaeus it would be necessary to wait for Paul Claudel "until . . . a similar language reappears in Christianity."[4]

Gethsemane, the site of anxiety from the Mount of Olives until it is incarnate in the flesh at Golgotha, is not simply a *passage*—a passage in the gospels or a passage from the world to the Father. It is also, and above all, the place of trial or an ordeal for a Guide or *"Passeur"*—Christ. He *traverses* first, from end to end, the anxious and mortal Being-there of our particular finitude, taking on board suffering (*pâtissant*)—suffering in his body—a world that is subject along with him to the ordinary law of corruptibility of all living things. Heidegger's *Being and Time* reminds us that "as soon as a man comes to life, he is at once old enough to die."[5] But it would be a mistake, or at least inadequate, to hold along with Heidegger that Christians do not truly undergo anxiety about death (and even less the meaninglessness of suffering) because Christian anthropology has "always already viewed death in its interpretation of 'life.'"[6] To counter this notion is a central point for this book. Far from the many psychologizing interpretations of Gethsemane, and this time on the *metaphysical* ground where the gospels are confronted by contemporary philosophy (Husserl, Heidegger, Sartre, Camus, Levinas . . .), the Son teaches us in his body, positively and in the unique language of the "Word made flesh," exactly what it is to be one of humankind, when the human being, in human flesh, suffers from no longer understanding God.

PART I

The Face-to-Face of Finitude

From the Burden of Death to Flight before Death

§1 The Burden of Death

Is there a "Christian meaning" in our anxiety concerning death? It is a crucial question but, initially at least, insoluble: we are after all human beings before becoming believers. The anxiety of a Christian faced with death is, first of all, as I see it, *quite simply anxiety about death—death as it is sent to the Christian*. It is not that there is a *Christian meaning in anxiety concerning death*. If we rush into the question, we are in danger of neglecting the necessary and serious analysis of the problem of meaning. Moreover, since it is clearly not self-evident that there is meaning here, to insist that there must be meaning is not to respect either God or oneself, or our contemporaries. Not God, first of all, because he himself, in Gethsemane and Golgotha, intentionally lived through a certain anxiety about death. Not myself, because external juxtaposition of meaning on my life or on my death can cloud my judgment and is often used to cover up its striking meaninglessness. Not my contemporaries, because they rightly recall for me what is clearly its meaninglessness, even when for myself, I would prefer to deny the evidence. Initially, then, there is nothing left for the Christian, or indeed for all human beings, in the idea of one's death, except the absolute meaninglessness of one's own life. This is an inescapable perspective that undermines us from the inside, in the double sense that it both eats away at us and destroys us.[1]

No pastoral letter addressed by a bishop to clergy or laity, whether a definitive testimonial or just irretrievably conservative (the one thing often simply being the reverse side of the coin to the other) will meet humanity in the fullness of our flesh if it does not explore such depths. There is no "small remnant of Israel" left today, any more than there was in the past, that does not need to come to terms first of all with what is true for the great "remnant" of all humanity. The *choice* (or *election*) of a possible sharing of anxiety over death along with Christ cannot turn into a privilege of some kind for the Christian only, into an "easing" or "release" from the anguish (*angustia*) of facing one's own death. As opposed to what are in effect falsehoods from Greeks such as Socrates, Epicurus, or Epictetus, the Bible already symbolically sets up, on different grounds, a universal "dread of the day of death" that weighs on all the children of humankind "from the day they come out of their mother's womb, till the day they return to the mother of them all" (Si 40:1–2 JB). Contemporary humanity joins up with the realism of the incarnation for all humankind, especially insofar as contemporary ideas include getting in touch with ourselves and reaching down into our own depths. If I try to explain and analyze the anxiety of humankind, I primarily recall struggles of my own. Even St. Paul wished at one stage to be "accursed," indeed to be separated from Christ, to rejoin "for the sake of my own people, my kindred according to my flesh. They are Israelites" (Rom 9:3–4). Maybe we do not live "according to the flesh" (Rom 8:13), but surely it is also important for us today not to give up on those whom Bernanos calls our "brother humans," those who share our flesh?[2] Along with them we come forward to the gates of death, and it is thanks to them moreover that we can live and inhabit our own particular anxiety concerning death. Only in terms of the weight or consequence we give to death can we estimate the weightiness that should be accorded to resurrection—our own and that of Christ.

§2 Fleeing from Death

As we all know, or at least as we all feel, there are many ways of fleeing from death. But is it just the prerogative of philosophers to effect such a flight? Christians are not exempt from the temptation: far from it. The escape routes worked out by Epicurus or Epictetus are so well known that we hardly need to rehearse a rebuttal here. We should perhaps remind ourselves simply that for Epicurus it is our lack of experience of death that prevents us from talking about it.[3] As far as Epictetus is concerned, a transformation of our opinion of death allows us to overcome it.[4] But in the long run adroit thought-play of this kind is neither intellectually nor emotionally satisfying. Both philosophers simply gloss over anxiety with rationality and multiply twofold our metaphysical question, our *why* in the face of the absurdity or meaninglessness of death. Christians are often convinced that they have privileged access to anxiety, as well as the secret of how to overcome it, and that their flight from death is more subtle because it is not strikingly obvious, if not in their own eyes, at least in the eyes of their "fellow human beings." A double positioning in Christianity hides, in my view, both death and the impossibility of overcoming it. The first position (rather "conservative"), tends toward Pelagianism.[5] It reaches its summit in nineteenth-century pietism, when it is supposed that we can gain salvation through the double merit of enduring suffering and obedience to the virtues. According to this view, in becoming in some way myself through the exercise of my liberty and its exertions, which are what determine the extent of my salvation, I guarantee in this world that I will have an afterlife in death. This suppresses the ineradicable anxiety that exists on this side of death.[6] The second position (rather "progressive"), tends toward Origenism.[7] It culminates today in a faith that is undoubtedly often strongly confirmed and that goes so far as to suggest an absolute affirmation of grace and divine redemption and thus a denial of all human liberty. In this view Christ's Resurrection and his victory over death are so total that we can forget the possible self-condemnation of humankind by humankind and humankind's inevitable "confinement" in sin. Precisely because there is a hell that confines me and lies to me [*enfer-me-ment*], making me believe falsely that it is nonexistent, should I not hold on to the idea of hell? Should I not ensure that it remains a *question* for me, a question that is addressed to me, and is indeed *my* question?[8] A place that is probably empty of the supposed unpardonable sinners, it nonetheless emerges as a possible horizon of all my thoughts and all my acts; and perhaps I shall myself, and by myself, be one day a prominent guest and figurehead in such a dwelling.[9] The probability of a "restitution of all things" (*apokatastasis*) thus leads to nothing if it invalidates both the solidity of my existence and the exercise of my freedom.[10] So while the first position (Pelagianism) allows too much to humankind and not enough to God, the second (Origenism) attributes too much to God and not enough to humankind. The one is flawed by an excess of freedom (or of merit) and through the lack of grace; the other by excess of grace (or redemption) and through a lack of freedom.

2

The Face of Death or Anxiety over Finitude

§3 Death "for Us" Humans

This double flight of Christians in the face of anxiety about death has its roots in an unwavering Christian tendency to see death, even if only biological death, within the horizon of sin. Is the only way for me to achieve salvation by enduring a series of sufferings? Or should I be unconcerned about making an effort to obtain salvation because of the boundlessness of divine mercy? And in either case, would the death of Christ not remain a *death of redemption* rather than of *communion*?[1] But still another question crops up. Christ very certainly dies for my sins (Rom 8), but doesn't he also die through the pure and simple humanity that he shares with me—that is to say, by virtue of his very ordinary participation in the law of corruptibility of all living things (the principle of entropy)? If he dies "for our salvation" (*propter nostram salutem*), as the Nicene Creed expresses it, is he not dead also and first of all "for us men" (*propter nos homines*) simply through sharing our fleshly humanity, as even the terms of the creed suggest?[2]

The Son having chosen to "come to (human) life," or to be born at Bethlehem remains then, like all humankind, *always already old enough to die*—whether by a natural or by a violent death: we can take up in the Christian context the famous Heideggerian formula that he quotes from a Bohemian peasant: "As soon as man comes to life, he is at once old enough to die."[3] But how can we consider the incarnation of the Son as man without first of all feeling that it is a real and total communion with the suffering and death of humankind as such, independently of all sinful characteristics? Or, to put it another way: how can we explain in Christian theology an eclipse of human finitude that then enshrines death forever, not simply spiritual death but also biological death, as the consequence of a transgression whose atonement on the cross then leads only to viewing, in Heidegger's phrase, *"death together with its interpretation of 'life.'"*[4]

§4 Genesis and Its Symbolism

Everyone knows, or recognizes today, that the myth of Adam in Genesis has symbolic rather than historic meaning.[5] But, as I see it, the symbolism does not stop there, in a general interpretation of the whole narrative and its sources. It operates more precisely in the hypothetical link between original sin, suffering, and death that we find in the verdict most often misunderstood, or at least misrepresented, in the book of Genesis: "You will die of death" (Gen 2:17).[6]

It is by no means certain that this sentence does not first of all outline a death that is primarily spiritual: that is, the separation of human beings from God that I would identify as "anxiety about sin," but not over finitude. The theologian Gustave Martelet suggests, "In symbolising sin by death, the Bible does not intend it to be taken for granted that biological death comes only from sin."[7] And the charge of heresy against Pelagius by the Council of Carthage (418), because of his supposed uncoupling of biological death from original sin, reminds us simply that between sin and death there is a symbolic link of "signifying" rather than a relation of effective "causality." Apart from registering the boldness and theological pertinence of new perspectives, we need also to explore the metaphysical consequences to its limits. We cannot just stick with simple epistemological considerations whose obvious validity (as in the hypothesis of evolution) is not enough on its own to account for the metaphysical.[8]

If it is appropriate that we finally stop "harping on about original sin to explain that we die,"[9] that is first of all because dying cannot and should not, any more than physical suffering, tell us simply about an impairment or failure in humankind, even in the hypothetical first humans, the couple Adam and Eve. While the argument still rages today—and can be read between the lines in differences between the *Catechism of the Catholic Church* and the *French Bishops' Catechism for Adults*,[10] it would probably not be profitable to develop it any further here. We all know, or feel, that neither sickness nor death can decently be derived from an original transgression without a distorted image of humankind and of God (vengeful even so far as to transfer onto a third party, his own Son, misdeeds of which the Son was not the perpetrator). And it is not a question of denying here so much the reality as the efficaciousness of sin, when it is completely taken in charge by Christ on the cross. Separating sin from consequences that in no way belong to it (physical suffering and biological death) shows it in its true nature, spiritual this time: it is the auto-enclosure of the self by the self that is *imprinted* or *grafted* upon a finitude that is not in itself sinful.

§5 The Mask of Perfection

If I am to rejoin and theologically accept the irreducibility of my own finitude, then I must finally give up both a pure ideal of perfection and the simple statement of my own imperfection. Neither the one nor the other in fact is sufficient, on its own, to establish the true meaning of my Being-there, which is always in relation at first to the horizon that is opened, and limited, by my own consciousness.[11] Inhabiting my own particular finitude, far from being a desperate search for a supposed perfection that neglects the incompleteness of my condition, consists simply, and independently this time, of any consideration of sin, in consenting to make my way, or we could say traverse (without ever going beyond it) into a potential *growth*. Irenaeus reminds us that, "as it certainly is in the power of a mother to give strong food to her infant [but she does not do so], as the child is not yet able to receive more substantial nourishment; so also it was possible for God Himself to have made man perfect from the first, but man could not receive this [perfection], being as yet an infant."[12]

The creation of humankind in this sense, even if it was good or "very good" (Gen 1:31), was not, insofar as it was a theodicy (i.e., a justification of the ways of God to humankind), the *most perfect possible*, in the sense at least of an ideal of a wholeness that had still be to be satisfied, solely in the eyes of humankind.[13] We can recall here the Rousseau-type idea of perfectibility, in which the possibility of improving, or of progressing, appears to be still better than being or definitively remaining the best.[14] But nothing guarantees in fact that the best *in itself* would have to be, or would describe, the best *for us*. Moreover, the desire for plenitude or perfection remains precisely one of the masks put on by the serpent, and thus also by sin—"You will be like God" (Gen 3:5)—to make us regret the efficacity of the finitude inherent in our condition, which is there even before any sinful transgression. It is probably our greatest sin, where the serpent exactly discovers our weakness and rushes into it, that we cannot accept not being like God (that is to say, "perfect" in the sense of an achieved plenitude), and on the other hand reject our own original imperfectability (which is far from simply signifying perfection or imperfection). Everything goes into reverse in such a perspective—sin now consists less for humankind in a falling from some ideal of perfection than a refusal of an original *perfectibility*, by which precisely human beings could have been said to perfect themselves.

Thus today we should give up the myth of a Golden Age, or of a Garden of Eden where humankind fell from grace. It is as outdated as it is trivial, even though it may remain strongly present to our consciousness. Paul Ricoeur suggests that "all the speculations on the supernatural perfection of Adam before the fall are adventitious contrivances that profoundly alter the original naïve, brute meaning; they tend to make Adam superior and hence a stranger to our condition, and at the same time they reduce the Adamic myth to a genesis of man from a primordial superhumanity."[15] We need to accept that we must, if not negate, at least overcome our ordinary conception of how we are created in the image of God (*imago Dei*) with these supposedly extraordinary attributes of his infinity in us.

§6 The Image of Finitude in Man

Far from these disconsolate and regretted infinities, of which the trail of Cartesianism paints only too famously the ultimately caricatured version,[16] the profundity of the image of God in us can be read today in the profundity of our nature, even at the heart of our corruptibility, as long as we see that it is simply natural and not *de facto* immediately sinful. According to St. Gregory of Nyssa, "Man . . . was made in the image of God . . . not part of the whole, but all the fullness of nature together."[17] We are in fact "in Christ" (*en Christô*), as the apostle says (Eph 1:3) as our own place and as the place we derive from originally, and not just in the sense that "as we have borne the image of the man of dust, we will also bear the image of the man of heaven" (1 Cor 15:49). Rather, from "before the foundation of the world" (Eph 1:4) and along the lines of the wonderful side-by-side (or "*côte-à-côte*"—rib-by-rib) of Adam and the Word incarnate, as we can see illustrated, for example, in the carvings on the North Portal of Chartres Cathedral, we can and must dare to read our own finitude in what is announced, and indeed undertaken, for the Word. As Karl Rahner suggests, we can read the "natural character" of our death in what is "also the natural character" of his death.[18] Through his incarnation, then, as we shall later see (Chapter 11: Suffering Incarnate), Christ teaches us first of all to be human beings—that is, precisely, not to flee from our own finitude. He teaches us how we can also, with him, "abandon" ourselves in death. The distortion of the image, or what we might legitimately call here the "sinful stance," can in no way be deciphered through the fact of the corruptibility of humankind—that is to say, through the extreme indications of finitude that are natural to us: physical suffering, disease, aging, and death. Although in fact such phenomena do affect our supposed integrity, they would not in reality have meaning (or meaninglessness) for us except insofar as they are shown to be capable, through our own eyes as through the eyes of others, of revealing our ordinary *manner* of living. That is, either we accept humbly to be "un-made" of ourselves, or we still nourish ourselves with secret ambitions of total power over ourselves and over the world. In other words, far from denying the unbearable existential weight of physical suffering, of illness, age, or death, a phenomenological recentering on the mode of lived experience of such things reveals their true and inherent meaning, as well as what they tell us, and above all reveals something about ourselves.[19]

The distorted image of God in humankind, or the sinful mode of the human being, is thus read less in finitude itself (suffering, aging, death) than in the refusal to accept it as such. Becoming like "gods," according to the spurious recommendations of the serpent (Gen 3:5 JB), is in this sense precisely not to be in the image "of God" according to Yahweh's plan (Gen 1:27). While the one (the serpent) makes a rejection of human finitude itself the site of temptation—along the lines of Olympus, so desired by the Greeks, the other (Yahweh), with the specificity of the God of Israel (*the* God), consecrates the acceptance of our Being-there and the weakness of our flesh (*bâsâr*) as the place of ultimate glorification. The agony of Christ is thus above all ours, especially in that it confirms a *weakness* chosen by God that will be forever and forever manifest, and that we bear—we also—in us, even in our own flesh.[20]

As for redemption, when the incarnation is in no way simply effective reparation but is rather the scene of its most perfect expression, this cannot and must not obscure the project of election [of God's people] and filiation, which anticipates and goes beyond it. Redemptive salvation is given to us as an extra—an overflow of a gift that precedes it. The term "redemption" describes an ontic [real or factual] property that we "have" or "receive" (historically), of the existential that we "are," at least in the eyes of God, in the very fabric of our being (election and filiation): "We *have* [*echomen*] redemption," St. Paul insists (Eph 1:7); but "he [God] chose us in Christ before the foundation of the world *to be* (*enai*) holy and blameless," and "he destined us for adoption as his children" (Eph 1:4–5).

The sole and unique project of God the Father, even before the founding of the world, is that we shall receive sanctification *in* Christ (*en Christô*) and become *for* him (*eis auton*) and *through* his Son Jesus Christ (*dia Iêsou*

Christou) his adoptive children (Eph 1:4–5). And the project, from Father to Son, in the Son and by the Son, is revealed to humankind.[21] In opposition to a certain Christian tradition where "everything having to do with the senses and the imagination in mystical experience is held to be fundamentally questionable in the extreme,"[22] it is important here to see buried in our Adamic nature, and taken on as it were beforehand in the figure of the "Word made flesh," that weakness chosen by God and reflected in our own weakness, his corruptibility in our corruptibility, his finitude in our finitude, and his death in our death. In the astounding aesthetic vision of Michelangelo, inscribed on the ceiling of the Sistine Chapel, this is translated theologically, going even so far as to spread the simple visibility of Adam in the Word incarnate to a "visibility," at least in iconographical terms, of the Father creator: "With great daring [Michelangelo] *transferred this visible and corporal beauty to the Creator himself.* We are probably witness to an extraordinary piece of artistic audacity, since it is impossible to impose the likeness proper to man on the invisible God. Would this not be blasphemy? It is difficult, however, not to recognize in the *visible and humanized Creator, God clad in infinite majesty.*"[23] The immutable image of a nature originally corrupted or impaired in us—in the double sense of a blessed impairment [*altération*] from an ideal of perfection (necessary incompleteness) and of an original constitutive *otherness* [*altérité*] of our being (election and filiation)—makes our originary finitude into the true meaning of the *imago Dei* inscribed in us. And whoever tries to deny the first (our finitude) concedes in reality also a rejection of the second (the image of God already inscribed in us by our finitude, as it was prefigured in Christ). ✳

We can read in the rejection of the configuration of humankind by God through finitude a sinful attitude specific to humankind. Humankind that is not content with being created in the image "of God" sets itself up as the equal of the supposed total power "of the gods"—a power as vast as it is falsely liberating from the human condition. In short, if it is probably useful in theology (and theology is even more advanced than philosophy on this question), to rediscover the obvious fact of the *natural character of death*, it is still also necessary to draw final metaphysical consequences from it: the establishment of the image of God in mankind by way of the finitude of Adam. And we should see that this is a perspective prefigured in the uncreated Word and recapitulated (*anakephalaiosis*), indeed transformed, in the act of the Resurrection of the incarnate Word.

Anxiety about death, or about the disappearance of the self, is not simply the basis of the "contemporary neuroses" in existentialist philosophy or the sign of a "sick or frail faith," as it is referred to in the astonishingly reductive comments of Hans Urs von Balthasar (who never distinguishes anxiety about death from anxiety about sin).[24] On the contrary, such anxiety is the sign of the total engagement of the Son with the non-sinful finitude of humankind, something he prefigures already in his person, and already before the creation of the world, a real power to inhabit and live within its limits, even if these limits are both summed up and taken on (in the sense of being recapitulated)[25] in the final act of Resurrection by the Father.[26]

§7 Finitude: Finite and Infinite

This finitude of the Word, shared with humans most fully through Christ's incarnation but also prefigured already in the act of Creation [by God] "in his image" (Gen 1:27), does not conflict with either the finite or the infinite. It transgresses rather and does away with any mundane duality to indicate here the limited and contingent horizon of an existence "on a human scale." We must therefore be careful not to confuse the "finite being" with one who "lives in finitude." The former (the finite) requires reference to another—the Infinite—of which he or she regrets being simply a limitation and desires afresh some kind of infinity (conceivable, as we shall see, by the act of the Resurrection rather than by the Creation). The latter (finitude) is happy simply with "Being-there," facing death and definitively anchored in an existence that is devoid, at least to begin with, of an elsewhere.[27]

Heidegger underlines in this respect, guarding in advance against any wrong-headed interpretation of the "facticity" [or "thrownness"] of our being, solely in terms of sin, that "the fallennness of Dasein" must not be taken "as a 'fall' from a purer and higher 'primal status.' Not only do we lack any experience of this ontically, but ontologically we lack any possibilities or clues for Interpreting it."[28]

§8 Finitude and Anxiety

The phenomenology of death does not then, strictly speaking, obstruct the horizon of finitude, as when someone who has been shipwrecked tries to see into a distance so obscure that he or she hopelessly waits to cry out, "Land ahead!" It recalls simply that such a horizon remains always irresistible and unfailingly already there. However much I proceed toward my death, the horizon of my own finitude will not cease to present itself upon the horizon, an escape route so insurmountable that it reveals nothing out there except the present in which I meet it and that encloses me on all sides.

The *value* of the horizon of my finitude is thus paradoxically that I find myself always *without value*: not in the sense that, being valueless, the horizon would go beyond the limits of my finitude; far from it. It is simply that no other criterion apart from my own way of regarding the horizon could precisely give it a value.

"Beyond good and evil," or outside all systems of moral values, we have to recognize along with Heidegger (interpreting Kant) that "in order to designate the finite in human beings it might suffice to cite any of our imperfections. In this way, we gain, at best, evidence for the fact that the human being is a *finite creature*. However, we learn neither wherein the essence of his *finitude* exists, nor even how this finitude completely determines the human being from the ground up as the being it is."[29]

It is thus appropriate in philosophy, as also probably in theology, to return to the pure and simple facticity of our Being-there (*Dasein*) described in *Being and Time*, because it is only that facticity, initially at least, that we know. The "ontological Interpretation of death takes precedence over any ontical other-worldly speculation."[30] If then, Heidegger insists, "our existential-ontological Interpretation makes no ontical assertion about the 'corruption of human nature,' [it is] not because the necessary evidence is lacking, but because the problematic of this Interpretation is *prior* to any assertion about corruption or incorruption."[31] *Anxiety over finitude* points simply to anxiety about being mortal, independently of my value judgment as to the good—or evil—basis of such mortality. The death of Christ (neither good nor bad from the point of view of the ordinary corruptibility of all living beings) surely belongs above all to the anxiety that was necessarily contemporaneous with his incarnation, which he experiences as mortal rather than being simply (even if to some extent correctly) what "made him to be sin" (2 Cor 5:21) for the atonement of our sins.

§9 The Eclipse of Finitude

The neglect in most interpretations of Gethsemane of a consideration of Christ's anxiety over finitude derives theologically, as I see it, from a non-separation of sin and death—as though for the Son to be anxious in the face of his own death stemmed uniquely and necessarily from his adoption of our sinful state, since he is, in St. Paul's words, "made . . . sin" without himself being a sinner (2 Cor 5:21). Nobody would want to call into question the validity of the Pauline proposition here, but I would simply point out that it concerns anxiety about sin, and death in relation to redemption, rather than communion. And this should not stand in the way of understanding the other, no-less-concise formulation of St. Paul as apostle to the Gentiles: "While we were still weak [*asthenôn*], at the right time Christ died for the ungodly" (Rom 5:6). Why should we once again convert the debility of humankind and of the apostle into powerlessness in the face of sins? Should we not rather see that the simple weakness of our corruptible being shows itself, within the horizon of death, as definitively incapable of building up a "kingdom within a kingdom" at the heart of the universal law of the living and its inescapable principle of entropy?[32]

The death of Christ for the ungodly does not threaten finitude, except insofar as he lives in finitude and incarnates it, independently of any sinful characteristics. The Augustinian perspective on sin and its "atonement," setting aside the excessive and popular accusations currently made against St. Augustine, would probably not suffice on its own as a justification for the incarnation of the Word.[33] It is rather that the Word made flesh, as we find in the theology of the first fathers of the church, invites us to enter into our own divinization. Far from denouncing human finitude, the incarnate Son consecrates it and transforms it by living within his anxiety until the very end. Because of the "natural character of death," which we find also in Christianity, we could also probably maintain, *in contrast to Heidegger this time*, that a Christian following Christ can and must, perhaps as a matter of priority, experience up to the end the anxiety of our own finitude, without however already putting "death together with [our] interpretation of 'life.'" Theology finds thus at its heart a certain "type of distress," not simply at sin, but rather more at finitude—even that which has been made precisely and paradoxically the subject matter of contemporary philosophy and that the Word himself "recapitulates" (*anakephalaiosis*) along with everything else, in his flesh. As Martelet says, "That sin alone does not explain the incarnation opens up to human history a horizon that we cannot ignore. In fact, not simply being the redeemer, Christ can respond to a type of distress that is not just sin, but is certainly finitude: distress in suffering and at our natural death in the important uncontroversial sense of this word. Undoubtedly it was above all to alleviate an intrinsic defect in our finitude that God became incarnate, but this was in order to involve us in the ultimate Glory of his Life."[34]

§10 The Face of Death

To accept that we see *death in front of us and to enter into its proper finitude* is not therefore for the Christian, as for others, the same thing as *coping with death*. The attempt and the temptation to try to conquer death belongs, as we shall see later, when we look at "anxiety over sin," among those objections raised, perhaps legitimately, by contemporary philosophy when it encounters Christianity. <u>Seeing death in front of us comes back on the contrary to letting the face of death appear. Fernando Pessoa, a little crudely but correctly, recalls to us that "we are death," or we are *made of* death.</u> "The very act of living means dying, since with each day we live, we have one less day of life remaining."[35] We must not allow death (which makes us, as it continually unmakes us) to lead us into believing the lie that it is simply accidental and that it just happens unfortunately in our own lives. Heidegger's famous "Existential Analysis of Death,"[36] which I can only suggest here, aims to unmask the way in which "Death" is encountered as a "case" in the world. The "one" of "one dies" "is the 'nobody'"—and today probably even more than in the past, apart from the spectacle of death, dead bodies are mostly seen "from afar" or "seen in the distance" (*télé-visé[s]*).[37]

As long as death is simply seen "in the publicness with which we are with one another in our everyday manner," as a "mishap which is constantly occurring," as a "well-known event occurring within-the-world,"[38] nobody truly dies *for me*—not just dying to save me, but quite simply and commonly, dying "in my own eyes." Is it the same when the person dying, indeed the dead person, is someone close to me: in the term used by the gospels, my "neighbor"? Heidegger, for his part, suggests going so far as to identify the lived experience of such death as that of "someone or other . . . neighbour or stranger."[39] The question regarding one's neighbor is so important to the Christian that Christians sometimes agonize more— often at the cost of a total misunderstanding of the necessity of loving one's neighbor—over the death of another rather than over their own deaths. Indeed, it is perhaps another way of fleeing from one's own anxiety about death. "To die with you or not to die" in the context of an accident, or "to die in your place so as not to survive you and be alone" in the agony of an illness: these are the cruel and insoluble dilemmas that arise, in such a way that we can never escape from them, both for Christians and probably for all humankind.

§11 To Die "with"

If Christ himself wept over the death of another—his neighbor from Bethany, Lazarus—he did not spare him either his suffering or his death. Why, "having heard that Lazarus was ill," did Jesus stay "two days longer in the place where he was" (John 11:6)? Why, when, as Lazarus's sister Martha says, "If you had been here, my brother would not have died" (John 11:21)? Heidegger suggests in a very different context, *"No one can take the Other's dying away from him,"*[40] and perhaps not even Christ could do so. At the heart of his earthly pilgrimage the Son must also acknowledge his estrangement from the death of another, even if it is the death of his closest friend. According to Heidegger, "The dying of Others is not something which we experience in a genuine sense; at most we are always just 'there alongside.'"[41] And the tears that follow (John 11:35) hardly stem in reality from a sense of bitterness or failure (as if Christ had effectively arrived too late); rather, he shows through shedding these tears his impossible mastery over a finitude that is forever corruptible, though not necessarily sinful. When Lazarus awakens from death (because, according to Christ, his friend "has fallen asleep" [John 11:11]), is it not probably because the sleep of the dying one is simply seen within the horizon of the future awakening of One who is living—in other words, the Resurrection? Lazarus, by contrast, sleeps precisely because he has penetrated into the silence of his own finitude. And awakening him does not break through all sleep, because one day, once again, he also will have to experience his death definitively. As far as Lazarus is concerned in this text, to be awakened (*exupnizō*) is not the same as to be restored to life (*anisthêmi*); a clear distinction is made: "I know that he will rise again in the resurrection on the last day," the disconsolate Mary says, though she understands only too well the difference between an awakening and an immense, far distant sleep (John 11:11 and 11:24). Would it not thus be necessary—though this implies a retroactive reading of the gospels—to await the act of Resurrection, when the thaumaturge, or worker of miracles such as awakenings from death, shows himself as the definitive conqueror of sleep? Christ is surely weighing up the significance of sleep for all finitude and for himself, so that he does not make a full demonstration of his powers of awakening—a demonstration that would necessarily be deficient until he had definitively taken charge of his own sleep. Lazarus woken has at least not died, and the stay accorded by his awakening will not be enough to spare him all sleep. A death that will still be "his" remains at the end, and beyond any reappearance or revivification.

Should we say that one could not die "for" others, as Maximilian Kolbe is said to have done, taking the place of a man with wife and children at Auschwitz,[42] or as Uriah the Hittite did, killed on David's instructions (2 Sam 11)? Is Christ truly dead *for us*, just as the sacrificial lamb is supposed to die *in our place*? Does Christ undertake, by way of an opportunity for our redemption, an ultimate act of reprieve for our lives? What are we to say of a sacrifice that is spared the Christian, but goes so far as Christ's death—or at the very least the anxiety that it generates? "Of course someone can 'go to his death for another,'" Heidegger says. "But that always means to sacrifice oneself for the Other 'in some definite affair.' . . . Dying is something that every Dasein itself must take upon itself at the time."[43]

The crucial aspect of the death of my neighbor for me—that he or she dies in front of me, in my place, or through my fault—implies that what is already at stake is my responsibility for the other, but this poses problems that only an ontological and existential inquiry can hope to resolve.[44] Probably it is enough to translate the ontological anxiety over death into an ethical problem to unscramble this. If death refers first of all to "the death of those we love," because, as Marcel says, "to love someone . . . that is to say: you shall not die,"[45] it is nonetheless true that a detour by way of *my* death and *my* anxiety shows us a necessary passage, not simply as to how best one should live through one's death (*ars morendi*, or the art of dying of the Middle Ages), but also how to accompany the other in his or her death.[46] The day and the hour will also come for me—as it does for Antonius Block, the disillusioned knight of Ingmar Bergman's film *The Seventh Seal* (1957). In Bergman's film Block can only play at killing the living or saving the dying until the hour of the Seventh Seal, when the character Death rises up before him.[47] The bell will also toll for me, in my own face-to-face with death, when the heart of this combat will be *my own*, and solely mine. In Albrecht Dürer's engraving of *Knight, Death and the Devil* (1513) the Knight and Death in reality only face one another in order to show their true faces.[48] But what about the Christian today—when the face of death rises up before him, as it does for the crusading Knight—who does not give up on his Christianity? Is Christ not already the victor in this terrible game of "loser takes all," where humankind faces death in an impossible "check-mate"? Could Bergmann's Knight, for his part, really have forgotten that?

3

The Temptation of Despair or Anxiety over Sin

§13 Inevitable Death

There is nothing more morbid or humiliating, it must seem, than always to be thinking about death, never mind whether this is, as in Montaigne's essay, "at the stumbling of a horse, at the falling of a tile, at the least prick with a pin."[1] What was seen in the past simply as the "misery of man without God" (Pascal) describes today, in a familiar inversion, the human condition in modernity, whether or not separated from God.[2] One can think of one's own death and the total disappearance of the self while appearing not to believe in it (Socrates), or again with resignation (Epicurus and Epictetus), or in the hope of finding some justification (Pascal), or in revolt (Camus), or even with tenderness (Péguy); but none of this will cancel out the ineluctable and unsurpassable character of death. As for Christians, if they do not take the tragedy of their own deaths and the deaths of others seriously, they can be quite appropriately criticized by a philosopher such as Jean-Paul Sartre for retreat or evasion, in the name of values that are supposed somehow to exist, when they are faced with the "possibility of choice" in their lives, a possibility that moreover belongs to humankind and solely to humankind.[3]

[margin handwriting: it is not disbelieving in it but displacing it from any position of supposedly existential primacy]

[margin handwriting: death adds urgency to choice, that much is true, but when primary it totally destroys that choice and produces bleak and nihilistic fatalism]

§14 The Conquest of Sin

Not only nonbelievers fall into despair in the face of the finitude of their existence. Death is in fact also paradoxical for the believer in that it marks at once what is most certain as event and what is least understood as far as its nature is concerned. Knowing of my future death as a fact does nothing to diminish its unknowability as action; on the contrary, it strengthens it.[4] Here precisely the *temptation of despair* comes close to anxiety over sin.[5] One who is certain in the knowledge of the advent of a being, but at the same time does not know *who* will come, or *when* this will be, may in fact find that such slender knowledge turns into excessive despair. There is also a great temptation, and particularly for Christians (who should know what a blind alley it is), to cling to and bury themselves in the certitude of a coming of which in reality they know nothing. And this is precisely the sense in Genesis of "you will die of death" (Gen 2:17). To "die of death" [in French "*mourir de mort*"] is not just to die: if it were so the repetition in the Hebrew of Genesis would not be necessary. It rather implies to *suffer death* so far as to die of it. It is not simply "you shall die" ("*tu mourras*"), as in the translation of the Bible into French by Louis Segond (1910), nor "you shall most surely die" ("*tu mourras certainement*"), as in Augustin Crampon's translation, *La Sainte Bible* (1923), and even less is it "you must die" ("*tu devras mourrir*"), as in the French ecumenical Bible, the *Traduction oecuménique de la Bible* (1987).[6] The instructions of God to humankind in the Garden of Eden are in reality as follows: "On the day you eat from it [the tree of the knowledge of good and evil], suffer to die of death." What I am looking for here is an interpretative translation that is closest to the literal sense of the Hebrew ("you will die of death"), in that it shows it is not just a question of dying (biological death), but of suffering death (spiritual death). On the other hand, it should show that anxiety over a possible transgression remains not simply before the non-sinful finitude of humankind (anxiety over death), but also because we suffer from not knowing *how* to live through this finitude and thus lock ourselves into it (anxiety over sin).[7] We should not substitute here the idea that "one dies *because* one has sinned" for the true sense of the divine judgment, which is rather that "to sin is *just* to die." To do so would be to grasp nothing about either sin or death from Genesis.[8]

Anxiety over sin—and thus also, quite simply, sin—*grafted* or *fed into* biological death, takes up in reality a *position*. It is like an army that conquers a previously neutral territory without ever having been the sole cause of the battle.

§15 Sin and Anxiety

In this sense, and in this sense only, can one speak of the "symbolism" of spiritual death in biological death.[9] When it is certain that someone is in fact doomed to physical death, consecutively after sin (a connection that, as I have tried to show, is empty or inane), that person's death will be none-theless a *manner of living*—sinful or blessed. It will be the person's own death and not just a signature on the act of (biological) death. Uniquely from this point of view, for Christians as well as for others, as we shall see, "death" refers above all to a "mode of being of life" rather than just "being-at-the-end of life." Such a mode or way of living one's life prohibits, above all for the believer, either despair over death (Camus), or the attempt to overcome death by a supreme act of consciousness (Heidegger), or an avowal of inalienable and inviolable liberty (Sartre). It is there precisely in con-temporary philosophy that an attitude is established that is probably quite rightly called *sinful*, an attitude of self-enclosure in our own finitude. The "radical no" that the Christian must, according to Hans Urs von Balthasar, pose against this anxiety does not show, as I see it, human beings taking in charge their existence with their horizon blocked by death (anxiety about finitude): it shows in reality the different ways of taking on, or freeing oneself, from such a burden (anxiety over sin). We need, then, to insist upon this: when Joseph Huby says, "Sin is related to spiritual death but is not the essence or *raison d'être* of biological death,"[10] this is not to sup-press the notion of sin, it is to *pick it up* and *reveal* its true nature. That nature is the separation of humankind from God in an auto-enclosure in finitude—a finitude that is not in itself sinful but that includes the desperate anxiety that marks a death (spiritual this time), anxiety over not knowing *how* to live through that finitude. And death, if it is not the re-sult of sin, then becomes at least its symbol.[11]

§16 The Temptation of Despair

To ward off the temptation of a withdrawal or self-enclosure into one's own finitude, the medieval tradition in general and St. Bonaventure in partic-ular reintegrated despair rather than anxiety and death into the structure of sin: "There is a sin [*si est peccatum*] which fights against mercy [*quod im-pugnat misericordiam*], it is despair [*desperatio*]."[12] Because despair is di-rectly and sometimes deliberately in opposition to the Holy Spirit and divine mercy, it leads to an enclosure within oneself and a distancing from God that is no less than the precise definition of sin (*mortal* sin).[13] A fasci-nation with death and the enclosure of oneself in anxiety are for the Chris-tian typical of temptations and prototypes of betrayal. Despair is true death—spiritual here—because it is directly contrary to God's beatified and redemptive intent for humankind.[14] Sin and redemption rather lead to anxiety over sin than to this primary form of anxiety, though they do

How can a manner of living death contain that apparently central point—that moment—which marks it as death?

yes!

sin

the relation between sin and that attitude marked by mortality

sin is in the despair that leads to the self's auto-enclosure not suppress the face-to-face of suffering and death that is particular to anxiety about finitude. One or other modality is freely chosen (blessed or sinful), as far as our *manner* of living, or of dwelling in sin, are concerned. Anxiety about finitude is intermeshed with anxiety about sin, and either gives it meaning (blessed) or snuggles up into a kind of meaninglessness (auto-enclosure). Deciding upon one will leave the other in suspense, since the first (anxiety about sin) stems from the second (anxiety about finitude). As Gabriel Marcel says, "It is not enough to repeat what would be a truism, that since we exist we are subject to death," nor even that "I am at risk of feeling that I have been drawn towards death"; it is rather that death leads me "to see the world as a dream, where in the final analysis death has the last word."[15]   Yes, this is the risk

The fact that the Resurrection frees us, or at least should free Christians, from such anxiety about sin, does not in fact spare us from its counterpart: anxiety about death. Is it not true, as Charles Péguy suggests, that the "ready-made soul"—through the "catechism," through "history," and even through the "calendar"—always already sees "the divine service of Good Friday in the light of Easter"?[16] And is this not the affirmation of meaninglessness on the edge of meaning, the placing of "death together with its interpretation of 'life'" that Heidegger pointed to? When will we finish, in both Christianity and theology, with what Sylvie Germain calls an "off-the-peg belief, all hemmed and buttoned up, guaranteed pure truth, lined with hatred and starched up with a good conscience"?[17] Theology of redemption searches intensely for meaning in the world and in humankind, but does it not forget sometimes, perhaps right from the start, the profound meaninglessness of both—the meaninglessness that the Word, precisely, comes to dwell in, in his flesh?

When the Word comes to dwell in Flesh, it comes to dwell in meaninglessness (flesh ⊃ meaninglessness)

4

From the Affirmation of Meaninglessness to the Suspension of Meaning

§17 The Life Sentence

It is not enough simply to affirm that the denial of meaning still entails giving some meaning to meaning. Against this affirmation, which is as well-known as it is pedestrian, Camus already found a response: he carefully distinguished the lived "feeling of the absurd" from the abstract "notion of the absurd."[1] The argument that there is a meaninglessness that makes sense only works in terms of "the most widespread spiritual attitude of our enlightened age: the one, based on the principle that all is reason, which aims to explain the world."[2] Does this mean that we have to resort to some kind of irrationalism based on a negation of meaning—an absolute meaninglessness? Certainly not. But it does, however, point up how few reasons have been produced by reason itself as to whether "life is or not worth living"; and Camus reflects bitterly, "I have never seen anyone die for the ontological argument."[3]

Why and for whom did Christ die? And who among Christians today would go so far as to die in order to bear witness to their faith in Christ? Against suicide—which, according to Camus clearly shows that [for the person involved] "life is not worth living"—can we say that Christ is still, for the Christian, a reason that makes life "worth living"?[4]

§18 The Christian Witness

Is the believer, then, sent back to questions that, despite their apparent simplicity, are given new importance through their place in contemporary philosophy (existentialism and phcnomenology in particular)? And do these questions send one back, as in the earliest periods of Christianity, to the possibility of martyrdom? We should not delude ourselves here. The "witness" (*marturion*) of the Christian today, even when there is a question of death agonies, no longer involves overcoming anxiety about death in the name of the supposed immanence of the Resurrection, since the ideal of an apostolic life for our day cannot simply content itself with a carbon copy of the first Christian communities. Neither can this witness find its meaning through some sacrifice of the self in the name of a kind of paranoia, brought on because the Christian is faced with a world that is atheist or indifferent to God and that assails it on all sides. On the contrary, witness in our time takes the form of a humble recognition of a reason for *living* that could also be a reason for *dying*—when certainly other reasons, probably equally respectable, could also be worthwhile in their own way. Avowing meaninglessness evidently does not suppress the question of meaning: on the contrary, it innervates and exacerbates it.

§19 Meaninglessness and the Suspension of Meaning

The real challenge as far as anxiety over death is concerned, both for Christians and others, resides not so much in a revolt against meaninglessness (Camus and Sartre) as in the way in which the search for meaning is read as either the possibility of its negation or its affirmation (Heidegger). The anxiety, which is not simply what Heidegger calls "*existentiell*" [i.e., ontic or factual] in the way it confronts the meaningless or the absurd, reveals to us in reality what Heidegger calls the "*existential*" [i.e., the ontologic or theoretical] aspect of humankind—that is, "Dasein's existence structure" or "Dasein's characters of Being."[5]

We can grasp Heidegger's distinction in the present context if we think of the difference between the book of Job and that of Ecclesiastes [or Qohéleth]. Job protests about what he no longer actually has (houses, work, children . . .) without giving up on his search for meaning, even when this leads into meaninglessness (his outrage and his praise of God even when there is no reason for praise). But Qohéleth, in Ecclesiastes, complains about what he has (wisdom, pleasures, work . . .) precisely because he finds no meaning in it (going thus from the vanity of all creation to the vanity of vanity itself).[6] *The absence of things but the presence of meaning*, even if in actual negation—in praise or rebellion (Job, Camus, Sartre)—is less important to our contemporaries than the *presence of things and the absence of meaning*, or at least its suspension—in silence, vanity, or anxiety (Qohéleth, Heidegger). That is the source of the famous and apposite contemporary analysis, often philosophically based, of a shift from atheism to unbelief, of a shift from the denial of God to indifference on the part of humankind.[7] Plunging into or getting to the bottom of this absence, which is not the same as the negation of a presence, leads also to "looking back wearily" or to "mankind . . . turning its will *against* life," occupying the space where moderns enclose themselves in such a way that they are unable to escape. The weariness is what Nietzsche described so well as the modern form of "passive nihilism."[8] It is not trivial then, nor is it just a recuperation, to demand (of the Christian) *theologically* that he or she render back Job and Qohéleth (Sartre, Camus, and Heidegger) to God in his role as the Father. Because it is precisely the Son, in his road toward death, who lives through the double ordeal of a rebellion against meaninglessness and the suspension of meaning. That experiment can be read paradoxically along two lines—not simply Heideggerian but also in rather more evangelical terms. It can be seen as the *fear of our decease* and as *anxiety over death*.

Christ Faced with Anxiety over Death

§20 Two Meditations on Death

The road to the Kingdom, which passes through a narrow gate, is at the same time a road of anxiety and a "difficult passage" (*thlibô* in Greek [squeezed, pinched] and *angere* in Latin [to distress, cause pain]): "For the gate is narrow and the road is hard [*tethlimenê*—anxious] that leads to life" (Matthew 7:14).[1] The Bible does not avoid this problem of anxiety, as Socrates or even the Buddha does: on the contrary, it faces the problem. Moreover, the Bible even sanctifies it in the necessary passage toward life associated with the suffering of a "woman in labor" (Isa 13:8). A comparison with labor also comes up in the cry of the "daughter Zion" (Jer 4:31) in the presaging of the Passion in John's Gospel (John 16:21), in the terror at the prospect of the day of judgment in Isaiah (13:8), and in the plight of the woman who gives birth at the moment of the Seventh Seal in the book of Revelation (Rev 12:5).[2] Throughout the Christian tradition anxiety points first of all to a narrow *passage*, as in childbirth, and not simply to a *wall* blocking the road ahead for modern man. But if Christians see this passage as a road, do they not risk among other things avoiding its obstructions too easily? If, as Kierkegaard maintains, anxiety, through faith, teaches us to rely on providence ("Anxiety as Saving through Faith"),[3] isn't that precisely because the route one actually traces through anxiety is not the same as the route one has decided upon in advance, a route that would have an inescapable and happy outcome? The cathartic and educational effect of anxiety on Christians is not that it protects their faith; on the contrary, anxiety exposes it because it tests it. Christian faith is not what Christians give themselves, but what they receive. According to Karl Barth, who follows on here from Kierkegaard's ideas, anyone who would claim to *have* faith, to be capable of believing, would certainly not believe.[4]

In the same way that anxiety leads Christians to a kind of abandonment of the self as a condition of their faith, so treatment of death is an index among contemporary philosophers of the extent to which they hold on to or abandon the self. Everything depends upon the *way* in which the philosopher or the Christian allows himself or herself to contemplate death to allow its true countenance to appear. Anxiety over death thus becomes a key site where the question of meaning arises, both for the Christian and the philosopher. Ridding oneself of the tensions that modern humankind suffers over the problem of a morbid and humiliating anxiety does not entail, either in philosophy or theology, that I always regard my life as dependent upon my death (as though at any moment I were going to die). Rather the opposite—it means that I give attention to death as dependent upon my life (because I know that one day I must die, it is incumbent upon me to give meaning to what small time remains for me to live). Maurice Merleau-Ponty tells us that "consciousness of death is, however, neither a dead-end nor an outer limit. There are two ways of thinking about death: one pathetic and complacent, which butts against our end and seeks nothing in it but the means of exacerbating violence; the other dry and resolute, which integrates death into itself and turns it into a sharper awareness of life."[5]

Thus, as both Heidegger and Merleau-Ponty make plain, we should not confuse the fear of decease with anxiety about death.[6] Fear of decease—which goes from life to death—remains above all psychological (psychoanalysis speaks in this respect of the death drive), while anxiety about death—which reaches back from death toward life—allows an experience that will above all be metaphysical to emerge (which is why we come across the very famous, but frequently misunderstood, phrase "*angoisse métaphysique*"—that is, metaphysical anxiety). What will this double experience of fear and anxiety be like, for Christ and for Christians? Is it enough, like Eugen Drewermann, to "psychologize" the anxiety to find what is authentically Christian?[7] Is Christ's anxiety in the face of his own death simply psychological? Or is it also, and more significantly, metaphysical?[8] The narrative of Gethsemane carries in it the trace of a double ordeal, both psychological and metaphysical, at least in the terms it uses: "And he took with him Peter and James and John, and he began to be struck with terror *and* amazement [*ekhambeisthai*], and deeply troubled *and* depressed [*adêmonein*] (Mark 14:33 AMP).[9]

[margin note: faith cannot be "had": it is a gift, tested by way of anxieties/trials]

[margin note: fear of decease vs. anxiety about death]

[margin note: where the psychological + metaphysical meet in angoisse]

§21 Alarm and Anxiety

The Greek word *thambos* points to amazement or dumbfounded recoil when faced with something unexpected, while *adêmonia* points to a state of disquiet and interior torment of one who is frightened.[10] This biblical distinction is precisely clarified in Heidegger's work, where we find an equivalent term, phenomenological this time, for dread or alarm (*Erschrecken*)[11] as a modality of fear (*Furcht*), distinguished from anxiety (*Angst*) as a specific opening into our having-been-thrown into the world.[12] *+ the closedness of a world* *⚹*

Thus it is useful to show how the "alarm" of Christ at Gethsemane (*thambos*) maintains in him precisely a feeling of fear (*Furcht*), indeed of alarm in the Heideggerian sense of the term (*Erschrecken*). And it is useful to bring out how he is gradually driven into anxiety (*adêmonia*) as a kind *anxiety in* of putting into abeyance of his being in the world as such (*Angst*). Then *abeyance of* the sense emerges, fully phenomenological, as it seems to me, of a Christly *angst?* entry into death that goes so far as his self-embedding in the flesh.

5

The Fear of Dying and Christ's "Alarm"

§22 Taking on Fear and Abandonment

The experience of fear (*Furcht*) typically starts off by making someone draw back from something that is "dreadful" and "harmful" that has broken into their world (a killing, an accident, illness, a death sentence). It leads to the opening of a new modality of the person's being, which reveals at once the precariousness of existence, an "endangerment" (*Gefährdung*), and the self's feeling of abandonment (*Überlassenheit*). Finally, there may be a wish to share this in the way of being fearful *with* or *for* someone else.[1]

"Alarm" (*Erschrecken*) points to that specific modality of fear that implies that the threat has come suddenly, approaching us as "something well known and familiar."[2] On the other hand, "dread" (*Grauen*) goes beyond familiarity and, when encountered with suddenness, may lead to terror (*Entsetzen*).[3] Because of the common characteristic of fear as an *act of drawing back* when it is shaped by alarm or dread, to be fearful, or to suffer fear as an internal human possibility, is not pathological here; it remains above all psychological. Neither is having fear specifically something that applies to the timid or to "cowards."[4] It is a determining factor in the *Dasein* or the very being of a person as such—and it is above all what the Word comes, as I understand it, to take on in his incarnation.

§23 The Cup, Sadness, and Sleep

What happened, then, to Christ's "alarm" (*thambos*) at Gethsemane? Doesn't his incarnation include suffering step by step all the characteristics of fear? Doesn't becoming-man in his being as the Son (*Menschwerdung*—incarnation) have to proceed as a form of drawing back before a finitude that, properly speaking, is not possible for him to take on? The "cup" (*potêrion*) that Christ knows from the start of his Passion he must drink down to the lees (Mark 10:38)—but before which he draws back in his agony—confirms that in the garden at the foot of the Mount of Olives *he is afraid* in the face of his death, at least in the way in which we all recoil before something threatening: "*Abba*, Father, for you all things are possible; remove this cup from me" (Mark 14:36).[5] Charles Péguy reminds us, citing Corneille's *Polyeucte*, that "the Christ once feared to die."[6] We forget this too often, changing immediately the *prospect* of the Resurrection as a modality of our lives into the *hope* of a being-of-life-after-death. The purported certitude then becomes enough to blank out how it is that first of all "we are in the world."[7]

Christ's "alarm" is then preeminently *the feeling experienced in the face of a threat of something well-known* that, coming nearer in a familiar world, causes the one who experiences it to draw back. The threat is the punishment of crucifixion inflicted on all political agitators in a Roman province.[8] The contemporary ideal of "he was not seen to go" is in singular contrast to the blessed "feeling the approach of death" that was so much wished-for in the seventeenth century and was probably also felt by Jesus through his long journey up to Jerusalem.[9] This alarm (*thambos*)—translated sometimes also by "tremble" ["*frisson*"][10]—has nothing in it, for Jesus at least, of dread or terror. The excess of what takes place is not such that the Son of Man has to enter into the convulsions frequently experienced by those condemned to death on the scaffold. Only the characteristics of *anxiety*, and not those of *alarm*, as we shall see, and as the gospel text underlines, truly show us the perspective of an annihilation of the self, as Christ's sweat becomes "like great drops of blood falling down on the ground" (Luke 22:44).

The condition of fear lived through by Jesus in Gethsemane confirms, and is then made very obvious, in a double feeling he has, both of the vulnerability of his existence and of his being abandoned to himself (*Überlassenheit*), as is attested by the mention of a "soul . . . sorrowful [*perilupos*] to the point of death [*eôs thanatou*]" (Mark 14:34 JB). In a way, sorrow displaces death here as the imminent event that is basic to the

Being-there of humankind (*Dasein*), opening up at the approach of this threat. But the overwhelming sorrow (*peri-lupos*) that submerges the very being of the person who suffers does not cause him to give up on himself, as would be the case for dread and terror. What is most important here, up to his death (*eôs thanatou*), is not so much the event of death itself as the tension of living through the abandonment of the self to the self, in the imminence of the approaching end.[11] Without indicating a total giving up, the sorrow "to the point of death" points to a fatigue, at least a psychological fatigue, of one who in his fear sees himself forsaken by those he loves.

Which is why, at last, there is a final effort by Christ to share with those close to him what we could call here a "*fear*," because this condition includes in itself the *desire still and forever to live with and for others*: "Stay here while I pray" (Mark 14:33 JB), Jesus says to his disciples on the Mount of Olives, and he takes Peter, James, and John with him so that they "wait here, and keep awake" (Mark 14:35, JB). And at this point precisely we find a rupture: he lives through his recoil at the cup ["Father . . . take this cup away from me" (Luke 22:42 JB)] and his sorrow at being abandoned, but fear runs him aground at the very moment of its ultimate verification. There is no sharing with anyone else, no sense, as the German proverb has it, that "two is an army against one." Three times he comes close to his disciples, and three times he cries out with the same sense of being abandoned, "Are you asleep? . . . Are you still sleeping?" (Mark 14:37–41). Why is there this impossibility of the sharing of fear in the narrative of Gethsemane? Could we not suggest that death, in philosophy as in theology, has to signify not only "the end of existence," but also and above all a "truly human way of existing"? We might ask whether Christ's passage through the modalities of fear is enough to tell us all about his death—about his assumption of humanity and the project of salvation of the Father as effected by Jesus. Does the fear of death at Gethsemane tell us more than simply the death of one faced with the possibility of "being at the end" of his or her existence?

§24 Resignation, Waiting, and Heroism

To answer the aforementioned questions we need to bring out more closely what "ending an existence" means—for all humankind as well as for Christ. From characteristics like fear we move on then to the various ways in which all humans envisage "Being-at-an–end," or their own decease.[12] The end of life denotes first of all an act of *disappearing* or *vanishing*, just as in "after the rain comes good weather," or, as one says, the bread is "finished" once it has been eaten. In dying, therefore, one is resigned to no longer being, either in that one has had one's time or that one has to go through the inevitable acknowledgment that "there will be others after" (Péguy).[13] This same end can also be seen as a road that ceases, or as a road that is blocked when there is a public notice of road works. Death in such a case would no longer be disappearance or vanishing, but simply a diversion or a passage. All kinds of hope remain still possible here, and nothing would prevent us from believing that this is not the end of the road, even though nobody had ever come back to show us the new thoroughfare. And after all, some people aim to sign off the end of their existence, like the artist who completes and perfects a painting with a final gesture. Bloody or heroic, and sometimes both at the same time, death in this case may put the seal definitively in people's memories on a total conformity of thoughts and acts. The hereafter of death counts for little when by my act of sacrifice, I survive myself by myself, in a here and now, or in a hereafter, that is heroic and unforgettable. The three modalities of "decease," or the ways in which it is possible to envisage the Being-towards-the-end of my existence, or the existence of others, are then (1) a resignation in the face of my disappearance, (2) a waiting during this interruption, and (3) a heroism in the accomplishment of death.[14]

§25 The Silence at the End

What do we know then of the death of Christ, of his decease or his Being-towards-the-end, such that we can decipher it in a way that he himself could also perhaps have regarded it? Paradoxically, the gospels tell us nothing that could decide in favor of one or other modality of the end. If, as we have seen, we have enough evidence in the scriptures of the way in which he envisaged the approach of the end—the alarm in his recoil before the cup, the self-abandonment in his sorrow, and the search for help from others before the emerging threat—nothing is said, at least in relation to Christ himself, concerning the *nature* of his end (disappearance, discontinuity, or accomplishment) or his way of overcoming it (resignation, expectation, or heroism). And this shows us that Christ, as we shall see, probably does not himself know the nature of what his end will be (the meaning of his own death) nor the way in which to go beyond it (either as worker of miracles or in powerlessness); but it is also because in his person he has to some degree renounced taking everything upon himself. Finally, an Other, his Father—with him and in him—overcomes his end.

§26 The Scenarios of Death

Textual silence as to the particular nature of the end and the possibility of overcoming it remains so often unbearable for Christians that they do not hesitate, as in the apocryphal gospels, to make up the script of a violent death, one that would have been inconceivable for Christ, even though it would have been common at the time.[15] There have been many attempts to suppress the silence of Christ and invent an ending. The first efforts, now outdated, suggested the proclamation of a stoic act by a Christ who was resigned, knowing himself to be unknown to humankind, but who through his death would pay dearly the ransom for their sins. They suggested *resignation to his death and disappearance*: no trace of hope or joy remaining even in Jesus himself. We read of the sad obedience of a sacrificial lamb led to the abattoir through the whim of a vengeful and angry father. A second version, still current, claims *the certitude of the Resurrection* and Christ's affirmation of a clear consciousness of himself and of his destiny with which, as the Son, alone among humankind, he complies immediately, because of his permanent participation in the beatific vision. He knows better than anyone else, even better than his executioners, the place, the day, and the hour of his end, as well as of his Resurrection on the third day (See the anticipation of the Passion in Mark 8:31; 9:31; 10:33–34). In this version, the certitude of a future Resurrection not only will overcome the fear of death, but at the same time will suppress it. The "divine comedy" (not in Dante's sense), will end with the event of the Resurrection. And in this sense, as the remote spectacle of the Son continues, we are supposed to leave it to the "master beyond" to direct the role of agony and death in the world as they march on to their conclusion in the world down here. The two scenes of the Mount of Olives and of the "place of the skull" (Golgotha) then disappear very quickly in a proclamation of the Resurrection made to the farthest reaches of Judea and to all of Samaria.

A final way of inventing an ending that manages to overcome anxiety—not specifically Christian this time but still often subtly developed among believers—is the affirmation, straight out, of a complete conformity between the thought and actions of Christ right up to his death. In other words, it suggests *the heroic completion of his life in his death*. In this version Jesus exposed on the cross opens up the way of Nietzsche's Overman, that of surpassing the self, and of a self-realization where there is the affirmation of a creative wish to live even in death. The famous offer of his life even through his own death will then disguise, with difficulty here, the triumphant heroism of the man who, believing he is giving us his life, in reality takes it back, all the more in that he has tried to give it meaning through his death.

§27 The Triple Failure of the Staging

None of these versions, then—resignation, certitude, or heroism—truly fits Christ or stands up to a full examination of the teachings of the Magisterium, the gospels, and an understanding of the Son's mission. As far as the first is concerned (resignation to his death and disappearance), *Gaudium et Spes* [*The Pastoral Constitution on the Church in the Modern World*, promulgated after Vatican II] corrects, or at least rectifies, the perspective of the Council of Trent, unilaterally based on the notion of atonement. The Council of Trent says that the Son, "by His most holy Passion on the wood of the cross . . . made satisfaction for us unto God the Father" ("meritorious cause"),[16] but *Gaudium et Spes* adds, "To the sons of Adam He restores the divine likeness which had been disfigured from the first sin onward" (the admirable exchange).[17]

The second version (certitude of the Resurrection) tries to compensate Christ for the commonplace mode of his death as if, in a way, he could not and was not supposed to die in the same way that we (also) shall die. In this version, only seeming to die (a form of Docetism),[18] it suited him personally not to disappear except in the certain knowledge of his own Resurrection. But if Christ were "protecting" himself against his death by Resurrection, much as climbers protect themselves against falls with metal spikes driven into rocks, would he then be dying an ordinary death—the death of all mankind? It is not enough to suggest, along with Karl Rahner, that "a genuinely human consciousness *must* have an unknown future"[19] nor even, along with Hans Urs von Balthasar, that we have a "faith in Jesus Christ" (Gal 2:16) for whom "the hour at the horizon of consciousness" is not the same thing as consciousness of what hour it is.[20] Such propositions, revolutionary and no doubt appropriate in their time, have led others to inquiry and exegesis of the meaning of the consciousness of Jesus when he is faced with life and death,[21] but we need today to push these questions to the limits and recognize, theologically this time, that the physical death of Christ, being neither an exception from ordinary death nor simply a consequence of sin, can only speak to us from within the common deaths of all humankind. It speaks of a death that the complete human condition would probably bear witness to right from its origin and that the Word made flesh comes to take on as such. Charles Péguy explains: "He [Christ] was going to have to undergo death, ordinary death, the death that we have in common . . . the death of all men, the death of all the world, the fate we have in common, the death in common with all the world; the death of which your father died, my child, and the father of your father; the death that your father, your young father, suffered when you were ten months old; the death your mother will suffer, one day, at one time; and your wife, and your children, and the children of your children; you yourself at the centre."[22]

The third and final version—*heroism in the accomplishment*—is one of the possible wrong turnings in a semantic theology that, through focusing on the performativity of language, sees in the death of Christ purely and simply a conformity between his words and his acts.[23] There is, however, nothing specifically Christlike in Christ's death seen in this way. Socrates and Gandhi were also able to sign off their lives by such acts of death. To suppress the idea of divine foreknowledge in the person of the Son, going so far as to make it a true "death of a man" does not contribute anything new to the consecration of such a death as heroic and exceptional. On the contrary, the death of Christ remains all the more inexhaustible when it is seen first of all as a commonplace and ordinary death. Each one of us can say it is a death that not only encompasses the characteristics of our own specific death, but also that it takes on the characteristics of all deaths, in that for all of us even to be born and to live comes back to accepting that we die.

§28 From Alarm to Anxiety

It can then be argued concerning fear, to conclude with the meaning of Christ's alarm, that it possesses "its own heuristic power" and that it is enough "to consider the fears that are previous to our own desires in order to establish what is really important to us."[24] What is true for all humankind is certainly true for Christ: in his own *fear* of death (on the cross), which is not simply fictive (Hans Jonas), but properly speaking real (Heidegger),[25] the depths of his being are revealed. Like one of humankind, and as a man, Christ draws back before the cup. He feels the precariousness of his situation and seeks to share that feeling with others. On the other hand, like anyone who refuses to accept the weakness of his or her human condition, he can neither be satisfied with, nor resign himself to, his own disappearance. But neither can he reassure himself about his Resurrection or perfect himself through heroism. It is as though, fleeing his decease with alarm (*thambos*), he has not yet plumbed the depths of his humanity or of all humanity. He faces anxiety and anguish (*adêmonia*) before the void that is opened up by the question of the meaning of life, once posed on the threshold of death. The triple failure of resignation, certitude, and heroism to ensure success in this ending only reveals how impossible in reality it is to master death and how death is insurmountable. The awakening of the consciousness of Christ before the immanence of his ending and the question of what it conceals thus opens up already, and as it were in advance, toward a new mode of temporality in which Christian eschatology anticipates all those later phenomenological realignments concerning what Heidegger calls the "*ecstases*" of temporality.[26]

6

God's Vigil

§29 Remaining Always Awake

Heidegger, at the defining moment of his break with theology (1920–21), starting off from a reading of the writings of St. Paul, and before his famous description of the "*ecstases* of temporality" in *Being and Time* (1927),[1] identifies a mode of temporality that is particular to "original Christianity." He talks of an insurmountable tension between the "already there" and the "not yet," between the first coming of Christ in the flesh and his second coming in glory.[2] In contrast to the Jewish *Eschaton* (the "end of days," waiting for the Messiah as a future event), Heidegger thinks that Christian eschatology changes factual temporality, and temporality in terms of events, into an originating and "ecstatic" temporality [i.e., including "the phenomenon of the future, the character of having been, and the Present"].[3] Claude Romano explains that "having-been-ness, (*das Gewesenheit*) determines the present of the believer and it is temporalized authentically starting off from his or her future."[4] Phenomenological consideration of temporality has a regenerating power for the whole of Christian eschatology, and in this respect the fundamental transformation consists less in a preoccupation with the *when* of the day and time of the coming of the Kingdom than its *how*. That is to say, it is concerned with the "manner of being a Christian before God (*Vollzugzusammenhang mit Gott*)" when the day and hour comes.[5] The First Letter to the Thessalonians reminds us: "Now concerning the times and the seasons, brothers and

sisters, you do not need to have anything written to you. For you your-
selves know very well that the day of the Lord will come like a thief in the
night. . . . So then, let us not fall asleep as others do, but let us keep awake
and be sober" (1 Thes 5:1–2, 6).

At the dawn of his Passion, would Christ not in reality himself already
be, like one of the "wise virgins" or bridesmaids in the parable of the wise
and foolish bridesmaids (Matthew 25:1–13), awaiting the coming home
still *on the alert*? And he would also be on the alert at the heart of the darkness of the Garden of Gethsemane, when certain among his own follow-
ers could not and did not know how to keep their lamps burning. If he
will stand waiting behind the door, at the hour when the knell is sounded
for our deaths, was Christ not beforehand the one who first stood on that
threshold, at the Father's door, as his last cry rang out? In the Passion, as
in eschatology, "what counts is not *when* the parousia, or second coming
of Christ, will take place—because the Son himself does not know the day
or the time—but it is rather *with what predisposition* the Christian [and
Christ himself as precursor, we might add] must wait so as to remain open
to this second coming. What counts is to remain awake so as not to let
oneself be surprised by he who will come like a thief in the night."[6] The
authentic Christian experience, distinguished in advance from the inau-
thentic experience by Heidegger, can be summed up as a "holding oneself always on the alert," not because one is *waiting for a future event* that
is always still to come, but because the future remains in reality always
already something that *can at any moment* orient one's present.[7]

§30 The Passage of Death, the Present of the Passion, the Future of the Resurrection

On the strength of such a phenomenological view of temporality, whose
traces can be found in an exemplary fashion in the Christian tradition, all
the *ecstases* of time receive at one stroke, as it were in an about-face, a new
identification. As with the gospel writers who reread the whole of the life
of Jesus in the light of his Resurrection (prolepsis),[8] the *past* of the death
of Christ indicates to us not so much the theological aspect of the event,
even of what actually happened (the act of the decease of the prophet Jesus in approximately 30 A.D.). Rather, it indicates the manner in which it
was seen by his consciousness as it took place: in other words, the act of
offering and introspection through which he embarks upon his death—or
better, as we shall see, tries to radicalize his death as the unsurpassable horizon of all life and thus also of his own life ("Father, into your hands I
commend my spirit" [Luke 23:46]). As the Son offers himself in an ultimate

way to the Father with his last cry, the *present* of this act indicates, in a specifically Christian temporality, not only what occurs in the now (I am going to die), but above all the accomplishment of the gift of presence in an instant (*Augen-blick*), or at a time that is sufficient in itself to determine the whole of what is to come ("When the hour [*hôra*] came, he took his place at the table. . . . Then he took a cup . . . he took a loaf of bread" [Luke 22:14–19]). Since the hope of resurrection, as we have seen, shows for Christ himself, as also for us, less the hope of a being-in-life-after-life than a manner of being in life in one's own life, a possible *future* opens up to the Christian. And this is because, far from continuing always with a future that is present but not yet actualized (one day I shall be resurrected), Christians welcome rather the *ad-vent* now, for themselves, of what is particularly possible for them. The Christian can say, if from today I live in my resurrection, then I accept being stripped of my supreme egoism, and I receive instead a new and radical otherness ("It is no longer I who live, but it is Christ who lives in me" [Gal 2:20]).

The existential modalities of a possible renewal of Christian eschatology illuminated by a phenomenological establishment of temporality are then as follows: (a) the *past* of the death of Christ, as the *passage* of an act of consciousness, or as a way of seeing the end, in a modality that is specific to it (the oblation or offering); (b) the *present* of his Passion as a total *gift* of the self (a present as gift), in a moment or at an hour that can shape all the future; (c) the *future* of the Christian as a *coming to (ad-vent to) one's self* of one's own individual possibilities in the welcome of the Other in one's self.[9] The Son, faced with his own death, already and in advance of any later phenomenological perspectives, inaugurates a new type of eschatological temporality according to which the *when* of the end counts less than the *how*, the now of the day and hour counting less than the giving up of the self at that time and at that hour. We find the appropriate question by Jean-Luc Marion brought up again in our emphasis on the anxiety of Christ, faced with death as his horizon: "Do the Incarnation and Resurrection of Christ affect ontological destiny [i.e., on the level of Being or metaphysical considerations], or do they remain a purely ontic [i.e., physical or factual] event?"[10]

§31 Theological Actuality and Phenomenological Possibility

If we move from eschatological and religious considerations of the end to the purely descriptive analysis of the "Being-towards-death," we find that phenomenologists, and Heidegger in particular, ordinarily accept a "methodological atheism" that is purportedly rigorous in all good phenomenology.[11]

Accusing the Parousia, or Second Coming of Christ, of remaining forever, as actuality, "an event that will come," Heidegger rejects Christianity itself on account of its impossible reduction of this event to the possible. Claude Romano explains that "instead of an immediate being-awake, awaiting the Parousia of Christ, [Heidegger] substitutes Being-towards-death as authentic resoluteness. . . . For the presence of God is substituted mortality as a possibility of my Being."[12] But does this double substitution of "Being-towards-death" for "being-awake," and of "mortality" for the "presence of self," really release us in a trouble-free way from the perspectives opened up specifically by Christianity? Surely the God of Christians is precisely and paradoxically a God who, in his Son, to say the least, *dies*. He thus lives through, to the very end, the sense of an absence, of a kind that simply living through expectation would not eliminate. Doesn't the rejection of Christian eschatology in the name of a passage to the Being-towards-death neglect the legitimate sense of a death of God in Christianity? Isn't there, after the *alarm of Christ* and the fear of decease, in the figure of the incarnate Word himself, the necessary labor of *anxiety* over death? Christ lives through such anxiety, so relevant to him that he will embody it even in his very own flesh. And in his living through anxiety we find confirmation that the Heideggerian formula, according to which the Christian cannot fully experience anxiety over death because Christians have "always already viewed death together with its interpretation of 'life,'" is definitively false.[13]

7

The Narrow Road of Anxiety

§32 Indefiniteness, Reduction to Nothing, and Isolation

In a list in *Being and Time* that is not exhaustive, Heidegger enumerates three characteristics of anxiety (as he does with fear, with which it is often contrasted).[1] What anxiety is anxious about, unlike what causes fear, remains "completely indefinite." "Anxiety" does not know "what that in the face of which it is anxious is." And it springs precisely from this state of affairs. What it is "in the face of" is first of all *"Being-in-the-world-itself,"* or the Being-there (*Dasein*) of the human being, so that nothing, even if there were a supposed threat, could justify its fear.[2] In an expansion of this begun in *Being and Time* (1927), then reconfirmed in the lecture "What Is Metaphysics?" (1929), what anxiety is "in the face of" not only afflicts individuals; it operates on the totality of beings so that "the world as such" becomes for them the site of their anxiety.[3] Not only is there "nothing which is ready-to-hand or present-at-hand," but there remains "nothing ready-to-hand within-the-world."[4] This reduction to nothing, then to *the Nothing*, makes the totality of beings in some way insignificant. "The nothing becomes manifest in and through anxiety,"[5] not in the Sartrean and "existentiell" sense of meaninglessness struggling with the absurd, but in the phenomenological and "existential" sense of the suspension of meaning.[6] Heidegger says "anxiety leaves us hanging, because it induces the slipping away of beings as a whole."[7] As Jean-Luc Marion adds, the immobile moment is "like a ship that, vertical at the moment of foundering, seems to freeze between sky and sea."[8]

The indefiniteness of that which causes anxiety and this reduction to the Nothing of all beings leads then, at the end of the process, to *isolating* the one who is anxious. Even more than fear, anxiety is isolating, not simply in the sense that drawing back before a given threat sometimes leads to failure in one's hope of sharing things with an other, but insofar as anxiety keeps one in an existential *"solus ipse"* [the self alone].[9] And in this existential *"solus ipse"* anxiety knows full well, independently of all experience, not to open up to an other—to an other also lost in the general shipwreck of the totality of beings. Such solitude brings *Dasein* "face to face with itself as Being-in-the-world."[10] It only fully plays its singularizing role, however, when it confronts death, as it does time and again. And that is death considered rather as "manner of living" than just "the end of life."

§33 The Strait Gate

What then of the anxiety and the anguish (*adêmonia*) that Christ lives through in Gethsemane: "And a sudden fear (*ekthambeisthai*) came over him, and great distress (*adêmonein*)" (Mark 14:33 JB)? According to Heidegger, citing St. Augustine, Luther, and Kierkegaard, metaphysical anxiety finds its place, not to mention its roots, in the theological field: "The phenomena of anxiety and fear . . . have come within the purview of Christian theology ontically and even (though within very narrow limits) ontologically."[11] Uniquely, within these very narrow limits—those probably of the narrow road (*angustia*) to Gethsemane—there is nothing artificial or excessive in the attempt that I consider theologically well-founded to describe here a *metaphysical experiment by God* in which he shares the extremes of human anxiety in the face of death.

As Dietrich Wiederkehr points out,[12] the dialogue of Jesus as he enters into his death is not simply *existentiell* (ontic); it also takes on an *existential* (ontologic) meaning for us. To die and be resurrected indeed not only exposes Christ to the meaninglessness of his existence in the face of the *reality* of his decease (as for a Sartre or a Camus), but also and above all leads him to question whether there is even a *possibility* of meaning when everything, including himself, plunges into an absence or suspension of meaning rather than into absolute meaninglessness. *Anxiety over finitude*—already distinguished from anxiety over sin and very precisely defined as a "structure that is specific to humankind," neither an accident of nature nor a consequence of sin—appears in an exemplary and paradigmatic fashion, in the agony of Christ at Gethsemane. The gospel narrative indicates above all that the agony is existenti*al*, and as we shall see, going *further than*

Heidegger, and even against him, this existential is only truly embodied when it is also incarnate in "flesh."[13]

§34 Anxiety over "Simply Death"

As I have tried to emphasize, anxiety and anguish (*adêmonia*) point in Greek to a state of deep distress and interior torment, to something that goes far beyond the reaction of recoil to something unexpected in alarm (*thambos*). We might ask once again whether Christ does not just recoil in *fear* when faced with death—though we must resign ourselves to being unable to define here the exact nature of the "Being-towards-the-end" of his existence (see §24: Resignation, Waiting, and Heroism).

Should we say rather that Christ enters progressively into an *anxiety* concerning his "being in the world as such," when nothing either on his part or on the part of his apostles could determine precisely the object of his anxiety? Certain theologians agree that we can recognize in the Gethsemane episode a solidarity between Christ and sinful humankind.[14] Others (or sometimes the same writers taking another perspective) identify the Son so closely with the problem of sin that they affirm, in a final *substitution* that relies upon a rereading of the poem of the Suffering Servant in Isaiah 53, how, in atoning for our sins, the Son does not simply die *for us*, but also dies *in our place*.[15]

These two perspectives (solidarity and substitution) are probably wrongly opposed to one another. Apart from the problem of deciding which is correct or sorting out the balance between them, we should ask what death is in question here, if it is not still and always that which is the consequence of sin. And, furthermore, what anxiety is in question, if it is not solely anxiety over sin? Once we detach biological death from its causal, but not symbolic, link with sin, could we not say that Christ would also for his part really have lived through anxiety when faced with "simply death [*mort tout court*]," not as an accident of Creation, or a product of the supposed Fall, but as the total and definitive assumption of human finitude given to us by God? Many questions arise here, as we have seen, which are not so much a denial of the reality of sin as a revelation of its true nature: sin as a (spiritual) self-confinement of humankind within a finitude that is not itself sinful.

§35 Indefiniteness (Putting off the Cup) and the Powerless Power of God

The onset of anxiety and of anguish (*adêmonia*) at Gethsemane comes above all for Christ—to take up again Heidegger's first identification of anxiety—within an *indefiniteness* concerning what his anxiety is "in the face of." That is, according to the gospel narrative, in the act of putting off "the cup," or in surrender to the fear of death. From "If it is possible (*si possibile est*), let this cup pass me by" (Matthew 26:39 JB), the Son moves in a metaphysical dialogue with his Father to "If this cup cannot pass by (*si non possibile est*) without my drinking it, your will be done" (Matthew 26:42 JB). In making such a crossing from positive to negative, the Son in a way surrenders and submits himself: "He sees himself already drinking," as Charles Péguy so rightly underlines for us.[16]

Precisely in such a surrender the Son rids himself of fear (*Furcht*) and enters into anxiety (*Angst*). Far from simply confirming the act of supreme obedience to the Father and of the divesting of the self, what this also shows, in the famous formula "not what I want, but what you want" (Mark 14:36) is first, and also in the most ordinary way, that the Son does not know— or better we might say, *no longer* knows—what he himself wants. Not, certainly, that he falls into some weakness or absence of will when faced with the imminence of his death—obviously not if one considers the force of his surrender—but, on the contrary, simply in that the cup as object of his will and reason for his fear (the cup that he begs to be taken away) "undoes" itself of its own accord. It is *un-done* (*dé-faite*) first of all in the way that a tangle in one's hair becomes sorted out. The cup ceases to concentrate in itself the that-about-which of fear and now gives meaning to him. Second, it is undone or defeated (*défaite*) as an army admits defeat. The cup can no more justify a victory of some kind over death in the sense that, through it, Christ would gain sway over his empire, even if that were negatively, through an act of retreat or of fear. The cup of the fear of death becomes progressively and almost instructively distanced from the Son as he implores for alleviation of what he is going through at Gethsemane. The surrender of his will to the Father opens up the kenotic (or self-emptying) route of the indefiniteness of his anxiety. For him, no longer knowing what *I* want becomes above all like accepting the indefiniteness of what an *Other* wants, if not for me, at least with me. The question of the meaning of life as measured by the yardstick of death then takes over positively here from a morbid and humiliating affirmation of the mean-inglessness (the non-sense) of life imposed simply in a perspective of death. In order that the Son give up his life in his death, without resigna-tion or certitude or heroism, will he not, himself, have to enter into a radi-cal questioning of the meaning of his own life? Is there still a "reason for living" at Gethsemane that would also be a "reason for dying"—as Camus phrases it, talking about the problem for all humankind, but thus also for the Son of Man?[17] Strangely, the total and radical absence of a reason for living and dying, at least in Christ's agony, is shown with great force in his cry of dereliction on Golgotha: *"Eloi, Eloi, lema sabachthani?,"* or "My God, my God, why have you forsaken me?" (Mark 15:34). Without going any further into the specific meaning of being forsaken here, we should note from the outset that it points to a failure for the Son himself, at least from the human point of view, in all attempts to give meaning to his own life. As Hans Urs von Balthasar says, taking up the medieval question of the *timor gehennalis* (fear of hell),[18] as applied to Christ, "Christ was not certain of his salvation by any other means than his prayer of supplication."[19] "It is accomplished [*telestai*]" (John 19:30 JB) are the final words of Christ on the cross given in John's Gospel. Does this not at first glance indicate "that is the end"—at least of his existence in this form, and of any heroic claim to some kind of trace of his life in his act of death?[20] He who "saved others" (Mark 15:31)—calming the storm, casting out demons, curing the sick, and restoring sight to the blind—becomes suddenly unable, as the priests and scribes at Calvary rightly state, to "save himself" (Mark 15:31). It is not just a drawing back from the cup as a simple fear of dying. Rather, the "Being-in-the-world" of the Son as such, which has shown at other times the *absolute power* of God, is caught here in agony between sky and earth, on the scaffold of the cross.

Contemporary Jewish theology faced with the Shoah—a replication for Christians at least of the cross, and quite simply of the scandalous and unjustifiable death of the innocent—finds an acknowledgment of the "powerlessness of God" at Auschwitz, a God who not simply does not wish to interfere, but could not.[21] This is a long way, it is true, from the Jewish theology of the "strong hand,"[22] or from Western theodicy,[23] which are sometimes unduly providentialist (i.e., trying to show God's will as evident in all events in the world). Surely the anxiety of the Son already opens up, as it were in advance, onto such powerlessness, onto the figure of a God so much given over to the hands of us humans that he needs them, if not so that he can exist, then at least so that he can reveal himself to them. Etty Hillesum writes in her war diary in the last days of suffering before her death, "I shall try to help you, God, to stop my strength ebbing away, though I cannot vouch for it in advance. But one thing is becoming increasingly clear to me: that You can't help us, that we must help You to help ourselves."[24] Would it be appropriate then in Christian theology, as in many recent reexaminations of the Jewish mysticism of Isaac Luria and his hypothesis of the withdrawal or "hiddenness" of God (*tzimtzum*), to give up on the notion of the absolute power of God?[25] We could certainly suggest this if we put God's power alongside simple psychological domination or pure metaphysical causality.

In a perspective that is strictly speaking Christian and specifically Trinitarian, however, the absolute power of the Father shows itself paradoxically all the more because his strength is manifest in weakness and his wisdom in foolishness (1 Cor 1:25 JB): "For God's foolishness is wiser than human wisdom, and God's weakness is stronger than human strength." Powerless absolute power, the divine *omnipotentia*, in fact maintains a real theological meaning even, and above all, in the depths of the silence of God—from the drama of Auschwitz to the hopelessness of Gethsemane and the agony of Golgotha. The "all-powerful" God of Christianity (*pantokrator*) is not, first, that which "dominates all" in Greek theology, as in Latin theology. It is he who has a hold on (*kratei*) or supports all things (*ta panta*). He is *omnitenens* (holding all things) rather than *omnipotens* (all powerful).[26] The mistranslation of the Hebrew term *El-Chaddaï* in French as the figure of an "All-Powerful" [*Tout-Puissant*] God has been quite rightly criticized,[27] but nothing indicates that we need necessarily bid farewell along with Hans Jonas to the "old theological categories" or the "traditional concept of God" to destroy forcefully all-powerfulness and enter into the problem of the truth of some kind of powerlessness.[28] Probably this would be to fail to recognize these categories themselves as well as the tradition they embody, at least as far as the Christian tradition and the narrative of Gethsemane that backs it up is concerned.

To say, for example, that "we cannot uphold the time-honoured (medieval) doctrine of absolute, unlimited divine power" simply because "omnipotence is a self-contradictory, self-destructive, indeed, senseless concept" is to forget precisely that this same medieval tradition takes great care to distinguish the absolute power of God,[29] which allows him to do everything (*potentia absoluta*), from the conditional power that in reality only authorizes him to do that which respects the order he has deliberately established or ordained in the world (*potentia ordinata*). To put this another way, we can start from a judicious comment by Hugh of Saint-Cher (c. 1200–1263) that is precursory in this respect: "God through his absolute power [*potentia absoluta*] could do everything himself . . . even as far as damning Peter and saving Judas," but, "in his ordained power [*potentia ordinata*], that which pertains to the conditions or to the laws with which God has clad things, and as long as these conditions subsist, God cannot contravene them—which he would have done if he had damned Peter and saved Judas."[30] Not even insofar as there is a law of redemption does the Father exempt his own Son from the most fundamental law of incarnation—

that is, from a taking on of flesh (*in carne*) by God in humankind that goes so far as to take on unsurpassable finitude. Might God in fact have been *able* to intervene for the inmates of Auschwitz when he *could* not intervene for his own Son at Gethsemane or on Golgotha? To say, along with Hans Jonas, not only that he did not want to, but that he could not, is not simply—and perhaps rather too easily—to acknowledge a pure and simple powerlessness in God, along the lines of some kind of genius divested of his strength by an originary and willed erasing of it.[31] It is first of all and more subtly to grant that this powerlessness itself, precisely when it is at its height as conditional power (*potentia ordinata*), consists in not breaking the rules that God himself has fixed and to which he then submits. Thus, when Hans Jonas insists that "the very existence of [something other than the possessor of that power] would already constitute a limitation" or a counter-power,[32] William of Auxerre (c. 1150–1231) has—as it were in advance—a response (and the whole of Christian theology in the Trinitarian tradition would go along with him). He says that "it is greater to be able to do something by oneself, and to *give to another* the power to do it, than it is to do that thing simply alone by oneself."[33]

The putting off of the cup by the Son at Gethsemane and the indefiniteness of his anxiety is not then a matter of developing "counter-powers" between God and humankind, or even in God himself, that would necessarily cancel each other out and be opposed one against another. They show, on the contrary, in some respect a Trinitarian *passibility* [i.e., capacity for feeling, especially for suffering] through which the "Being in the world" of the Son, solely as Son who is *all-powerful* in the image of his Father, actually comes to founder. From a desire of unconditional all-powerfulness (*potentia absoluta*), Christ passes progressively, and almost pedagogically by the route of his anxiety and of his anguish (*adêmonia*), to the recognition of another power, conditional this time (*potentia ordinata*), to which he must necessarily submit, even according to the law of his own incarnation and simply because he shares our human finitude. To expect of God, as Hans Jonas does, that he would show himself at Auschwitz, and to regret, at least negatively, that he did not do so, brings us back, as I see it, to the image of certain chief priests and scribes at the foot of Golgotha. On the one hand they desired unjustly that he "come down from the cross now, so that we may see and believe" (Mark 15:32), and on the other hand they falsely deduced, starting from this disappointment, that his true nature was never to descend from the cross, because then—that is to say at Golgotha as at Auschwitz—he did not descend, at least as we might have wanted or expected him to do. "You must say," the chief priests tell the soldiers, that "his disciples came by night and stole him away while we were asleep" (Matthew 28:13).

But the necessity for a renewal of theology, whether Jewish or Christian, should not occlude the riches of its past. While certainly God would plead for our help not to fade away in us (Etty Hillesum), rather than for it to be revealed that he does not exist, he nonetheless does not leave off being God *"all-powerful,"* since the full extremity of his power consists precisely in complying with an originary powerlessness. It is such powerlessness that remains always woven into human finitude, with its law of corruptibility to which God himself, right to the end and without ever disposing of it, consents.

Passing from absolute power (*potentia absoluta*) to conditional power (*potentia ordinata*) and not to impotence or powerlessness—such is the true turnaround that strictly speaking "sets in motion" the Son in his conviction that there is a Father who is *absolutely* omnipotent and that produces a kind of vertigo in him. When we put back into place the cup of the fear of death, the reasons for his withdrawal disappear. Rather than the imminence of death, his filial relation itself, or rather the absolute nature of the power on which it is based, seems—at least at first sight—to be set aside. But without this power, his anxiety is such that it *no longer knows* what it is anxious in the face of. The nothing of anxiety in the nontaking of the cup gives way then to *anxiety over Nothing*. This new anxiety is deeper or at the same time more authoritative, since it exposes the meaning or the meaninglessness (the power and the powerlessness) of a life. The entry into kenosis (i.e., the progressive emptiness of the Son) confronted by the meaning or meaninglessness of his own life marks then precisely this passage from the nothing of anxiety to anxiety over Nothing. And it is appropriate once more that the Son, carrying with himself that humanity that is also ours, right to the end, in some way loses his footing [as in Heidegger's terms one "loses his head" faced with fear].[34] He verifies, and verifies for us, that any ground on which to rest will only find its true base in God the Father and never in humankind. "The receding of beings as a whole, closing in on us in anxiety, oppresses us," Heidegger says. "We can get no hold on things (*Es bliebt kein Halt*). In the slipping away of beings only this 'no hold on things' comes over us and remains."[35]

§36 Reduction to Nothing and Kenosis

The entry of the Son *into Nothing*—the second characteristic of anxiety—is confirmed in the freely undertaken kenotic act of the Son, according to the hymn of praise in Paul's Letter to the Philippians:

His state was divine . . .
[He] emptied himself [*ekênosen*]
to assume the condition of a slave,
and became as men are . . .
he was humbler yet [*etapeinôsen*]
even to accepting death,
death on a cross.

(Phil 2:6–8 JB)

If the Son himself, in the grip of his anxiety and renouncing his fear, "can get no hold on things," the *emptiness* or *Nothing of the kenosis* does not point to a loss of his filial relation as such (it will be, as we shall see, maintained at all costs); it is rather the end of the manifestation of his terrestrial all-powerfulness.[36] Without giving up on a close relationship with the Father and even at the heart of that unfailing intimacy, the whole of creation of the "totality of beings," taken up by the Word incarnate, finds itself carried along into this vast movement of kenosis and, according to St. Paul, "subject to vanity" (Rom 8:20 AV). As soon as he to whom the world was so much bound in his project of salvation renounces, along with his Father, the exercise of unconditional all-powerfulness (*potentia absoluta*), the whole of creation comes to submit for always along with him, although not necessarily in the way he does (who will come himself to teach it to the Father), to the conditional and ordained law (*potentia ordinata*) of finitude and of corruptibility. What anxiety plunges into nothing is no longer just the "Being-in-the-world" of the Son, who would not wish the world to remain as it was at the peak of unconditional all-powerfulness. It is "the world as such" in that impossible Christly capacity by which he, *himself*, gives it meaning. The created world seems "reduced to Nothing," since in the general shipwreck of beings it no longer means anything. The Son *holds no responsibility* for his own death, as it is precisely by his death (in which he obeys his Father according to the laws of incarnation and not simply the laws of redemption) that he enters into *the Nothing* of the meaning of life. In this absence of meaning, more an interrogation than an affirmation of meaninglessness, as Jean-Luc Marion says, "Vanity marks the world with indifference."[37] At the extreme limits of the kenosis of the Son and of the totality of the created world with him, what is revealed is the true and implacable meaning of Heidegger's "existential 'solipsism,'" or isolation.

§37 The Isolation of Humankind and Communion with the Father

I follow Heidegger in suggesting that the final characteristic of anxiety is, unlike fear, that it *isolates*. The way in which the disciples fall asleep three times at Gethsemane already marked out a failure as far as the sharing of fear is concerned. But we move from the loneliness of alarm (*thambos*) to the real solitude of anxiety and anguish (*adêmoneo*), from the failure in communication with the apostles to the acceptance of singularity by the Son. *Adêmonein* (Mark 14:33), according to Balthasar, indicates precisely "the horror which isolates" as a loss of all ties and attachments.[38] Rather than the fear of death, entry into such isolation constitutes in itself the true combat of Gethsemane. Christ's return three times to the sleeping disciples has no other aim than somehow to cross over this threshold.[39] But by the last time the victory has in fact been achieved: "You can sleep on now and take your rest. *It is all over*" (Mark 14:41 JB). What is it that is now over? Monique Rosaz and Édouard Pousset suggest, "It has to be that sleeping has changed its significance, so that Jesus says to the disciples 'you can sleep on now.'"[40] What is over (or done) in this indefatigable coming and going from the disciples to the Father is above all the entry by the Son himself into a total acceptance of the existential *solus ipse* of his own anxiety. It is the loneliness of an action when only he who undertakes it can really bear the load. Many contemporary theologians, most prominently Jürgen Moltmann, go so far as to connect this first relinquishing or abandoning of God by Christ the man at Gethsemane with a second abandonment, Trinitarian this time, of God (the Son), by God (the Father), on Golgotha. They thus interpret in a literal way "My God, my God, why have you deserted [*abandonné*] me?" (Mark 15:34 JB).[41] From such a perspective, Christ's isolation in his anxiety becomes extreme, more extreme even than any other human solitude lived through by those in communion with God. Moltmann says, "Jesus suffered and died alone. But those who follow him suffer and die in fellowship with him."[42]

But was it necessary for the Son to be relieved of his duties in this way and separated from the Father so that he might take on the solitude of his anxiety to its full extent? Must we, like Rilke in his poem "The Olive Garden," indeed, like Moltmann, think that the Son blames the Father for his abandonment, going so far as to repudiate him and deny him to himself?[43] I do not think so. The gospel texts themselves resist such an interpretation. At the heart of the many appeals of Christ to God, in fact, the Father does not cease to be there for his Son, but on the contrary becomes even more so: above all when he cries out to *his* God—that is to say to the God of the Son—in his words, *"My God, my God, why have you deserted me?"* (Mark 15:34 JB); and again in the appeal to *"Abba,* Father" (Mark 14:36)—to whom the Son begs that he "remove this cup." The term *Abba* in Aramaic indicates first of all the father of the one who speaks.[44] We see this also in the last words of Christ on the cross: "Father, into your hands I commend my spirit" (Luke 23:46). At Gethsemane and at Golgotha, God "is teaching himself, himself as man," as Charles Péguy so finely expresses it. The "'Our Father' (*Pater noster*) of the Sermon on the Mount becomes on this occasion '*My* Father'(*Pater mi*)."[45] However seductive the hypothesis of a double abandonment of the Son, first by humankind and then by God, may be, as far as I can see, it simply does not work (even if it would greatly simplify matters) as a way of resolving the problem of "existential 'solipsism'"[46] lived through in his anxiety at Gethsemane and on the cross.[47] That does not, however, mean that Christ did not live through extreme solitude; rather the contrary. It is just that such solitude had above all and uniquely to contain the transition from the unbreakable link of the Son and the Father, to what Eugen Drewermann calls the "widening gulf between Jesus and his humanity."[48] It is *not the Son* who loses his Father in doubting God, but *the man* who loses himself in Jesus in separating himself from God. We do not have to interpret the cry of dereliction made by Jesus on the cross as a sign of distress of the man in a death where God no longer replies to him and would be eliminated because of his absence. On the contrary, as Gustave Martelet says, this cry can be understood as "a lament made to be heard by God and answered in the Resurrection."[49] How far will humankind go in their rejection of God as he is in Jesus? That is the true question concerning Christ's agony. It is not "How far will God go in abandoning his Son?" (as though the debate no longer concerned humankind, and we were simply to make the Son into an expiatory sacrifice for the Father). "All that counts," Eugen Drewermann maintains, in what has now become classic theology, "is to remain human. But how can that be done if we have not encountered the kind of humanity that allows us to remain anchored in the truth?"[50]

§38 Of Anxiety Endured on the Horizon of Death

At the heart of this embedding of God in man, Christ in reality cannot and must not respond to the modalities simply of his own decease (resignation in the face of disappearance, certainty of the Resurrection, and heroism in his accomplishments). Precisely because neither he nor his disciples saw a justification for his end and saw no meaning in what appeared to be the meaninglessness of a disavowal of absolute power, it was appropriate that those close to him would set up a blank refusal of any possible sharing of his fear or his alarm (*thambos*) in the face of the cup that would come to him. His entry into anxiety and anguish (*adêmoneo*) thus opens an ineluctable, and in terms of the Trinity and of God a kenotic emptiness, or a plunge into the Nothing, where the surrender of glory by the Son to the Father, more than the filial relation itself, allows certain characteristics to emerge. As far as the anxiety at Gethsemane is concerned, we see *indefiniteness over what it is in the face of* ("not what I want but what you want" [Mark 14:36]). We see a questioning of the meaning of the power of God in the act of pushing back, in a negative sense, the cup of his decease, to his Father (Matthew 26:42). We see an *entry into the nothing of kenosis*, going so far as to renounce even that power (Phil 2:6–8), and a dragging down in the same movement and into the same shipwreck, of the whole creation subject to futility (Rom 8:20). We see the *isolation and extreme solitude* of the Son, not so much in an abandonment of the Son by the Father (who is always named as such) (Mark 14:34), but rather in the rejection of God in the form of Jesus by humans because of his powerlessness (Mark 14:41). The *fear of his decease*—a drawing back when confronted with the Being-towards-the-end of life—yields place to *anxiety over death* as a way of living life within the unavoidable horizon of the possibility even of its own impossibility. What is this *death* then for Christ himself—a death in which he sinks into his own anxiety? Is it not possible for him, unlike in his moment of fear faced with the cup, to stick to it? Or even to back away from it?

8

Death and Its Possibilities

§39 Manner of Living, Possibility of the Impossibility, and Death as "Mineness"

Notwithstanding that it is a further division into three (which only indicates in reality his exacting examination of the concept), Heidegger also reckons the modalities of death as tripartite—that is, "death" as distinguished from "decease."

(a) Rather than just the end of life, death points above all to a *manner of living*, a "way to be, which Dasein takes over as soon as it is." "As soon as man comes to life [as the poet says], he is at once old enough to die."[1] The "Being-at-an-end" [*Zu-Ende-Sein*] of decease gives place, in a metaphysical slippage toward anxiety, to the "Being-towards-the-end" [*Sein zum Ende*] of death. Death designates a current [*actuelle*] *possibility* of my being as a manner of living, which all the more distances it from the future *actuality* of the event. Humankind in the prospect of death does not simply see itself as *finished*, as we might casually talk of someone who has fallen before the enemy, or been disarmed, as being "finished" ("I'm done for: I'm finished"). We appear to ourselves, on the contrary, as beings that are finishing or dying in the future (*sum moribundus* [I am in dying]).[2] It is the unfinished state that paradoxically and positively opens up onto a whole set of possibilities as long as life is not yet ended.[3] To exist for the human is no longer to live life with the morbid and mortifying perspective of death; on the contrary, it is to come out of the self (*ek-sister*),[4] to open up, like a ripening fruit, onto the "not-yet" (*ne-pas-encore*) that it is up to us to become for ourselves.[5] Humankind only lives, as we might ordinarily say, because we are dying—and not dead. "Death, in the widest sense, is a phenomenon of life."[6] At the heart of this expectation, of this *surplus*, or *not-yet*, the possibilities of life only find meaning in their necessary confrontation with the ultimate possibility of our death.[7]

(b) With its imminence, which has nothing to do with unexpected ontic occurrences such as a "storm" (overflowing), or the "remodeling of the house" (metamorphosis), or the "arrival of a friend" (expectation),[8] death no longer designates solely a pure and simple possibility among many other possibilities of existence. On the contrary, it indicates ontologically a *possibility*, the only possibility that has for its principal characteristic that it can cancel out all other possibilities, in canceling the human being for whom all remains possible as long as this ultimate possibility has not yet happened. For Heidegger, "death is the possibility of no-longer-being-able-to-be-there. . . . Death is the possibility of the absolute impossibility of Dasein."[9] We can put this in Emmanuel Levinas's terms, leaving aside Heidegger's technical language (though such language is also often necessary). Death is then defined as "the impossibility of having a project,"[10] an impossibility in which, however, all the other possibilities of my being remain still suspended.

(c) Because this "possibility of impossibility" remains at the same time always "*mine*," as I have already stressed, "*no one can take the Other's dying away from him*."[11] The "mineness" of my death (*Jemanigkeit*) is disclosed, in the final analysis, as the possibility that is at once *my own*, most *absolute*, and most unsurpassable ("not to be outstripped") of my Being-there (*Dasein*). Always mine, death as the horizon of my existence shows above all what belongs to me (what is mine) in my "*ownmost* potentiality-for-Being."[12] In the light of the permanent possibility of impossibility for my being, I show myself to myself in my manner of living and organizing such an impossible possibility. The possibility most specific to me becomes then *ab-solute* insofar as, separating me etymologically from all relations with the Other in singularizing me (*ab-solutus*), it demands that I accept my death "authentically," that is to say, starting from myself and solely from myself. And if I get ahead of it, it is not, in the sense that, as in suicide, I take the initiative to try to hurry on its moment. On the contrary, getting ahead of it, I recognize solely that I neither can nor should live, in an imaginative fiction, beyond the horizon of a death whose certitude alone demands that meaning is attributed to it. The horizon of my death, which is the most specific and uttermost possibility, appears finally as *unsurpass-*

able. It is unsurpassable ("not to be outstripped") not simply in the sense that it is ineluctable, but to the extent that making me free for it can also mean getting ahead of it, even so far as to sacrifice myself (*Selbstaufgabe*). In such a sacrifice, which suicide in reality imitates like a perverse carica-ture, the free gift of a life represents what Heidegger calls "an authentic potentiality-for-Being-a-whole."[13]

The characteristics that I would stress here of this ultimate "possibility of the . . . impossibility" of my being that is my death,[14] for me, are: first, an "ownmost" possibility that shows what is mine; second, an "absolute" possibility that measures me in my capacity to take it on in relation to myself; and third, an unsurpassable ("not to be outstripped") possibility that renders possible anticipating it through the free sacrifice of the self. What this means is that I am sent back in reality, more and more, to a *way of living or of existing* in a world of possibilities, rather than just to a final event, definitive and actual, of the end of life.[15] What then is the situation that Christ faces with his own death—no longer simply plunged into the nothing of anxiety, but now also open to the *possibilities* that they release?

§40 Being Vigilant at Gethsemane

From the moment of the handing over, in a certain sense negatively, of the "fear of decease" or the cup of the Father ("Not what I want, but what you want" [Mark 14:36]), the death of the Son represents not so much a Being-at-an-end as the particular modality of his existence. And this is the pri-mary characteristic of "death," relative here to the act of "decease." On the eve of his Passion, and thus just as the ascent toward Jerusalem begins, Jesus refuses to reply to the question of *when* the downfall of Jerusalem and the destruction of the Temple will take place: "Tell us, when [*pote*] will this be, and what will be the sign that all these things are about to be accomplished [*sunteleisthai panta*]?" (Mark 13:4). To this question "when" of the eschatological end (*telos*), elucidated for us at present only in the light of the Epistles of St. Paul, not only does Jesus not reply, but he seems not to know himself: "But about that day or hour no one knows, neither the angels in heaven, *nor the Son*, but only the Father" (Mark 13:32). He then adds his own *comment*: "Jesus began to say to them, 'Be-ware that no one leads you astray'" (Mark 13:5—taken up again in 13:33). The Heideggerian hypothesis of an authentic Christian experience of re-maining always "awake and sober" because of a future that is not simply to come, but possible at any moment (see Chapter 6), would be confirmed then rather by an eschatological reading of the Epistles of St. Paul than by a phenomenological deciphering of the going up to Jerusalem described in the gospels.

But the authentic Christian experience of "Being-always-vigilant" marks exactly the exemplary experience of Jesus himself at Gethsemane: "Keep awake and pray that you may not come into the time of trial. . . . And again he went away and prayed" (Mark 14:38–39). The being always awake points not simply to the modality of the Christian at the Day of Judgment, but also and above all to that of most ordinary beings at every moment of life, in that the Son opens up the way for us, having been through this way himself at Gethsemane. As we have seen, never mind whether he is hanging on the cross, there is not (or is no longer) a Being-towards-the-end for Christ—at least not in the sense of "I am finished," coming from someone on a scaffold condemned to death.[16] The dying Christ, along with the believers who follow him, sees death as a *way of living* or a "form of existing." They are always already "old enough to die" once they "[come] to life," according to the implacable law of finitude—or old enough to be reborn once they enter the water of baptism in the hope of redemption from sin. Death then is all the more exemplary in that it raises the believer to what is quintessentially Christian: continuing to be "vigilant" in an unflagging relation with the Father. Remaining vigilant despite the fact that, not simply the world in general but even those closest to us, in the absolute void all around, sleep and doubt. In the same way, then, that the Son opens up to the Father, never ceasing to name him as such, even when his sense of abandonment is at its strongest, so the Christian *ek-sistence* formulates precisely a leaving of the self to go toward the Father as a modality of life envisaged within the horizon of death.[17] At the heart of this *ek-stase* and precisely by *ek-stasis*,[18] the Son gauges, for himself also, the amplitude of the final possibility of his death: that is, the absence of an *a priori* validity of the "Being-there" of his life confronted with death (the impossibility of having a project), and the nonassurance that there is a survival, or a more-than-life [a *sur-vie*] after death, (death viewed "together with its interpretation of 'life'").

§41 From the Actuality of the Corpse to Possibilities for the Living

On the way to accomplishing what he has to do, but not yet dead, Christ dying, or simply living because life is only a postponement of death, measures out the whole of his life within the horizon of his death. The ultimate "possibility of the pure and absolute impossibility of Dasein [Being-there]"[19]—second characteristic of death (§39)—opens up to Christ as it does to the Christian, positively this time, a whole set of things *possible* whose very impossibility now necessitates that they are given meaning. Jesus says to the disciple who, in Luke's Gospel, lingers after the decease of his father rather than following him immediately: "Let the dead [*nekrous*] bury their own dead; but as for you, go and proclaim the kingdom of God" (Luke 9:60). Such "deaths" (*nekroï*) point to the many "spiritual deaths" of those who will not come to find the life of the Kingdom, but before that they point above all in Greek at those who are actually dead from biological death—from the death of all the world: corpses. We might ask whether the implication of the reply by Jesus to the grieving son in this episode is that he should no longer take any notice of his own father's corpse. The obviousness of a negative response to that question should not, however, hide from us what is at stake here. Once more it is Heidegger who underlines that one cannot in fact treat the "deceased" either as a "mere corporeal thing" remaining there (*vorhanden*), nor simply as an inanimate corpse, just "an item of equipment, environmentally ready-to-hand" (*zuhanden*).[20] If death shows itself as a loss, it is above all "a loss such as is experienced by those who remain."[21] In this ordeal, it is those who remain who have priority, and only they who have to live through it. Roger Munier points out, "Death is not a pulling up or uprooting; it is not we who depart, it is those left over who remain."[22] Jesus does not insist to the grieving son that he should not feel or suffer, or that the rituals associated with death should not take place. The narrative of the death of Lazarus, if we consider it solely in the perspective of the care accorded to the corpse, would seem to confirm this. We find that Jesus himself, in fact, lingers and weeps over the tomb of his friend (John 11:34–36), and he bends down over the mummified corpse that is "ready-to-hand" (*zuhanden*)—that has already received all the usual treatment of the dead—"hands and feet bound with strips of cloth, and his face wrapped in a cloth" (John 11:44). He bends down over the body remaining there (*vorhanden*), which already has a "stench" because "he has been dead four days" (John 11:39). Far from a meaningless abandonment of the dead to themselves, then, the imperative to "let the dead bury their own dead" seems only to suggest leaving the actuality of one's own death (exemplified by the death of an other) to evaluate all the possibilities in one's life that are opened up, starting from that ultimate fact, "*the possibility*" of a future when there will be for me "*the impossibility of any existence at all.*"[23]

Neither Montaigne's "let us presently ruminate and say with our selves, what if it were death it selfe?,"[24] nor even the theological assumption of a final possibility in some form of redemptive grace (anxiety over sin but not over finitude), can manage, at least in the first instance, to maintain an openness. The *ars moriendi* (art of dying) of the Middle Ages above all—as a reflection of the possibility, the moment, and the manner in which my decease could be realized—lack the sense of my death as pure and simple possibility that there will be a future impossibility of my "Being-there," since these arts are concerned with the conditions of the realization of death rather than with questions operating upon it.[25] As for the theological notion, rationally based, of a "second birth" in the death and Resurrection of Christ, it necessarily produces, in addition, what Heidegger calls an "ontical assertion about the 'corruption of human nature'"[26] that, as I have already tried to show, through a distinction between anxiety over finitude (§8) from anxiety over sin (§15), necessarily escapes inquiry that is primarily existential-ontological.[27] There remains then, even at the heart of the tradition of Ignatius of Loyola, as in that of other great mystics (in particular St. Theresa of Ávila and St. John of the Cross), a specific usage of death. Death is used in setting up rules of choice, or discriminations, concerning its actual possibility. They open up, starting off from death and considering the ultimatum of a future impossibility that it poses to us, the sum of all the moments of our life: "I will consider, *as if* I were at the point of death," Ignatius of Loyola writes in his *Spiritual Exercises*, formulating a *rule* on making "a sound and good election," or choice. He considers that "procedure and norm I will at that time wish I had used in the present election. Then, guiding myself by the norm, I should make my decision on the whole matter."[28]

The imminence of one's death is not the point here. As we have already seen (§39), there may be ontic occurrences causing it, such as "a storm," the "remodeling of the house," or the "arrival of a friend." But death is not simply flooding, nor pure metamorphosis, nor impatient expectation: death in reality does not "live on" (*ne survient pas*)—in the sense of being the sole end of life (a decease). Or better, we might say, it only lives on, as actual possibility of my Being-there, insofar as it *organizes my more-than-life* (*survie*).[29] All my projects still hang upon the ultimate "impossibility of having a project." Death imposes a seal under which each of us shall necessarily be measured in a final and unsurpassable way. To make a "sound and good" choice "in this life" demands that I project retroactively the possibility of my death over the present in my life that it opens for me. And in this way the "not yet" or the "surplus" [*excédent*] that remains for me to live through and that makes my life guides, orients, and reveals my "*own-most* potentiality-for-Being."[30]

§42 The Death That Is Always His: Suffering in God; The Gift of His Life and Refusal of Mastery

I have already suggested, disagreeing here with Moltmann (§37), that the solitude of the man and not of God in Christ is all the greater in that the communion of Son with the Father is so strong. Death *isolates* Christ from all other human beings, so that he rejoins the depths of humanity that is in him. In its ultimate and last characteristic (§39) death remains, for him also, *always his* and *what singularizes him*. Through death the Word opens up toward his ownmost Being in the world, *remaining the Son*, "professionally Son," precisely and paradoxically to the bitter end of his anxiety. Charles Péguy writes, "Making this prayer as a man [which is addressed to 'my' Father] suddenly one does not know whether he may not be speaking all at once, very specially, particularly, almost professionally, as it were technically, as it were the Son of God."[31] It was convincingly put in the formula of the Scythian monks, and later taken up at the Second Council of Constantinople (533), that it is not simply the Son, as Son, but "one of the Trinity has suffered, or rather was passible [capable of feeling, especially suffering], in his flesh."[32] The "professionalism" of the Son *in his suffering* communicates to the "professionalism" of the Father *in his accompaniment* of the Son in this suffering. Thus we find the very relevant and finally "traditional" distinction, made by Moltmann, with which this time I am in agreement, between the suffering of the Son and the suffering of the Father: "The Son suffers dying [*erleidet das Sterben*], the Father suffers the death [*den Tod*] of the Son."[33]

Who, in fact, analogically and humanly speaking, puts up with the greatest suffering, the Son who dies or the Father who suffers from his death? Both Catholic and Protestant theology today, far from having a perspective on atonement that sees a Son heroically satisfying the wrath of a vengeful Father, have rediscovered the importance of the great tradition, stemming from Origen, that "the Father himself is not impassible [i.e., is not incapable of suffering]."[34] This is a formula that does not, however, signify, like certain excessively radical theologies on the Death of God, that the Father himself would have died with the Son. On the contrary, he suffers all the more from the death of the Son, since *he himself* does not die. And this is precisely because the Son dies in a profound communion with the Father that is at the furthest point from an abandonment of humankind, so that the death of the Son cannot be identified with the death of the paternal being of the Father.[35] The paternity of the Father and the filial nature of the Son's relationship with him in a way define and protect (all the better to sustain) what remains in a minor way of the now distant abandoning by the Son *of* his Father (Abba, Father) and not of the Son *by* his Father. At the risk, however, that we never get away from the pure and simple fact of the event of the death, we can say further that the "death" of the Son does not indicate—or not simply—some kind of thing (*quid*) or somebody (*quis*) that dies. Rather than just the existential annihilation of the Son, and with him of the paternal being of the Father, the crucifixion points to the existential form of being of the Son as a son. He is a son who, right up to his death, never ceases to address his Father: "Father, into your hands I commend my spirit" (Luke 23:46). The death of Christ is thus not simply "his death"; it brings into the light "his own self." Through it is disclosed his "ownmost" being in the world, which goes, within the contours of Mark's Gospel, from "Jesus Christ" to "the Son of God" (Mark 1:1). This will be the sense of the avowal of the centurion at the foot of Christ's cross, in the first human words to break the opaque silence at the death of the Son in his communion with the Father: "Truly this man was God's Son!" (Mark 15:39).

It is the "ownmost" possibility of the Son that characterizes him in his singularity and contributes also to his "absolute" possibility. (§39). His death is his own, as I have underlined, insofar as it reveals what is his own—that is to say, his divine filiation. But we might say that the Son of God, in his quality as Son, is he who neither can nor should die: "No one takes it [my life] from me, but I lay it down [*tithêmi*] of my own accord" (John 10:18). His death is *absolute* at least to the extent that it isolates him, defining him precisely in his being as Son of God. It is this *ab-soluteness* that requires him to take on his death somehow *authentically*, taking it upon himself, starting solely from himself. The gift of the life of Christ is proclaimed in the gospels when his death is still not imminent, or, we might say, when death paradoxically threatens the beneficiaries of life (the sheep) rather than the donor himself (the good shepherd). Only he, whose place was precisely not to die ("No one takes it [my life] from me"), imposes upon himself that firm decision to go to the bitter end with the gift of his life, to go as far as his death ("I lay it down of my own accord" [John 10:11–18]). We can say that this "resoluteness" [*Entschlossenheit*] of Christ, following here to some degree (but to some degree only) Heidegger's view, does not point to "a quality of 'judgement' nor of any definite way of behaving, but something essentially constitutive for Being-in-the-world as such [for *his* being in the world?]."[36] And we might describe that "something essentially constitutive" as the offering of his life through his death, not simply as reparation for our iniquities but also, and above all, as submission to the ineluctable law of the corruptibility of all living things. In the same way as death shows us a way of living rather than the end of existence, the gift of himself by Christ shows us the modality of being in all his life rather than a final and heroic act of his death. To lay down or to give [*tithêmi*] and not to take or take from [*airô*]: to "divest oneself by oneself" and not "to be divested by another": that is what for the Christian shows the "truth of Dasein which is most primordial because it is *authentic.*"[37] And that truth is above all the truth of the Word, made flesh through and through in his pilgrimage on earth.

The death of the Son as "ownmost" possibility, in his filiation with the Father, and as "absolute" in his gift, appears then (along the lines of the third Heideggerian characteristic of death, as "possibility of the absolute impossibility") to be "unsurpassable" as a free sacrifice (§39). It would seem appropriate here to hope for a new deployment of a true theology of this deliberate or intentional consent on the part of Christ, something very distant from the simple emphasis on the historical inevitability of his death that we find in so many modern and contemporary perspectives, from Renan to Jacques Duquesne.[38] In deliberately accepting the extreme possibility of sacrifice of himself (*Selbstaufgabe*), Christ in effect "anticipates" his own death, making his consent (a consent that theology has chosen to see as obedience or submission to the Father) into the personal modality of his life. But this very celebrated obedience of the Son until death, and "to the point of death—even death on a cross" (Phil 2:8), is not simply a matter of an ordeal followed by redemption, though such a view has been at the heart of a certain Pauline theology of sacrifice. It is above all, in a more commonplace and perhaps more exemplary way, the sacrifice of the flesh and of the incarnation. As the author of the Epistle to the Hebrews puts it, "Sacrifices and offerings you have not desired, but a body [*sôma*] you have prepared for me" (Heb 10:5).[39] It was not enough, then, in Tertullian's impressive phrase, that Christ "carried the cross (*crucem gestare*)";[40] it was also necessary for him to carry the flesh (*carnem gestare*). Further, and so as not to dissolve away the corporate nature of the incarnation simply by citing the exemplary nature of the redemption, I would emphasize that it is because, as Tertullian says, Christ "came in the flesh, and by the process of human birth,"[41] that he accepts "tasting death, and . . . rising again from the dead."[42] His flesh that is born will also at once be a flesh to die, indeed to be resurrected, so that it does not neglect (as we shall see in Chapter 11, and here I disagree with Heidegger) to incarnate the lived experience of anxiety even in flesh. It is only flesh that is capable of expressing anxiety in all its radicality.

The "sacrifice of the self" of Christ (*Selbstaufgabe*) when it is "carried" in this way, indeed given birth to (*gestare*), in flesh that will show the sacrifice, cannot go any further in indicating some kind of "possibility of

existing as a *whole potentiality-for-Being*."[43] Here, precisely and definitively, the Heideggerian route, with its perspective of anxiety seen solely
through a *consciousness* of the horizon of death, diverges from the other
route, specifically Christian this time, which sees an *incarnation* of lived
experience that is existential and includes the insuperable characteristics
of the flesh that *carries* it. The body experiencing anxiety in fact always
suffers it as a burden, rather than being able to master it, or get the better
of it.

Like a woman giving birth—to return afresh to the biblical notion of
anxiety—Christ accepts his death, even as far as the ultimate possibility
of a sacrifice of the self, less to rise above it than to offer himself and abandon himself to it. A specifically Christian liberty has in fact the paradoxical aspect that it deliberately renounces any Promethean-style direct
confrontation of the human and death. No trace of independence, or of
self-mastery, or of absolute "potentiality-for-Being" is found in the liberty
of the gospels. On the contrary, there is simply the recognition of a bond
of free dependence on the Holy Spirit and of filiation with the Father: "For
you did not receive a spirit of slavery to fall back into fear, but you have
received a spirit of adoption. When we cry 'Abba! Father!' it is that very
Spirit" (Rom 8:15). This refusal of "supreme lucidity" or "supreme virility"
in Christianity, as in Judaism,[44] definitively rejects the post-Nietzschean
perspective, presented also in *Being and Time*, of those who are above all
masters of their own death.[45] Paradoxically, when *Being and Time* takes
up the subject, making as if to lead us toward a relinquishment of the self
to let the face of death emerge passively, it *concludes* actively as I see it—in
the double sense of rushing forward and of overshooting the mark—with
a face-to-face where only the total assumption of the self by the self would
necessarily pronounce the last word.[46]

§43 The Flesh Forgotten

Plunging, then, gradually into the anxiety of Gethsemane, Christ on the
ascent to Jerusalem and Golgotha envisages his death successively as a *way*
of living his life and no longer as the end of life. He substitutes thereafter
a "*how* is it possible to remain always vigilant?" for the "*when*" of the final
Parousia, or Second Coming. In the "*possibility* of the absolute impossibility of Dasein,"[47] he converts the problem of the corpse (Lazarus, or the
son in mourning), into a call to give one's life ("Get up" and go to "proclaim the good news to the whole creation" [Mark 14:42; 16:15]). As a
possibility that is solely his, or "his own," he takes on, first, what is "ownmost" to him as Son of God, who does not ever break off his relationship

with his Father ("Abba! Father!"). Second, he assumes this possibility as what is most *absolute* to him, what singles him out as the shepherd of his sheep in a life that nobody can "take" from him (*airô*), and only he can lay down or give (*tithêmi*). Finally, in what is a radical and unsurpassable step, he anticipates his own sacrifice in giving total consent to his Father, crying out (as we also, adoptive children, cry out), "*Abba*! Father!"

But neither before nor after this taking on of what are in effect the Heideggerian characteristics of death, and as it were to turn his back on them, does the Son ever try to overcome or defy his own death through an act of will (which would, as I see it, have been doomed to failure), or by an act of "supreme lucidity" or one of "supreme virility." Putting aside all theological considerations, the roots of such Promethean ambitions, which attempt to go beyond death and fully to take it on, lie probably, as I have already suggested, in Heidegger's neglect of the flesh or of bodiliness in general. But is it not characteristic of anxiety—as it often becomes physical suffering—that it is inscribed in the flesh, where precisely and necessarily all overcoming of the self by the self remains fundamentally impossible? Unlike the notion of an absolute power that, according to Heidegger, ignores the body itself, the gospel narrative knows better and brings to light the dictates of an *incarnation of the anxiety (or anguish) of the Son in his flesh*. "In his anguish he prayed more earnestly, and his sweat became great drops of blood falling down on the ground" (Luke 22:44).

PART **III**

The Body-to-Body of Suffering and Death

§44 Disappropriation and Incarnation

Since Christ knowingly and definitively takes on all the characteristics of anxiety and death, we cannot any more maintain, along with Heidegger, that because Christians have "always already viewed death together with its interpretation of 'life,'"[1] the Christian does not truly experience anxiety over death. A simple phenomenological reading, or rereading, of Gethsemane is enough to provide evidence to the contrary. All the same, we might want to ask *who* exactly it is that, when "a sudden fear [*ekthambestai*] came over him, and great distress [*adêmonein*]," was "sorrowful to the point of death [*eôs thanatou*]" (Mark 14:33–35 JB). The many factors that lie behind Christ's anxiety, even if it is his and specific to him, are still not enough to establish the full extent of his singularity. Christ, on the one hand, as we have seen (§43), on the horizon of his death as well as in the anxiety over his finitude, declines to accept a *"whole potentiality-for-Being,"* "supreme lucidity," and "supreme virility." He cannot then take credit (uncover his ownmost) by taking credit for his own death (making it his own). What is specific to him, as we shall see (§49), comes back on the contrary to a disappropriating—not because the event is inappropriate for him, as we have seen (§40–42), but simply in that it is not appropriate that he should, in himself, carry *alone*, humanly and definitively, the burden of his death in an existential and unbreakable solipsism. On the other hand, the Son, albeit he is always the Son of the Father and "professionally

69

Son" (§42), does not cease to take his anxiety to its furthest extent in making it incarnate in his flesh. Where the Heideggerian formula fails in some way to implant the anxiety "in the flesh," Christ on the contrary puts into action his assumption of the flesh—in Charles Péguy's term, "*encharnement.*"[2] He does this at Gethsemane as at Golgotha, undergoing it in the extreme in the fleshly body-to-body of his Passion (*patior*). The Being-there of Christ cannot then just be restricted to the perspective of finitude, however unsurpassable that might be, and however much it might be a specifically human manner of existing. It was still necessary for him to experience this limit of finitude in his flesh and psychologically to bear the burden of it. If in fact *Dasein* (Being-there) is separated too far from the mode of being of objects that are "ready-to-hand," available (*zuhanden*), or of beings that are "present-at-hand," extant (*vorhanden*),[3] if it has, as Didier Franck suggests, strictly speaking "no hands,"[4] then it is difficult to see how philosophically it could *incarnate* the feeling of anxiety and still less how, theologically this time, it would be *resurrected* in the flesh. "To give hands" to the Being-there of Christ who is neither "ready-to-hand" for his adversaries (the guards, for example, trying to seize him), nor "present-at-hand" for his disciples (Thomas the apostle wanting to touch him or Mary Magdalene at the tomb recognizing him), is in a way, as we shall see, to allow him to carry through his incarnation to its endpoint, in a Resurrection of a body that is "imperishable" (1 Cor 15:42). Neither the heroic appropriation of the Being-there of a Christ enclosed in the existential solipsism of his own death nor an ontological account of anxiety that neglects the flesh of the one who suffers is adequate to describe the specificity of Christ. He alone, without any exaltation or pain, falls to the earth, as it were to rejoin his own sweat that is falling upon the earth like "great drops of blood" (Luke 22:44). And, "going a little farther, he threw himself upon the ground [*epi tes gês*] and prayed" (Mark 14:35).

§45 Embedding in the Flesh and Burial in the Earth

The earth (*gê*) does not in fact gather up the prayers of Christ's soul (*psuchê*) (Mark 14:34 JB), except insofar as his body (*sôma*) makes clear his appropriation of flesh (*sarx*): "Take; this is my *body* [*to sôma mou*]" (Mark 14:22). But in this incorporation, he says, "Keep awake and pray . . . the spirit indeed is willing but the *flesh* (*sarx*) is weak" (Mark 14:38). The embedding in the flesh at Gethsemane is thus furtively anticipated, in a fall that is a kind of burial in the *earth*, in the *humus* of the garden of the Mount of Olives (Luke 22:44), and then again at the depths of a "tomb which was hewn in stone" (Luke 23:53 JB), but that will be found to be empty (Luke

24:3). To throw himself to the ground is probably also for Christ to experience that he is not just a man standing up and has not just "knelt down" (Luke 22:41); he is on the earth, as though bent beneath the weight of his own finitude. The *divinization of the human* that has been so rightly honored in our day, in an apposite return to the theology of the Greek fathers (Irenaeus, Athanasius, Clement of Alexandria) needs to be counterbalanced with the complete *humanization of the divine* that was typical of Latin theology (less, however, as we have already seen, in the distancing of the Father brought about by sin than in a full assumption of a finitude that is not sinfulness, and where sin consists precisely, and solely, in a shutting oneself up in finitude). At the height of incarnate suffering, what is shown even as far as the Son is concerned, as we shall see, is not the purifying ambition of a suffering being, but rather the impossible mastery of that which, not deriving from the Son (pain), makes possible the full recognition of the Other in him (the Father). And it is that Other in him who is alone capable of breaking the existential circle of the solitude of his own death: "Unless a grain of wheat falls into the earth [*eis tēn gēn*] and dies, it remains just a single grain [*monos menei*]; but if it dies, it bears much fruit" (John 12:24).

9

From Self-Relinquishment to the Entry into the Flesh

§46 Suffering the World

Christianity definitively places in opposition to a Nietzschean and post-modern perspective (one viewing anxiety over death as the site of self-fulfillment and "great health,")[1] the radical and unsurpassable experience of suffering—if not as physical pain then as ontological suffering. "Anything built by activity," Husserl underlines, "necessarily presupposes, as the lowest level, a passivity that gives something beforehand."[2] An original passivity—a customary passivity according to the law of finitude—is what precedes and is the basis of all activity. And Christ incarnate, simply because of the fact of his incarnation, comes as I see it to share in this, for example, in the course of his last meal, and even when he gets ready to wash the feet of his disciples, when "he knew that the hour had come for him *to pass* [*metabê*] from this world to the Father" (John 13:1 JB). The probably hypothetical knowledge (at least as objective certitude) that "he knew" should not obscure for us the *suffering* in his Passover. "To pass from this world to the Father," for the Son, is not just to leave this world and pass toward other earths, or indeed to escape once and for all, in a distinctively Platonic fashion, from "steps and points of departure into a world which is above hypotheses, in order . . . [to] soar beyond them to the first principle of the whole."[3] To "pass" (from) this world (*metabê*), within the "metabolism" that the world imposes on those who pass through it, comes down at first glance, though not solely at first glance, to being subjected to an ordeal—to *suffering (from) this world* in its irreducible finitude and not to fleeing it in a passage of flight.[4] "Suffering is a pure undergoing," as Emmanuel Levinas says.[5] That is also the reason that, like any human being, Christ cannot count on fleeing scot-free from his inescapable immanence in this world or from a radical passage through his own corruptible nature (*meta-phusis*).

§47 Living in the World

Husserl, describing the "originary Ark, the Earth," says, "I could just as well think of myself as transplanted to the moon . . . or as a pilot of an airplane that flies off and lands there," since all beings in general "have ontic being only on the basis of my constitutive genesis and this has *earthly* precedence."[6] On the basis of such an "originarity" of the earth for human beings, even Christ neither can, nor should, at least in the first instance, pass too readily (from) this world to another world, quitting (the earth) where his own being in the world is rooted, and where (if not exclusively here) it even took its form. In this our "dwelling" on earth, *God is* or says "I AM," calling out of the burning bush to Moses (Ex 3:14), and Jesus answers, "I am he," as the soldiers fall to the ground in Gethsemane (John 18:6). "*Ich bin,* I am, *du bist,* you are," Heidegger tells us, means, "I dwell, you dwell. The way in which you are and I am, the manner in which we humans *are* on the earth is *Buan,* dwelling. To be a human being means to be on the earth as a mortal. It means to dwell."[7] Far from being a kind of faithless desertion, dwelling in the world for the Son at the hour of Gethsemane comes back simply to accepting being "shut in" here, "dwelling," and taking the world under his "care," even when everything will urge him to leave it.[8]

The humility of Christ's falling to earth on the ground of Gethsemane (*humus*) thus in a way moves to its completion his act of *dwelling* in taking on flesh (incarnation) from Bethlehem to Golgotha. St. Macarius says, "As God created the heaven and earth for man to dwell in, so He created man's body and soul for a dwelling for Himself, to inhabit and take His rest in the body as in His own house."[9] Experiencing the weight of the world, or the burden of finitude, the Word does not flee the dwelling in this passage. On the contrary, "the Word was made flesh, he lived among us" (John 1:14 JB), in suffering.[10]

§48 Otherness and Corruptibility

But the death of Christ in the ontological suffering of the world, his true dwelling, is only something that is *revealing* here (of how he has taken in charge our humanity in himself): it is not what is revealed (his being the Son of God). While he would never stop being "professionally son" up to the furthest point of his abandonment (§42), he still has to reach the point where, concretely and almost physically, his filial relation will at last be expressed. As all the theological tradition has maintained, his filial relationship holds good above all in the *kerygma* [the apostolic proclamation of salvation through Jesus Christ], which has often been wrongly interpreted, as we shall see later (Bultmann, Ebeling, Ricoeur), simply and unilaterally in hermeneutic terms, as an act of language. This has been done without letting it speak, better and otherwise than all discourse, in terms of the silent flesh or, in Husserl's phrase, the "pre-predicative evidence"[11]: "You that are Israelites, listen to what I have to say: Jesus of Nazareth . . . this man . . . you crucified and killed by the hands of those outside the law. But God raised him up, having freed him from death, because it was impossible for him to be held in its power" (Acts 2:22–24). In this proclamation (*kerygma*), two affirmations, so customary that their overweening necessity is concealed, run through the discourse of Peter at Pentecost. First, concerning Jesus, it is affirmed that this man—the Nazarene—is not resurrected by himself *alone*; on the contrary, an *Other* has pulled him away from the power of death: God (*o theos*), or in other words, his Father. Second, it is affirmed that his flesh would have "experience[d] corruption [*diaphtoran*]" if he had been "abandoned to Hades" (Acts 2:31). No escape, then, at least not *a priori*, for him at first sight, from the ordinary law of corruptibility of all living things or from the incarnation of his anxiety in suffering flesh.

§49 Self-Relinquishment

"My solitude is . . . not confirmed by death but broken by it," Levinas writes, implicitly in opposition to Heidegger here. "What is important about the approach of death is that at a certain moment we are no longer *able to be able* [*nous ne 'pouvons plus pouvoir'*]. It is exactly thus that the subject loses its very mastery as a subject."[12] In this "no longer able to be able" or losing "its very mastery" provoked by the approach of death, the human subject finds suddenly and paradoxically that death is never really his or her own in the sense of appropriation, or as a demarcation of property. Death precisely is a radical disappropriation of the self and the exact opposite of all appropriation. To put it another way, we could say that the phenomenon in itself of death only shows itself paradoxically in quitting *the self*.[13] But who exactly is the *other* who is solely in a position to break open the existential solipsism of the dying persons that we all are (*sum moribundus*)?

How can this *other* achieve what Heidegger calls "**freedom towards death**," so that we are *"released from the Illusions of the 'they'"*?[14] According to Heidegger, it is not Christ, or the Anointed One of God (*Christos*)—far from it. Nor is it the Total Other named Yahweh, according to Levinas. The *other* is on the contrary identically death itself: that which is not me but that comes to me—alienates me and takes my identity from me ("taking from" in the double sense of the destruction of my ego and the deconstruction of myself). Levinas says that the other "is not unknown but unknowable, refractory to all light . . . the relationship with the other is a relationship with a Mystery."[15] There is no reduction possible of the *other of death* to *my identity itself*, given that this completely other unceasingly destroys what I actually am, in its approach in a natural way (death through old age), or in a violent fashion (accidental death). Christ refuses any Promethean face-to-face with death in his leaving off fear as he moves toward anxiety ("Not what I want but what you want" [Matthew 26:39]). He denies any ambition of all-powerfulness and welcomes right to its end the Being-there of his death ("He saved others; let him save himself if he is the Messiah" [Luke 23:35]). In reality he already suffers, himself also, and here also (in his Passion), the burden of alterity and the estrangement of his own death. But if death overtakes us and spills over with *more*, as Levinas sees it (the passivity of dying), and as we probably find also in the Judaic view (the precession, or turning of the appeal back to the subject who hears it ["Hear, O Israel" (Deut 6:4)]), there is *still more* than that, or at least *it is otherwise*, in Christianity.

§50 Passing to the Father

In effect we return to the question of *who* exactly is this who, when struck with alarm [*effroi*], anxiety, and anguish [*adêmonein*], said, "My soul is sorrowful to the point of death" at Gethsemane (Mark 14:34 JB)? He is not simply, and despite the many Christian (and therefore infidel?) interpretations of Levinas, an ordinary person who allows a "visitation" from the outside, by the other who precedes him and overwhelms "the very egoism of the I" by means of "a face [which] confounds the intentionality that aims at it."[16] The "absolutely other" that is revealed in the Son at Gethsemane and on Golgotha is in Christianity neither uniquely the other of his finitude, totally exterior to himself (death), nor the Wholly Other in his infinite transcendence (Yahweh). While death *reveals* the man in a philosophical perspective (Hegel, Heidegger, Sartre), the death of the Son is accepted also, and decisively, in theology as what is *revealed* and *revealing* of the Trinitarian being of God. For the Son to pass from this world to the Father

(John 13:1) does not come down exclusively or, in Trinitarian terms, to experiencing a "taking on board of suffering" (*pâtir*) that can be set apart from the "passage." Passing is also, according to the most conventional rules of communication in idiomatic terms, and as we extend them to the Trinity, a matter of offering his passion for existence to the Father ("to pass from this world *to the Father*" [John 13:1 JB]). It is to make a kind of ford in the river, himself as ferryman or guide ("Passeur"), and to communicate an ordeal that has not been suffered simply as a result of sinfulness, but that is "natural." In Gustave Martelet's view, "The Son has become so completely man that he is capable henceforth of experiencing in his flesh (the worst of) the human, and to make Him from whom he came encounter it. Having become one of us, he is empowered by his humanity to disclose to the Father, in a way that is not simply divine but also human, this tragedy that is truly ours and that is above all only ours."[17] Along with the washing of the disciples' feet, which is the setting up of the Eucharist in St. John's Gospel (John 13:1–20), and then the transformation of the self (*métabolê*), what is happening at one and the same time and in the same movement is a *taking on board of suffering* (of the world) and the *passing* of this (to the Father). In suffering this world the Son conveys to the Father (a passage) the weight of finitude experienced in his death and begs now that the Father will also break the pain (*ôdin*), which will "teach" him—not because of his ignorance, but through a total communion with the Son's suffering—what its burden is: "But God raised him up, having freed him from death, because it was impossible for him to be held in its power" (Acts 2:24).

§51 Oneself as an Other

The otherness of the Son with respect to the Father, and of his humanity relative to God, cannot thus be seen, or not simply seen (in a Christian rendering) as pure exteriority to the Total Other, whether that implies death itself or the transcendence of Yahweh (Levinas). It is, on the contrary, taking up a famous phrase of Husserl's, at the heart of "transcendence in immanence."[18] According to Didier Franck, perhaps "the most important proposition of Husserl's *Cartesian Meditations*" concerns "the *intrinsically first other . . . the other Ego*,"[19] and we can identify that other with the figure of Christ. Finding in myself the figure of a God "more inward than my most inward part" (*interior intimo meo*), according to St. Augustine,[20] brings me back to deriving the *alterity of God in me* (the "economic Trinity," or God with respect to the creation) from *the alterity of the Father in the Son*, which was always already there for the Son and, above all, *more inward* than his most inward part (the "immanent Trinity," or God with respect to His own inner life). The reduction or suspension of the world in order to reconquer it (*epochê* or "bracketing," in Husserl's "phenomenological reduction") is wonderfully illustrated when Husserl quotes St. Augustine in the final sentences of the *Cartesian Meditations*: "Do not wish to go out; go back into yourself. Truth dwells in the inner man."[21] This reduction indicates, theologically, but in a reading that is also faithful to the methodological demands of phenomenology, that all the truth we receive only ultimately comes from the one who is *"the* truth" (John 14:6).[22] Far then from any *dialectic* between Father and Son, or between God and humankind, in which the play of opposites would subsume them under a superior unity, the Son in reality remains phenomenologically Son in his relation with the Father insofar as he is, and remains, "himself as another" (Ricoeur).[23] That is precisely as he is Son (receiving the gift of his life), linked to the Father (who generates the gift), and as he is man (sharing our finitude); but he offers himself to God (the author of a world that, so far as we are concerned, we can only experience in finitude).

§52 Destitution and Auto-Affection

The very famous statement of St. Paul to the Galatians, "It is no longer I who live, but it is Christ who lives in me" (Gal 2:20), not only speaks, in a purely ego-logical perspective, of what Jean-Luc Marion calls an "identity of the self with the self, or rather I with the I [that] can only be brought about . . . by the mediation of God."[24] St. Paul also indicates, and perhaps emphasizes, the design of a *life* that shows itself in me (using Michel Henry's terms) as "revelation of revelation, a self-revelation" or "auto-affection" of the self to the self.[25] Far from constructing an opposition between the destitution of Ego-ity [individuality] (Jean-Luc Marion), and the pure immanence of the subject to him- or herself (Michel Henry), it is important that the one is brought back to the other and the one brought back *by* the other. What is true here of the disciple in relation to Christ and the destitution of his ego (the economic Trinity) is in fact also true of the Son in the auto-affection of his relation to the Father (the immanent Trinity). Through the loss of his heroism as a subject doubly "undone" (or defeated), as we have already seen (defeat of the ego and the deconstruction of the self [§35]), the Son cannot and must not believe himself "alone in the world," or rather we might say "in *his* world"; that is something he would never have experienced, or at least never thought to himself. In the solitude and "mineness" of his own death, and because he is crushed and torn apart even in his flesh, what is revealed is the indwelling in him of an Other, capable of accommodating the burden of the finitude that he has put on.[26]

The alterity of death for me as a pure and simple exterior expression of finitude (Levinas) follows thus a path in Christianity that goes from the *alterity of the Father in the Son* to the *alterity of humankind and of God*—the one only fully being taken on in the incarnation in the other. Or, to put it another way, the Son, in delivering himself to the Other of his Father ("not what *I* want but what *you* want") remains the same ("God made man") and invites us also, because we are "adopted as sons" (Gal 4:6 JB), to divest ourselves of ourselves in order to recover ourselves, like him and with him, in the Other of his Father ("so that," as Michel Henry suggests, "humankind can become God").[27]

§53 Alterity and Fraternity

The Christian does not, as in Messianic Judaism, have to "bear the suffering of all" so that "each person acts as though he were the Messiah."[28] It is, on the contrary, because the Messiah is precisely never *me*—his suffering being first of all that of God and not simply my suffering—that the welcome I give him is as a pure and veritable "incarnate" alterity. Far from allowing each of us to see ourselves as like the Messiah in an *Old Testament* prophetic act, what particularly marks out Christianity is the alterity incarnate in one's neighbor, as though the branding of each sheep in the flock were individualized, "a brother for whom Christ died" (1 Cor 8:11 JB). To take up a formula from the work of Jean-Luc Marion explicitly directed against Emmanuel Levinas, the injunction to love one's neighbor does not designate the other as "just anybody." The other is "just such an other" (*tel autre*)—a particular other.[29] The *haecceity* (this-ness) of the other, in the sense of the most extreme singularization (*haec*), confirms all wrongdoing against one's neighbor as first of all a sin committed against God: "Insofar as you did this [or neglected to do this] to one of the least of these brothers of mine [to feed, welcome or clothe them], you did it to me [or neglected to do it]" (Matthew 25:40 JB).[30] We need then, at least in the eyes of believers, to make obvious the originality of the Christian message. On the one hand, as Balthasar maintains, "Christian brotherly love is the proof through experience of the fact that we love God."[31] And, on the other hand, sin as a lack of love for our neighbor is not so much weakness as such (like hunger, thirst, foreignness, sickness); it is rather an auto-enclosure of the self in a finitude that is not in itself sinful. And it is the absence of helping the other as we would need to do in order to break out of our solipsism. Christ is resurrected as the glorious Son of the Father, and at the same time as the brother incarnate of humankind. He converts the neutral alterity of death, first of all in naming it as a passage—not in the sense of a flight but as an offering of his passive suffering. And, second, he personally lives through it—succeeding in breaking up "existentiell" solipsism as well as "existential" solitude.[32] To die, for the disciple of Christ, comes down not simply to accommodating the other as such (Levinas), but also to accepting the challenge of definitively (and in a singularized fashion) breaking open the circle of one's own isolation. Thus and thus only can it be said, as with the grain of wheat, that "unless a wheat grain falls on the ground and dies, it remains only a single grain" (John 12:24 JB). To fall on the ground and die is not to remain alone. And this is the case whether we consider the Son abandoning himself to death up until he accepts the Father ("Not what I want but what you want") or we consider the disciple of Christ, welcoming the present of his life as a gift, this life of the Resurrected Son that can only come from his Father ("It is no longer I who live, but it is Christ who lives in me" [Gal 2:20]). Shown first of all in his flesh—incarnate or resurrected—the *life* of Christ demands of the Christian's *life* today that it is also incarnate, although in another mode, in a flesh that is singularized by love for our neighbor. Even Heidegger anchors the anxiety of death in the flesh, and even for Levinas, if "the face" is "neither seen nor touched,"[33] it is incarnate in a body that singularizes it. For the Christian theologian (Hans Urs von Balthasar) there is a "figure" (*Gestalt*), in the double sense of a "form" that defines it (*species*), and splendor that it radiates (*splendor*).[34]

§54 Entry into the Flesh

One cannot hope, then, as has been attempted in much contemporary theology, to renew the concepts of Christian thought, starting off from "the face" (in reality faceless) of a Levinas-style phenomenology. If we recognize and follow here the guiding and kerygmatic principle of St. Peter's address at Pentecost (§48), that Christ "abandoned to Hades" would also "experience corruption" in his flesh (Acts 2:31 JB), then it brings us back to accepting precisely the fleshly ordinariness of Christ who, definitively and independent of all ulterior speculation over the motives for the incarnation, would be dead if he had not been "freed . . . from death" (Acts 2:24) by God his Father. And for Christ, as well, at least in his own eyes, *nobody* dwells here—in the literal English language sense of the term (*no-body*)—if he or she is not a body, or does not have a body (*some-body*). We might ask again, in a question like the chorus of a song that never seems to come up with an answer, *who* is this, who, when "a sudden fear [*ekthambestai*] came over him, and great distress [*adêmonein*]," was "sorrowful to the point of death [*eôs thanatou*]" (Mark 14:33–35 JB)? Our question is particularly important in these circumstances—that is to say, when there is flesh destined for decomposition (*diaphtoran*) and death (*thanatos*), indeed when Pilate is "astonished that he should have died so soon" (Mark 15:44 JB). Moreover, there is the "corpse" (*ptôma*) that Pilate allows Joseph of Arimathea to have taken down from the cross (Mark 15:45 and John 19:38) much as we allow a sailor only a "mooring" [in French *corps mort*—or "dead body"] for his final berth. And there is the question of the "body of Jesus" (*sôma tou Iesou*) that Mary Magdalene says to the supposed gardener she would like to take away on Easter morning, as one might look for a package so carefully registered and deposited that one would be amazed to find it had gone astray. No trace of the *fleshly* life remains, at least after the recognition of the death, either in the "corpse" to be taken up (Joseph of Arimathea) or in the "body" to remove—to take or hand over (Mary Magdalene). The *corps mort* (dead body) of Christ is so much a dead body, as we have already seen, in the terms of St. Peter's address (Acts 2:31), that he would have "experience[d] corruption" if he had not been dragged away by another (in him) from the power of death: "God raised him up" (Acts 2:24). The commonplace proposition that nothing resurrects itself is thus not simply a recognition of the immanence of an alterity based in oneself that is the source of all identity (§53); it is also a matter of granting the humble and necessary demolition of the self, albeit for God in his capacity as Son of Man, with his corruptible flesh, until an Other (the Father) takes on, first for his Son and then also for the whole of creation with him, the decision to bring about a reconstruction or recapitulation (*anakephalaiosis*—or summing up of human life). It is probably necessary today, perhaps even more so than in the past, in order to guard against any resurgence of "Docetism,"[35] to recognize the total assumption by Christ himself of our corruptible flesh, and at the same time to allow his incarnation to express itself all the way through to its conclusion, even as that is a manifestation of his anxiety and his suffering flesh.

§55 The Anxiety "in" the Flesh

When we come to the very obvious but necessary implantation of anxiety *in the flesh*, it would probably not be wise to conclude too hastily that Heidegger completely neglected the flesh or the incarnation of anxiety. Anxiety, according to *Being and Time*, is "often conditioned by 'physiological' factors," so that it becomes a "problem *ontologically*" and "not simply with regard to its ontical causation."[36] The threat in anxiety, although indeterminate and something that we cannot localize, is still "so close that it is oppressive and stifles one's breath."[37] "Anxiety robs us of speech."[38] It can grab us literally, in its own terms, by the throat (*angustia*). But if anxiety robs us of speech, it is not primarily in that it is incarnate "in flesh," according to Heidegger's "What Is Metaphysics?," but simply that in the face of anxiety "all utterance of the 'is' falls silent."[39] The weakness of Heidegger's analysis of anxiety comes down less, as I see it, to his leaving out the body than to his inscribing it still and always in the unsurpassable horizon of being, indeed within the ordeal of its annihilation. Putting it another way, although, as far as Heidegger is concerned, anxiety could stifle one's breath (and thus also speech), it always remains above all an experience in the mode of language, even if it is the negation of all speech about "that which is." But that is precisely what the anxiety experienced at Gethsemane *denies*. It denies not simply the paradoxical angelism of Heideggerian anxiety, which is suffered uniquely in the interior depths of the consciousness. More than this, it denies the verbalization of anxiety through the horizon of "speaking," something that would only silence, through a kind of overflowing, what is actually uttered and displayed in the flesh.

§56 Toward Dumb Experience

Against all the presumptions that are far too hegemonic of hermeneutic theology today—and attempting to ensure that the horizon of a descriptive phenomenology does not overshadow the necessary process of utterance, without which after all it would not be accessible to description—I would say that Christ's "entering into agony" (*agônia*) does not so much verbalize the metaphysical ordeal of his anxiety in the mode of language as it shows it through his *fleshly lived experience*, experience in which his "sweat became like great drops of blood falling down on the ground" (Luke 22:44). Whatever way you look at it, putting aside all naive tendencies to exalt pain or all excessive spiritualization, Christ's flesh sweating "like great drops of blood" expresses itself in an extreme human consanguinity, above all in a nonverbal mode. This ties in well with one of the very first requirements of descriptive phenomenology: "Its beginning is the pure—and, so to speak, still dumb—psychological experience, which now must be made to utter its own sense with no adulteration."[40] The issue here is not one of the interpretation of speech, nor of the structure of languages, even if such approaches inherit the tradition of Dilthey, Heidegger, Saussure, Gadamer, or Ricoeur. In the face of suffering and with the existential experience of incarnate anxiety, words largely fall silent, precisely in that they take on body. "The Word became flesh" (John 1:14)—and commenting on this, Hans Urs von Balthasar says, "The first meaning of 'The Word became flesh' is quite straightforward: Word,[41] this particular form of personal utterance, known to everyone, takes on a form of being which, as such, is foreign to the word, for flesh as such does not speak."[42] In the sweating of his own fleshly substance (and again a long way from any naive or decadent tendency to exalt pain) the Word, speechless, experiences first for himself and in himself the unique speech of "Word [become] flesh" (John 1:14), which is the sole thing, as I see it, that can speak the meaninglessness (or non-sense) of speech—speech that is always *too much* in the light of the surplus and excess in all incarnate suffering.

The flesh itself is expressed rather than speech. Speech remains incapable, when all is said, of giving an authentic version of the flesh. "The Logos [the Word] became man, so that man might become Logos," as the fifth-century St. Mark the Ascetic writes in a letter to Nicolas the Solitary.[43] But it is not just a simple opposition, because the Word speaks in the flesh without just letting it think for him and with him. It is appropriate for the Word that he is enclosed thoroughly in his flesh, so as to lead his kenosis to its conclusion, through his solidarity with our flesh, not simply as redemption of our misdeeds. And thus, starting off from that flesh, and within that flesh—indeed both within and beyond any attempts at language—what speaks is, on the one hand, only what is seen in a rupture of the flesh (the open rib), and, on the other hand, it is what can only be understood in inarticulate discourse (the cry of the abandoned).

10

Suffering Occluded

§57 An Opportunity Thwarted

The Heideggerian occlusion of suffering, even more than its occlusion of bodiliness (*corporéité*) stems first of all and philosophically from an over-determined focus on forms of withdrawal that still empower speech (e.g., consciousness concerning death, fear, and anxiety) as opposed to types of excess that silence all discourse and only speak authentically through the dumb and silent experience of the flesh. Paul Ricoeur asks if, "having placed too great an emphasis on fear (*Being and Time*, §30) and finally on the anxiety stemming from being-toward-death, does one not neglect the instructions that a phenomenology of suffering would be most apt to dispense?"[1] Such a dissimulation or concealment by Heidegger of incarnate suffering arose nonetheless (like the charge of "always already view[ing] death together with its interpretation of 'life'") as a justified reaction against what had been the excessive overvaluation of suffering in theology. As opposed to the philosophical or theological ways we have already evoked of fleeing from death (§2), there are also modes, paradoxically and specifically Christian this time, of overdetermination of suffering. It is as though, in a masochistic way and in the form of a supposed recompense, a celebration of the spirit must necessarily correspond to suffering in the flesh. It would be impossible to count up the multiple misinterpretations of Holy Writ, sometimes still ongoing in people's consciousness (if not in theology?), that justify what Marcel Neusch refers to as "traps of Christian masochism."[2]

Instead of the God who "reproves the one he loves, as a father the son in whom he delights" (Prov 3:12), the more causal model of a vengeful God, along with the *pedagogic* virtues of the Father as educator, has often been substituted. We find mixed up with the Son who "became the source of eternal salvation for all who obey him" (Heb 5:9) the notion of salvation through the act of suffering and redemption through *obedience* to suffering. Beside the wish to "be imitators of God, as beloved children, and live in love, as Christ loved us and gave himself up for us, a fragrant offering and sacrifice to God" (Eph 5:1–2) we find a love of suffering and the perseverance of love, even through suffering. But despite all this, the Lord *does not send* suffering. He simply makes the best, along with humankind, of what occurs, and over which neither he (the divine) nor those to whom he addresses himself (humankind) either can or should dissemble their powerlessness (on the one hand intentional and on the other hand suffered). The Son, no more than any of us, *is not made purer* by suffering, according to a *catharsis* that would be well and truly Hellenic: he only obeys his Father in submitting himself, according to the manner of his own creation (conditional power), to the general law of corruptibility of all living things. God *does not want* humans to suffer: he simply requires of human beings that there should be no limit to love—even where there is suffering—because that alone (love and not suffering) remains credible or, as Balthasar says, "worthy of faith."[3] What has happened to Christianity, capable, as I understand it, unlike many philosophies (from Socrates to Heidegger) and indeed many religions (Buddhism, Hinduism), of truly handling suffering and formalizing a certain discourse about it, is that it has found itself thwarted or aborted because of numerous large-scale exegetic misunderstandings.

Is there a way for the Christian of today and for our theology to escape these traps? I would not want to be complacent on this point. One has only to look, for example, at the constant development of what has been called the "*salvific meaning of suffering*,"[4] at least from the point of view of the scandal it constitutes for those who do actually suffer. Putting aside the kind of polemic that we find in that literature, more or less scholarly, where authors try either to approve or denounce such attitudes, it is important in my opinion, as Paul Ricoeur has suggested, to develop a true "phenomenology of suffering."[5] Our guiding principle should be the pure description of Christly living, so well displayed before us at the heart of the gospels. We can leave aside, then, over-explanatory accounts, because it is necessary, almost at the most basic level, to relearn to *read* the gospels: that is, as Christian Bobin expresses it, if this reading is to help us "make room for suffering . . . to see the life in suffering in my life—simply to see it."[6]

Let us attempt, then, to return once more to our question as to *who* exactly it was, struck with alarm [*effroi*], anxiety, and anguish [*adêmonein*], who said, "My soul is sorrowful to the point of death" at Gethsemane (Mark 14:34 JB)? Because first of all he was "made man," getting down to this question means that we must also return, in our Promethean ambition, to try to find for ourselves an answer to suffering.

§58 Called into Question

When his disciples pose to him a genealogical question on the subject of a man who has been blind from birth ("Who sinned, this man or his parents, that he was born blind?"), Jesus replies with two negatives: "Neither this man nor his parents sinned" (John 9:1–3). And here he avoids a double trap. If it were the man who had sinned, he could not have committed the sin until he was born, and therefore would not have been blind at birth. If it were his parents' sins that created the problem, then it should have been them and not the man who was struck blind, and the punishment missed its target. Again, in a similar example, as far as causality is concerned, concerning other people who suffered in other circumstances—"those eighteen who were killed when the tower of Siloam fell on them"—when asked whether they were "worse offenders than all the others living in Jerusalem," Jesus firmly replied, "No I tell you" (Luke 13:2–5). Arguing for the absence of a cause does not mean, however, that he is not calling on us to pose questions. The French ecumenical Bible [TOB] translates Christ as saying to the man born blind, "I came into this world for a calling into question" (John 9:39), as it were to silence and end discussion of all our (supposedly "good") reasons for suffering. Could we not echo Heidegger that being human is precisely a matter of seeing in oneself "inquiry as one of the [essential] possibilities" and then undertake to remain "interested" (*inter-esse*), that is to say, caught up in it?[7]

§59 Toward a Phenomenology of Suffering

The questioning of the *who* (*quis*) of the physical suffering of the blind man, as well as of the *what* (*quid*) or *why* (*cur*) of the fall of the tower of Siloam, leads to an absence of response—or better, we might say, to a negation of any affirmative response. A true "phenomenology of suffering" requires methodologically (by the phenomenological method called "reduction") and, almost evangelically, that judgment on the question of *quis* and *quid* is suspended. As Heidegger puts it, phenomenology "does not characterize the what of the objects of philosophical research as subject-matter, but rather the *how* of that research."[8] And Husserl talks of "the 'object' in its How [*das Objekt im Wie*]," that is to say, "'the object' *in the How of its modes of givenness*."[9] Thus we could say that it is neither a question of "whose fault is it?" (genealogical question) nor of the "what" or "why" (causal questions) in suffering, to the extent that, as John Paul II suggests, it is difficult to render intelligible to us in what way "Christ causes us to enter into the mystery and to discover the 'why' of suffering, as far as we are capable of grasping the sublimity of divine love."[10] At most we might ask of Christ—taking all the necessary precautions when it comes to describing the suffering of another (and, besides, in this case, that of the Son of God)—to tell us in his flesh *how* he suffers, or, perhaps we should say, *how to offer* one's suffering when one suffers. As André Comte-Sponville says, although we ask, "Why?," "there is no reply (one suffers for no reason), neither is there really a question. The body screams, but does not question. We do, however, speak of the lessons of pain. . . . But pain teaches nothing except when it cancels out what one thought one knew. Its lesson is an anti-lesson: that all discourse, which would appear ridiculous, unbearable or cowardly, should cease in the face of pain."[11]

11

Suffering Incarnate

Let all discourse cease and let pain speak: that should probably be the first, and the most compelling, commandment of a "phenomenology of suffering." It would depend upon a mode of description (and not of explanation or analysis) that does not conceal either what is evidently the meaninglessness of pain or its unbearable presence.[1] Whoever suffers *inordinately*, that is to say, above all in bodily suffering, becomes wholly suffering, going so far as to be identified totally with that which he or she suffers ("he or she is nothing but suffering"). Suffering beings do not see (themselves)—or at least no longer see themselves—in the way that they know, or think they know, they are seen. Marc Richir explains that affect, "as one might say, leads excess in a different direction. It leads in the direction of a body so excessive as to be *invasive*—while, on the other hand, where our sensations are concerned, the excess of the body is exhausted through disappearing into the world."[2]

§60 Perceiving, or the Challenge of the Toucher-Touching

In fact, someone who perceives (that is, who seizes or discerns something by the organs of sense) experiences first of all the common tendency of our own bodies to lose themselves in things—like Aristotle's famous "impress of a signet-ring" on wax that then becomes a receptacle of perceptible form.[3] Touch the wax, and it receives an exterior impression that identifies what is touched with what has touched it. In the same way we identify what is seen with the one seeing it. So our flesh (*sarx*), according to Aristotle, amazingly long before Husserl or Merleau-Ponty, has to be defined first of all not in terms of bodily "substance" (*sôma*), at a distance from the soul or all other beings, but rather by the environment or "medium" (*meson*) first and immediately of ourselves to ourselves, in virtue of which we put ourselves in contact with the totality of the world and its beings, like "an air envelope growing round our bod[ies]."[4] This medium of (his) flesh, *element* rather than instrument (*organon*) or Middle Term,[5] is precisely what Christ suffers from, in my opinion, in his earthly pilgrimage. It constitutes his "true body" the world, or rather *his* world (called thus to become through filiation *our* world, as it is the world in which God manifests himself in the flesh). That is in reality, in the final instance, the true basis of the incomprehension of Christ's disciples in the episode of the woman with a hemorrhage. In response to his question shouted out to the crowd, "Who touched [*tis mou hêpsato*] my clothes?" (Mark 5:30), it is ironic that they can only reply according to the logic of good sense (and as if to blame him for a foolish question, or indeed a total absurdity): "You see the crowd pressing in on you; how can you say, 'Who touched me?' [*tis mou hêpsato*]" (Mark 5:31). But the banality of such a reaction, if it could be justified in the order of a lived experience of ordinary flesh, does not take account of the touch that the Son experiences here—something that differs in every way from the touching of the crowd that encloses him. For example, "Immediately" (*euthus*) that he is touched and once again before there is any attempt linguistically to justify or interpret it, Jesus perceives (almost passively we might say) that a "power [*dunamis*] had gone forth from him [*ex autou exelthousan*]" (Mark 5:30). On the one hand, the woman has been *suffering from* (*pathos*) these hemorrhages for twelve years. She has in the terms of the text "endured much" (*polla pathousa*), not simply from the sickness but also "under many physicians" (Mark 5:25–26). On the other hand, corresponding to this is the *suffering of the Son*, of a "power" [*dunamis*] in him and going forth from him—almost despite himself (Mark 5:30). It is not simply a matter here, to take up again the famous example from Husserl of a phenomenological corporeity (used so frequently by Merleau-Ponty), of the "toucher-touching," in the relation between the woman who touches and the Christ touched.[6] When the woman touches Jesus through his clothes ("who touched my clothes?") she does not jostle him with impunity, as in some kind of rough bodily bump, when passengers on a train collide with one another, in a hurry and squeezed together. On the contrary, her touching is animated and oriented by her intention that "if I but touch his clothes, I will be made well" (Mark 5:28). The toucher is inhabited by an aim, but an aim for something like a "caress" rather than a collision (in Levinas's phrase), "where the subject who is in contact with another goes beyond this contact."[7]

As with the caress that, as Levinas says, "does not know what it seeks,"[8] this woman surely does not really know that she is touching the Son of God. She does not purely and simply want salvation—as might be with a caress in a sexual relation that solely aims to awaken eros. Conversely, and much more profoundly, she tries to incorporate herself with the flesh of the Son by touching his garment. Merleau-Ponty tells us, "The thickness of the body, far from rivalling that of the world, is on the contrary the sole means I have to go unto the heart of things, by making myself a world and by making them flesh."[9] Along with Mary, who "anointed Jesus' feet, and wiped them with her hair" (John 12:3); Joseph of Arimathea and Nicodemus, who "took the body of Jesus and wrapped it with the spices in linen cloths, according to the burial custom of the Jews" (John 19:40); and indeed along with Christ himself, who "began to wash the disciples' feet and to wipe them with the towel that was tied around him" (John 13:5), Jesus the man *and* God, in this episode of the healing of the woman with hemorrhages, reveals himself, and is revealed, as constituted of the same "texture," or of the same "fabric," as humankind, in an intercorporality that has no other goal but to touch in the other (as when two hands come together in meeting or greeting one another) "the same power to espouse the things that I have touched in my own."[10] Humankind is incorporated so to speak with God (the woman with the hemorrhages, Mary of Bethany, Joseph of Arimathea and Nicodemus at the deposition from the cross) and God with humankind (the washing of the feet) by a touch in the form of a caress (rather than the collision or contact of bodies that remain in total exteriority). Wanting neither to seize nor to possess, these respective touchings, in the form of caresses, reveal silently, as Levinas says, "the anticipation of this pure future [*avenir*], without content"[11] That is precisely why Jesus "touched" replies to the woman with hemorrhages "touching" him: "Daughter, *your faith* has made you well." It is not simply that she "told him the whole truth" (Mark 5:33), as one might admit a wrongdoing, but above all that the truth she speaks reveals only, and all, the depths of the mode of being of her body: "If I but touch his clothes . . ." (Mark 5:28).

The bodies of the woman with hemorrhages and that of Jesus are thus in a way specifically "con-tingent" with one another, not simply in the ordinary sense, in the way that needed to be recovered in theology, of their common and inevitable corruptibility. Their con-tingence is shown, etymologically this time, as a con-tact or an "intersecting of fleshes" [*cumtangere* (to touch with)] by which silently, but more fundamentally, because the toucher-touching here is preeminently nonlinguistic, they come into a relation with one another, and are indeed precisely *in contact.*[12] Among such contacts [*prises de contact*] between humankind and God in the figure of the human-God, many show us, as we shall go on to see, the modes of the incarnate being of Christ—paradigmatic in this respect of what it is specifically for God just to live and show himself in the flesh of humankind: (a) by *auto-affection* of the self in his own flesh, above all in his intimate relationship with the Father; (b) by *embedding* of sensation in the world, perceived subsequently by means of signs that show him also in this (divine) manner of perceiving; (c) by the uncontrollable *excess* of perceiving over what is finally perceived, consecrating his incarnate suffering as the inevitable passage of the "body" that he *has* (or believes he has) into the "flesh" that he *is* or becomes definitively, at Gethsemane or on Golgotha.

§61 The Modes of the Incarnate Being

(a) The experience of *auto-affection* of the self in the flesh is above all that in which the Son shares in an unceasing reciprocal interiority (or circum-incession) with the Father.[13] "I was born," he says (a fleshly experience for Christ, though not only that), "to testify to the truth" (John 18:37). However, if he is always already born or rather engendered in the presence of the Father, we can say in opposition to any Arianist tendency that the truth and the life he testifies are not simply what he *has* (received), but also what he *is*: "*I am* the way, and the truth, and the life" (John 14:6). But if the Son, even in his flesh, testifies that his Father is the giver of Life, he must also testify that in himself and of himself he is "the living one" (Rev 1:18). In other words, in the terms used by Michel Henry, "The Son is revealed only in the Father's self-revelation . . . [so that] each appears in turn as the condition of the other."[14] In his own auto-affection of the flesh of a born human being, the Son's life is an ordeal, not simply like the life of the Father, but as it is manifest under the mode of corporality, specifically as *his* manner of being, as Word made flesh. Merleau-Ponty suggests, in another context, that what makes each of us unique is our basic ownership of our feelings.[15] Probably we can also find, in this fleshly auto-affection of the Son to the Father, as we shall see (§66), what makes both the uniqueness and the originality of the Trinitarian being of God, through a feeling where all the internal movements of the Son's "own body" are shifted off and *pass* on to the Father, even in the double sense of both suffering from them and passing them on.

(b) The *disappearance* of sensation into the world perceived or, in other terms, the incorporation of God into the world, is experienced, precisely by the incarnate Son, through the many kinesthetic experiences, or internal movements of his own body, through which he builds up the world (of God) and manifests there the *signs* of his divine glory. Thus he *hears* what his mother says and *sees with her* that there is no more wine at Cana (John 2:3); he performs a "wonder" that can be *seen* in the healing of the Royal Official's son at Capernaum (John 4:48); he *sees* a sick man lying by the pool in Bethesda, *speaks* to him of a cure, *waits* for his reply, and makes him *take up* his mat and walk (John 5:9); he *feeds* a large crowd by the Sea of Galilee so that they will physiologically (but not only physiologically) have something "to eat" (John 6:5–11); he *heals* a man blind from birth at Jerusalem "so that God's works might be revealed to him" (John 9:3); he *weeps* over the death of a friend (Lazarus) at Bethany, then he *calls* Lazarus to come out again into life (John 11:35–44). What is exhibited in these *signs*—acts and gestures that are frequently commented upon in exegesis, but ordinarily seen solely in the perspective of a heroic conformity between his acts and speech (§24)—shows also, phenomenologically in my opinion, and setting aside any problems of anachronism, exactly what there is of his flesh as "the body itself" or "the organic body" (*Leib*) much more than his body simply as corporal substance (*Körper*).

If it is an objective body or "object for this world" (*Körper*), my body also appears to me, first in my own eyes, but also in the eyes of the other, as *specifically my own body*, a subjective or phenomenal body, in Husserl's terms—"subjective from this world" or, in other words, my flesh (*Leib*). Fleshly vivacity, or liveliness (*Leiblichkeit*), according to Husserl, obviously does not signify simply the physical body (*Körperlichkeit*); "rather, the expression refers to the kinesthetic, to functioning as an ego in this peculiar way, primarily through seeing, hearing etc.; and of course other modes of the ego belong to this (for example, lifting, carrying, pushing, and the like)."[16] To put this another way, and this time in the context of theological studies, Christ is revealed to us first of all as "Son of man" in that he himself experiences "in *his* flesh" (*leiblich*), the *same* as we ourselves could live through and experience as the world on the basis of our own individual flesh: seeing, talking, hearing, feeding, healing, weeping. Should we not then try, in the first instance at least, to form along with Christ in his flesh (which is incarnate then resurrected), a "communitization" (*Vergemeinschaftung*), or a community of monads through which we are able also to constitute, with him and in our own flesh, even though not necessarily like him in his Trinitarian being, a "common world" between humankind and God?[17]

The totality of the sensory lived experience of his own body (*Erleibnisse*) for Christ is not what constitutes him, at least not in himself, as Son of God. *To see* for him is not in fact simply to recognize a lack of wine in a pitcher, but to experience this lack and respond to the appeal of his own mother that he let his Father act, "who is in heaven" (Wedding at Cana). To *cure* is not simply to act as thaumaturge [worker of miracles], but to arouse the expectations of faith and seek to fulfill them (the paralytic or the man born blind). To *feed* is not simply and exclusively to give bread to those who do not have it, but also to deliver Life in giving himself in the form of the "bread of life" (feeding the multitude and the discourse on the Bread of Life). To *weep* is not simply to lock himself into his own sadness, but to believe still in a possible power and presence of an other in himself capable of breaking the circle of our irreducible finitude (the raising of Lazarus). In short, and to rejoin here the ancient but very fecund theological doctrine of the "spiritual sense" (Origen, Bonaventure, Ignatius Loyola), the kinestheses of the earthly life of Jesus, which make his own body, or his incarnate flesh (as man), also go to constitute him in himself (as Son of God). Through him the entirety of the internal lived experience of his own body operates a double *passage*—of man (humankind) to God, and of the Son to the Father. The lived experience of the Son in *his* flesh will then also be the experience of the Father (through his unbreakable communion with the Son), although that will be in another way and in another mode, because it is not directly fleshly. To say here with Jürgen Moltmann that "the Son suffers dying [*erleidet das Sterben*]" while "the Father suffers the death [*den Tod*] of the Son,"[18] as it were in analogy with how a father suffers even more the death of his own son because he is not the one who is dying (§42), comes down then to holding, phenomenologically this time, that the Father, while not himself experiencing physical suffering in the flesh, nonetheless still feels [*(res)sent*] the internal lived experiences of his Son, which are passed on in turn to him (kinestheses, affect, and the lived experience of consciousness). In other words, the fleshly communion of the Father with the Son operates less by an exchange or reciprocity of bodies than by the conveying of *lived experience* of the incarnate body of the Son to that of his eternal Father by way, so to speak, of a "fleshly recipient" of lived experience in the flesh of the Son (and perhaps also in ours). And this is without the Father himself being in the flesh. Thus, we find, as we have already seen, the ordeal of anxiety over finitude at Gethsemane (carrying the burden of a non-sinful flesh) will be transmitted by the Son legitimately to his Father. It is not that the Father is unaware of the nature of what has been created, but simply that he has still not experienced it in the mode of the flesh of humankind (communication in different idioms) until the unbearable burden is broken at last, in the Son, by the bursting through of the Resurrection. The incarnate Son incarnates in this sense, and in a form that is both visible and tangible, the very *manner* of being in the world of

God through his flesh, even though he might not himself be exclusively and uniquely flesh. As Bonaventure says, "It is also clear . . . how in everything that is sensed or known, God lies hidden within [*patet etiam . . . quomodo in omne re quae sentitur . . . interius lateat ipse Deus*]."[19]

(c) The *living through* of incarnate suffering now brings in and contributes more in reality than all the experience of auto-affection or of kinesthesis of the flesh. Auto-affection reveals the Son uniquely in his *immanent* interiority (in his originary connectedness to the Father revealed in the act of fleshly birth). Kinesthesis shows him above all "*economically*" [i.e., within the "divine economy"]; it identifies him in his interactions with the world and with an other (seeing, hearing, healing, feeding, weeping), at once in the fleshly manner of being that belongs to humankind and in the manner of being fleshly—though not solely that—of God. Concerning suffering, Gabriel Marcel suggests that "surely this is being touched in point of what we have, in so far as what we have has become an integral part of what we are?"[20] Put in another way, and according to a fleshly lived experience shared in reality by all of us, I could say that when suffering is embodied for me in my body, then all that I *have*—or think I have—falls definitely out of question, and what is important is what I really *am*. According to a formula that I use here advisedly, to say "I have a body" amounts precisely to forgetting that one day, very certainly, "my body will have me." We have to face up to reality (admitting both a defeat and a dazzling victory that is not really mine): nothing remains of what I *have* when I consider what I *am* (have become) with respect to my suffering. My body is something in reality I never *have*: it is only what "I *am*."[21] This serves to remind us both of the ineradicable experience of a suffering body and theologically of the no-less-compelling words of Christ at his last supper: "This is my body"—*hoc est corpus meum* (Mark 14:22).

§62 The Excess of the Suffering Body

In contrast to perception, which goes all the deeper as it loses itself in the real world, incarnate suffering lived to the extreme carries, as we have seen Marc Richir saying, "excess in a different direction," that "of a body so excessive as to be *invasive*."[22] The invasion of the self by one's own body is experienced above all when something is lacking—or rather is lacking *for me*—because in reality everything is lacking once being goes beyond self-interested preoccupations and breaks the ordinary chain of utility. In Heidegger's terms, it is when equipment that should be "ready-to-hand" [*zuhanden*], or "present-at-hand" [*vorhanden*] does not come to hand, whether it is lost or useless, that on the one hand the general organization of my world becomes obvious to me (because something is missing in my organization), and on the other hand I experience myself as "having hands" (because with the lack of equipment what is shown fully and solely is the Being-there of my own poor hands—since they have nothing to take hold of—and I am thus in the tight spot where I am only these hands and can only see myself as such in my incarnation). When a hammer that was needed is missing, to take up a famous example from *Being and Time*, I see myself at once in my capacity as a hammering being. Setting aside the ironic aspect and coming back again to our attempt to work with phenomenology and theology together, we can say that Jesus, the son of a carpenter, would also have had to know very well what it is to *hammer* and would have known, as Heidegger expresses it, that when we consider "a cabinet-maker's apprentice, someone who is learning to build cabinets and the like . . . His learning is not mere practice, to gain facility in the use of tools."[23]

But far from Nazareth, and even from Galilee, things go differently and perhaps more seriously when in his incarnate suffering Christ encounters a lack not simply of things or of disciples to support him, but even more a lack *of* himself and *for* himself. It is not enough, after all, for any of us to make a show of the "I can" of our consciousness, or of our flesh, to establish the world intentionally through the spatiality of our own bodies.[24] When I suffer (in) my body, in reality *I cannot carry on*—and that is precisely because, as far as my extreme fleshly pain is concerned, *I cannot bear it any longer*. The body, "naked and indigent," is, as Levinas says, that which has to accept that the game has changed.[25] I, who have thought of myself as intentionally forming things (the world, myself, the other), discover myself, indeed through my corporality, becoming in fleshly terms totally suffering, to be suddenly and passively constituted in an "impossibility of retreat" or, as Levinas says, an "impossibility of detaching oneself from suffering."[26] Thus I fall short for myself or, rather, I fall short of myself, in the sense that the *me* in myself, believing in a way that I am incorporate in the world at the same time as perceiving it, finds suddenly of and for myself that I am not "incorporable." I am unknowable and unidentifiable through a rupture with my own body. I cannot lie to myself, though words seem to come quickly: "The content of suffering merges with the impossibility of detaching oneself from suffering."[27] It is exactly thus with Christ on Golgotha, forced onto the cross, as he is forced also into his own suffering, exposed to the same impossibility of detaching himself from suffering, confronted by the same incompleteness of being as by the fleshly finitude of all living things. In St. Augustine's words, "The cross, that is everything that Christian flesh suffers."[28] When the Son indeed "cries out"—nailed and exposed upon the cross even in the nakedness of his flesh—he resolves ultimately to be nothing *but flesh* (incarnate and suffering) and silences his speech definitively, even if that means solely addressing himself to his Father at the height of his abandonment. After this feeling of total abandonment—when he "cries out," in a shout [*boaô*], the *words* of his anguished anxiety, "My God, my God, why have you forsaken me?" (Mark 15:34), there flows out from him, or is dug out of him, from the flesh this time, the last and ultimate "loud cry," inarticulate because it does not reach to the level of discourse: "Then Jesus gave a loud cry [*apheis phônen megalên*] and breathed his last" (Mark 15:37). Beyond the words, Christ's flesh here is exposed and split open, breaking down in a "fleshly rupture." Charles Péguy talks of "the rupture that is done once, the rupture of tissues, the rupture of vessels, the rupture of the cords of life."[29] Only in this breaking up of the flesh does the curtain rise—or rather, as we read in the Epistle to the Hebrews, it is torn, "by the new and living way that he opened for us through the curtain (that is, through his flesh)" (Heb 10:20). And in Mark's Gospel we read, "The curtain of the temple was torn in two, from top to bottom" (Mark 15:38). Could we not say that, in a Christian way and specifically so this time, suffering has at last *unveiled the truth* (wounded or vulnerable [§65]) of the Being-there of humankind? Heidegger talking of "the original essence of truth" suggests it is something that "has been remembered. Unhiddenness [*a-lêtheia*] reveals itself to this remembrance as the basic feature of beings themselves."[30]

12

The Revealing Sword

If in suffering we are divested of the self and enter into the flesh, beyond the question "Why," and at the heart of self-incarnation, we need to come back, once more, to the "scandal" of suffering as such, to the "stumbling stone [*skandalon*]" (Rom 9:32) against which our feet collide. "In spite of all possible energy and notwithstanding the most cunning tactics," Maurice Blondel says, "how often pain flares up to the point where man is forced to regret he was born."[1] The distance remains immeasurable, as one knows, or least as one feels, between evil observed and evil actually suffered: "We may well accept and foresee fatigue, being fed up with work, the reversals of fortune, the betrayals of life; we still remain always surprised and crushed by them, otherwise than we had expected."[2] "Otherwise" and other: that is probably what the cry of the rupture in the flesh uncovers here—the cry of That One who in reality "[speaks] of the temple of his body" (John 2:21) when "the curtain" of his own "temple" was torn in two (Mark 15:38).

§63 Sobbing and Tears

Some people say, as we have seen, that they would choose to suffer themselves rather than let others suffer—indeed they would choose to suffer their own deaths rather than that of their neighbors or their spouses. Just as when I think about my own death, however, a world separates the *tears* I might shed over the suffering of a friend from how I actually *sob* at my own suffering.[3] My incarnate suffering, no less than my death, remains still and always my own, incommunicable and inexplicable. "Suffering with the sufferer" is not in this sense necessarily suffering; it is rather "to suffer suffering." We need only consider the distance that lies between the *tears* of Christ over the death of his friend Lazarus (John 11:35) and his "grieved and agitated" *sobs* at Gethsemane (Matthew 26:37) just before his own death. As in the case of a decease, these tears are always and only shed in relation to some kind of determinate event. More than suffering, they are shed for grief (singularized and localized like a wound, even if a moral wounding). The *tears of the weeping* Mary Magdalene at the empty tomb (John 20:11), those of the young man who wants to bury his father (Luke 9:59), or again those of Christ at Bethany faced with the death of Lazarus (John 11:35) are not so much weeping for someone (*quis*) or something (*quid*); rather they arise, like fear, when faced with the suffering or demise of a particular being. They do not show, like *tears shed when sobbing*, a being who in himself or herself "breaks down" and "opens up" all his or her person. In a way these tears are "nothing to do with it," because they do not know the "why" of their own weeping and because they achieve nothing other than accepting an entry into the Nothing.

I cannot agree, then, that we could separate, as is so often done, "physical pain" from "moral suffering," as if "taking possession" of one's suffering through the consciousness were somehow better than simply but fully "suffering" the pain in one's body.[4] More importantly, truly inordinate suffering, whether that implies the overflowing of the self by a radical suffering in one's being or, even more, the suffering of an other, remains always essentially "physical." Pain, on the other hand, as an evil that can be localized, belongs not only to a specific physical problem, but also has some of the characteristics of "morality," or suffering for another, when sobbing does not really come into it.[5] Gabriel Marcel suggests in a note of 1931 that "physical suffering . . . be regarded as the *prototype* or root of all suffering,"[6] and that is perhaps the last word, if not the first and only word, that can help us to elaborate a true phenomenology of incarnate suffering. Sustaining in this sense morally the possibility, indeed the quasi-certitude, of some future consolation, *tears* bewail, when all is said and done, their own pain above all, because they do not actually inhabit the (incarnate) suffering of the other so much as they are distressed in their present despair. Even though it often seems unbearable (but we do put up with it all the same, even against our will!) moral pain can often, not to say always, be detached from the pained being who undergoes it. The sufferer from moral pain gets on with living, or rather is able to put on a good performance, most often to the point where others have to believe in it (except, of course, when moral suffering is lived through in a pathological form and takes on exactly the same mode as physical pain with the same impossibility of withdrawing from it). Going further then, and perhaps also less overtly than the *tears of weeping*, we find that there are *tears of sobbing*, and they are characteristic this time of "physical suffering." Unlike what happens almost always in weeping over "moral pain," these tears make all distance from the self to the self definitively impossible. As Levinas explains, "Where suffering attains its purity, where there is no longer anything between us and it, the supreme responsibility of this extreme assumption turns into supreme irresponsibility, into infancy. *Sobbing* is this, and precisely through this it announces death. To die is to return to this *state of irresponsibility*, to be the *infantile shaking of sobbing*."[7] What then of the sobs of Christ at Gethsemane, which he shares with humankind—from his "supreme irresponsibility" to his own "infantile shaking"?

§64 Fleshly Exodus

The first experience of sobs, or of the gaping and indeterminate opening of his being in flesh, can be read in the avowal by Christ himself of the *weakness* of his own flesh: "Keep awake and pray that you may not come into the time of trial; the spirit [*pneuma*] indeed is willing, but the flesh [*sarx*] is weak" (Mark 14:38). This is neither the consequence of sin (as we have already seen) nor even the scolding of a teacher: neither instruction *ex professo* [from one with expert competence] nor sermon *ex cathedra* [from the chair, as in solemn declarations of dogmatic teaching]. The impossible overflowing of the flesh is shown here above all as "confidentiality" or "confession." As Charles Péguy reminds us, "This was a man speaking to men."[8] Following the suffering that Christ now *is* (has become), the Father is revealed to his own Son first and next to humankind, as Blondel says, as "other" and "otherwise": "Always something other than [one] expected."[9]

The Father is revealed:

(a) To the Son, and in particular at Gethsemane and Golgotha. Christ suffering, and being exposed in the flesh on the cross is not, or not any longer, at home [*chez lui*] at the heart of this suffering. He is no longer at home with the image of himself as a God so powerful that he can work through signs [or miracles] and exercise his power to reestablish some kind of lost integrity in the world. Blondel tells us that suffering "keeps us from becoming acclimatized to this world, and leaves us here with a kind of incurable discomfort [*malaise*]."[10] Being "at home with himself" in the circumstances comes back then for the Son as a *man* (and like all humankind) less to the question of offering up his suffering than to accepting that he will live it through and that it will be followed by the "*Exodus*" of his *wounded flesh*, all the more unbearable in that there will be a tearing open of the flesh that has to endure while he is powerless to cicatrize or heal it. But paradoxically, and *divinely* this time, he does not recognize himself as "at home with himself" until he is in the presence of an Other who precisely is not him—or rather who is only him (*alter ego*) to the extent that he remains other than him (*ego alter*). That is, his own Father, to whom he groans out his suffering, and "from the beginning till now the entire creation, as we know, has been groaning in one great act of giving birth" (Rom 8:22 JB).

(b) Next, God reveals himself to humankind, exposed on the cross. He shows himself as *other*—elsewhere and otherwise—than they expected: "They will look on the one whom they have pierced" (John 19:37). To "bear the cross" was not enough for the Son, as I have already emphasized (§42) for him to reveal this aspect of his divinity. According to Tertullian, he had also to "bear the flesh" (*carnem gestare*) so that he could "bear the cross" (*crucem gestare*).[11] That is precisely what provokes the astonishment of the soldiers at Golgotha: not seeing one more victim of torture, but suddenly to recognize in this one, who like others bears his cross, that he alone at the same time bears the flesh (of humankind and of God). And yet, paradoxically, they "pierced his side with a spear" (John 19:34). If there is then what Étienne Gilson called the "metaphysics of Exodus" at the heart of the First (the Old) Testament or the Second (the New) Testament,[12] it does not appear from any kind of statement on being (ontology), whether in terms of the "pure act" of existence (Étienne Gilson) or the "horizon" of all that exists (Heidegger).[13] Only an Exodus, or *fleshly voyage*, of Christ— of the kind that one does not know where it is going or whence it comes— impresses its mark in reality on the suffering being of Christ. And it does so in a way that is eminently non-sinful as, without any resistance, Christ abdicates from himself and gives himself up wholly and deliberately to the sole and simply obvious fact that "now it is necessary to go." It is indeed a voyage at the heart of (the) flesh. God says to Moses at the Burning Bush, "I am who I shall be" (Ex 3:14—[translation of the TOB: "Je suis *qui je serai*"]). That is, God is starting on the route that his flesh will one day take, at the heart of the history of Moses, a route that will become his own history, like the history of Moses, and will be told, as Péguy recalls to us, as "a story that has happened to the flesh, and to the earth."[14]

§65 The Vulnerable Flesh

The radical impossibility of remaining in command of this voyage shows the extreme vulnerability of the flesh of Christ, the wound (*vulnus*) in his side, pierced and torn open like a curtain in the temple of his body. "He had just suffered the experience in himself, he had just come to understand," Charles Péguy says, "and then all at once he knew what this frightful temptation was; what this *"angoisse"* was, frightful and in his own body; he knew what the weakness of the flesh was, the infirmity of all flesh."[15] The opening in his flesh pierced by the spear (John 19:34) and the stigmata of his hands wounded by the mark of the nails (John 20:25) remain from the experience and are what make him recognizable in his Resurrection. "Put your finger here," he says to Thomas, "and see my hands. Reach out your hand and put it in my side. Do not doubt but believe" (John 20:27). The wound in the flesh (*vulnus*) belongs thus and probably forever to the very being of God. Paul's sufferings, through some lack or nonfulfillment, do not reach this Christ-like level of suffering. He writes, "In my flesh . . . what is lacking in Christ's affliction for the sake of his body, that is, the church" (Col 1:24). Jesus, on the contrary, as Pascal says, "will be in agony until the end of the world,"[16] but only so far as the *vulnerability* of his flesh indicates his nature itself and his radical destitution—his most ordinary being, as it were disappropriated of everything, including (as we shall see) even the act of appropriation itself. Jean-Yves Lacoste writes, "It is only at the hour of his death or at that of his birth that the man appears to us *entirely* in the guise of the destitute, as one to whom every right of possession is denied or as one who has yet to appropriate anything."[17] Without shame or resignation, then, but rather in the total nonmastery of the self that follows from incarnate anxiety, the Son returns to a "state of irresponsibility." In this state being responsible for oneself would not imply bearing one's own suffering, nor even (as we shall see later) that of another. As opposed to all false heroic and non-Trinitarian handling of his suffering at Gethsemane, a very positive *irresponsibility* in the Christian scheme comes back to reveal Christ himself, and perhaps also reveals him to himself, as incapable of bearing in Promethean fashion *all* suffering, even his own, so that he offers or *passes on* the suffering to the Father.

§66 The Non-Substitutable Substitution

It is not enough in Christianity, as I have so far tried to show (§53), to bear the "suffering of others" in such a way that "each person acts as though he were the Messiah."[18] On the contrary, it is because the Messiah is above all *never* me—his suffering being first and foremost that of God and not simply *mine*—that his reception by me belongs to a pure and true "incarnate" alterity. Jürgen Moltmann emphasizes that the cross of Christ is not the same as the cross of his disciples. What the disciples had to take on themselves was not his cross but "their cross." According to Moltmann,

"Jesus suffered and died alone [or, as I understand it, in communion with God at the depths of his abandonment by humankind]. But those who follow him suffer and die in fellowship with him."[19] To suffer and die "with" the Son does not mean that one does not any longer suffer and die, nor does it take away the "mineness" of suffering and death. Christ suffers and dies *for* me and *with* me: he does not suffer and die in my place. The true "place" of suffering for the Christian comes down first of all to accepting that one take *one's* place—not instead of [*à la place de*] Christ, but *with* Christ, who is suffering and resurrected *with* me, and not *without* me. Like a guide or ferryman [*Passeur*] taking in charge the one who passes or whom he guides [*le passant*], Christ transforms, starting from today, the meaning of my suffering, so that I am able to make it (along with him) the modality of my own life. It becomes, as it were, the place of reception of an *elsewhere* or an *other* of my life—indeed it is the *other of my suffering* and the *other of the Father* in my life. If there is then a substitution that is possible in Christianity and radically rejected in Judaism (Levinas), it does not in any way involve an exchange of places, as if one were suffering oneself what God suffered, or indeed as if enduring the same suffering as God would necessarily guarantee that one then obtained some kind of salvation.[20] The substitution consists solely, but in a complicated way because of the simple heroism of the subject concerned, in accepting that we do not engage with suffering *all alone*. We are not besieged by the incarnation of suffering, close to our own bodies, in the stronghold of our "great health,"[21] which we believed we could master and dominate. Suffering is something that is (supposedly) unfinished, that surprises and displaces all living beings, that has always still conformed to the law of corruptibility of all living beings. We are, as Heidegger says, "at once old enough to die," "as soon as [we come] to life."[22] I must thus accept that I inhabit the special region of my own finitude, philosophically because *I am thrown into it*, and theologically because the One comes who, to the bitter end, has taken on this burden and "pitched his tent among us" (John 1:14 JB, note 1b). Such at least is the substitution, not "impossible," but non-substitutable, of which Christians neither can nor must allow themselves to be deprived. To be deprived of the substitution would for one thing risk losing Christ himself here and for another would entail confining us, this time perhaps forever, in the pure unbreakable solipsism of suffering and dying flesh.[23] "Hell," rather than simply looming at the horizon of my freedom, where I would perhaps be the first guest, denotes a potential denial of Christ at the very heart of my suffering, the "absence of every other," indeed the perpetuating of my suffering in "a death that could not even put an end to it."[24] My responsibility for the other does not then make me "even responsible for the other's responsibility." In Christianity "to be me" does not imply that I carry an extra burden of responsibility. Rather, it allows me to have one responsibility less—precisely because *one individual* has carried, even as far as "supreme irresponsibility," that responsibility, in passing it, or perhaps we should say in delivering it, to his own Father.[25]

§67 The Act of Surrendering Oneself

Christ offers himself on the cross, passing over to the Father without however ever *passing over* the Father. He does not just "give," nor does he just "give himself." What happens is more like an exchange of different procedures, and it would be false to say that one or other method was "good," since they operate only under a common reciprocity. Conversely, and in a total asymmetry this time, Christ delivers and surrenders himself up. He delivers: Just as a "good deliverer" finally brings us to safe harbor, never mind who is the recipient or what the cargo is (above all when it is a question of "unloading" the burden of finitude). He also surrenders himself up: this is like pulling himself together and also resigning himself from himself, not simply the "prisoner" tracked down or in a corner from so much injustice (figure of sin), but also one of the "wretched," or a "pauper," exhausted and wounded by the burden of his condition (figure of finitude). Beyond any reciprocity and even any profit from this gift, Christ *delivers* not simply what he is himself, but also the act of giving and surrendering (giving of the gift). We follow in his footsteps, albeit in another mode (because what dwells within us is the knowledge of his Resurrection). In giving, indeed in giving and surrendering himself, the donor always strives in reality not to forget and to remind whoever might have forgotten that in giving he has surrendered himself. The gift, conversely, is not truly given until it is aban-*don*ed ["*donner*"=to give], remaining indeed at once gift and separate from the gift. St. Thérèse Couderc writes in a letter, "Surrender oneself: it is even a greater thing than sacrificing oneself; it is more than giving oneself; it is even more than abandoning oneself to God. Finally to surrender oneself is to die to all of oneself. It is for me no longer to be occupied with myself, except in keeping myself always turned towards God."[26] As with my birth, that could never have been given to me unless it had been handed to me by others (my parents), and given to another (the "Father who is in heaven"), so the Son, "breaking down" and "opening up" his sobs as he presents himself to his Father, does not become fully himself—either for himself or afterward for us—until he *delivers* his being as a gift, even literally abandoning it.[27]

§68 Toward a Revelation

The anxiety about our own deaths and the suffering that is incarnate (or, as Péguy sees it, "*encharnée*" [in-fleshed]) in our own bodies lies very far from this abandonment, which is as it were inscribed in the pierced side and the flesh offered. But it is from them that we receive finally the ultimate and probably the only possibility of a "Christian meaning." Without fleeing suffering (and death) in a fearful escape into the beyond or trying to confront it heroically in the here and now, the Christian recognizes that, on the one hand, suffering remains to some degree supremely unacceptable; on the other hand, the Son himself can carry it through to its finish by not taking it all upon himself—or, perhaps, we should say *for* himself. He chooses to do what is probably most difficult, handing over responsibility to his Father ("Not my will but yours be done" [Luke 22:42]). Christ invites us also to this "gift of the gift"—a gift not simply of ourselves but also of our will to give—each in our own passage (both in a *passive* taking on board of suffering and in a *passing* on of the gift) through our own suffering and our own deaths.

Maurice Blondel underlines that we can take the measure of a person according to the *welcome* he or she gives to suffering, because suffering is the imprint of the other in us.[28] Suffering remains, one might say, at least for me, if not for the other, that which tears me apart rather than, as the untenable alternative has it, something that reveals me to myself in my own and everyday being in the world. Either I "welcome" the figure of the other in suffering and death (as in the non-sinful Passion of the Son) or I "refuse" the presence in everyday reality of this other in myself (suffering, death, the other, God), and I then necessarily, indeed definitively, "revolt" at the hour when I come to suffer. Blondel's "revealing sword" [suffering that "cuts through life"], the suffering endured in my flesh, makes me see how, and how much, in my "great health" also, I have neither forgotten the Guide (the Son—the *Passeur*), nor the destination, the addressee, of my *passage* (the Father).[29]

§69 Useless Suffering

All the same, nothing at the heart of such suffering taken on board (*pâtir*), or such a passage, shows that it is enough to give (oneself) or indeed to make the gift (to deliver oneself up) to become positively acceptable or "give-able (*donable*)." It goes almost without saying that my unworthiness does not mean that I cannot be accepted by God, but simply the act of giving, particularly of giving this gift, remains still and always a supreme possibility for the Donor—and for him principally it is good in that it is not made alone (because his act of giving is not done without me). We should not, or should no longer, require suffering to invoke (albeit in terms concealed under the Hellenizing concept of catharsis or the Judaic concept of sacrifice) the supposed benefits of purification through suffering. I would hope that we can agree today to recognize that it is neither necessary to suffer mentally or bodily (even though such a suffering may be a possibility) to gain our salvation. One would hope that this—finally—goes without saying. But the very specific Christian perspective of a "usefulness," or at least a "fecundity" in suffering, is such that it very often transfers the ambition of salvation to the virtues of purification once suffering is present and acknowledged, not just sought after. In fact, many mystics (Francis of Assisi, Thérèse of Lisieux, John of the Cross), indeed even among our contemporaries (Marthe Robin, Jacques Fesch),[30] where we can discount any instrumentalization of suffering, witness the effectiveness of suffering that may "lead to conversion."[31] Such experiences, however, do not cancel out either the absurdity or the futility of pain. Rather than disguising the cry of protest that arises from pain, in reality they exacerbate it, to the point sometimes of endorsing a suffering that is all the more intense because the ascetic ideal is so exacting. One cannot simply deny the validity of the hypothesis of catharsis (or of the purifying effect of suffering), but for the subject it remains solely within the horizon of the lived experience of his or her *own* flesh, and it remains within the spectrum of *his or her* own conversion. It cannot and should not be extended to the fleshly lived experience of other people—also and above all because what one might say to invoke and justify the supposedly purifying virtues are in reality nothing but an attempt to forget the unforgettable. Such talk ignores the overwhelming auto-affection of the person who, here in front of me and very often "under my own eyes," suffers in his or her flesh, often so far as to be reduced only to suffering in an inexorable impossibility of withdrawing from it.

Incarnate suffering is then something that only I experience for myself, and nothing sanctions it. If I start justifying it when somebody else has to suffer or stand up to suffering, he or she can only point to the contrast with my "great health." Levinas maintains, "The least one can say about suffering is that, in its own phenomenality, intrinsically, it is useless: 'for nothing.'"[32] In other words, and avoiding what might seem simplistic here, as I see it we can say that the person "nailed to the bed" (suffering) is also "nailed to the cross" (cornered in his or her suffering): he or she is like Christ (hung out or exposed in his flesh) and with Christ (grappling not only with sin but also with the burden of his own finitude), but not identical with Christ (because only Christ will take suffering on board [*pâtir*] even to the end of his own suffering, leading to his *passage* to the Father. Just as the Son gives no response to the *who* on the subject of the man who has been blind from birth (John 9: 1–41) or to the *what* of the accidental suffering of the victims of the fall of the tower of Siloam (Luke 13:2–5) (§58), so in reality he does not receive a reply for himself from the Father as to the *why* of his own suffering or his abandonment: "My God, my God, *why* [*eis ti*] have you forsaken me?" (Mark 15:34). Opening the eyes of the man born blind by a miracle is not the same as deleting all the man's suffering, even if in this case it was exemplary: in reality we all also suffer, or suffer-from [*pâtir*], a certain alterity from the finitude in us, even if it is to different degrees. To aid the man to "receive his sight" (John 9:18) is only to help the man to see what he has never yet seen, precisely because he did not see. It is "so that God's works might be revealed in him" (John 9:3). The healing of the man born blind, like the surrender of the Son on the cross, is not backward-looking, as it were, confirming the why of his sufferings, or thinking that they would be rooted at the heart of sin in his origins. It is a putting-forth to the future. It turns toward the question "for-what" [*pourquoi*] is the Son living, as son, and passing (going from) this world to the world of the Father. "I do not know whether he is a sinner," the man healed of his blindness answers finally, when questioned about Jesus. "One thing I do know, that though I was blind, I now see" (John 9:25).

It is useful in the phenomenological mode, but also as a central part of theological inquiry, to go back to the source of a problem in what Heidegger called a "step back" [*Schritt zurück*]. My discussion so far has entailed going back to the notion of sin as self-enclosure in a finitude that is not itself sinful (Part I). This has then led us down a long path, to the "why" that has no reply in Christ's anxiety and his death at Golgotha (Part II). And all this was to prepare the "realm" of "what constitutes the source of this entire thinking":[33] the presence of the other in me (Part III).

The presence of the other is in the form of a triple reception. It is seen, simultaneously, in the body-to-body of suffering and death for the incarnate Son (finitude), at the heart of the Son's passage to the Father (taking on board suffering [*pâtir*] and passing), and through the Son's act of offering, without justification or reciprocity, of himself to God as well as to humankind (gift of the gift). When words are silent, the flesh speaks, and what springs up is the "infantile shaking of sobbing,"[34] that of the child without-speech (*in-fans*). The child is at once vulnerable in fleshly terms and receptive. Hans Urs von Balthasar quotes the words of Novalis written shortly before his death: "To be childlike: That is best of all. Nothing is more difficult than bearing one's own weakness. God helps with everything."[35]

Conclusion: The *In-Fans* [without-Speech] or the Silent Flesh

Husserl talks of "'my' flesh, that which is most originally mine": it is what has always been at once most my own and most close to me. From this, he says, "The one that I am (*as a child*) is the first and is immediately appropriated."[1] In other words, there is nothing that moves me in my flesh or stirs up my affect, coming from myself (kinestheses of the body) or still in myself (feelings), that does not take over my own original establishment of my world through my flesh, "as a child." Finitude in its face-to-face (Part I), anxiety in Christ's assumption of it (Part II), and suffering, like death, in a body-to-body (Part III), send us back to what each of us on our own has seen, to the return of responsibility through supreme irresponsibility— that is, to the mode of being of childhood. The "*infantile* shaking of sobbing" belongs *metaphysically* (in a passage or change of condition [*meta*] that is not at all psychological, of a *phusis* [nature] at the peak of its immanence) to one of those experiments that God poses as a challenge, then and newly, in a radically original and constitutive way, to his own flesh as well as ours.[2] The infant [*in-fans*] is in reality one who is "without-speech," who does not speak [*infari*] because he or she (still) does not know how to speak.[3] Adults often, or almost always, try to help a child as "spokesperson," as though not knowing how to speak must mean, straight off, not being able to speak: "People were bringing little children [*paidia*] to him in order that he might touch them; and the disciples spoke sternly to them." Jesus, however, seems to know very well that for him (and perhaps only for him) to touch is better than speaking. Because these children are brought to him first of all "in order that he might touch them" (Mark 10:13). The "still dumb . . . experience" that "must be made to utter its own sense" in phenomenology,[4] as in theology, according to my understanding, remains first of all and at its origins that of *touching*. St. Bonaventure writes, "His supreme delightfulness touched [*astringitur*] in that He is the incarnate Word dwelling in our midst [*corporaliter*], offering Himself to our touch, our kiss, our embrace [*palpabile, osculabile, amplexabile*], through ardent love which makes our soul pass, by ecstatic rapture, from this world to the Father."[5]

"Do not hold on to me" (John 20:17), says the resurrected Jesus to Mary Magdalene, who has come to "take him away" (John 20:15). We can put any simplistic explanations aside and see this in terms of a touchstone for later developments (see my *Metamorphosis of Finitude*, Part II). Then we could say that the Resurrected One does not let himself be "seized" any more in his body (*Körper*) as an object (corruptible) of the world, but only "approached" in his flesh (*Leib*) as subject (incorruptible and constitutive) for this same world. More, while he can say that a "ghost does not have flesh and bones as you see that I have," Jesus certainly appears to the Eleven in "flesh and bones" (Luke 24:39). Is this simply because it is said that he "ate in their presence" "a piece of broiled fish" (Luke 24:43, 24:42), as if objectively the body of the Resurrected One could experience some form of hunger? Or is it not rather that in the process of eating, independently of that hunger of the body and solely through the diverse kinestheses of his (resurrected) body, what was revealed was "the thing itself" ("in person," or "in flesh and bones," as Husserl was rather oddly to say)? Indeed, what is recognizable at the Resurrection is the *manner* or *mode* by which previously Christ also ate or established this same world through his (biological) body—his body that holds unfailingly to, and indeed is embedded in, his (phenomenal) flesh. "That disciple whom Jesus loved said to Peter, 'It is the Lord!' When Simon Peter heard that it was the Lord, he put on some clothes, for he was naked, and jumped into the lake" (John 21:7). When the women come to the tomb in the early morning of Easter day ("Paschal" day), they are suffering [*pâtissant*] because of a *passage* that is not as yet understood, but they see with their own eyes and hear, even from the mouth of the angel, that Jesus of Nazareth, the crucified one, now resurrected, "Is not *here*," but "is going ahead of you to Galilee; *there* you will see him" (Mark 16:6–7). Thus, in the final analysis, could we not say that theologically what is broken open through the resurrection of the flesh is the impossible yet so much longed-for total apperceptive transposition of the here (*l'ici*) to the over-there (*là-bas*) that we find in (Husserl's) phenomenology?[6] In the Resurrection we see how it can finally and legitimately be said of Christ that he "lives in me" (Gal 2:20) without any competing notion that he "does not live in you." Putting together the suffering (Part III), as well as the finitude (Part I) that is taken on by Christ through his anxiety (Part II), we can say that the Resurrected One leads us in a way toward an *elsewhere* and consequently invites us to live *otherwise*—without however leaving the basis of his flesh, which always is and has been (from his birth to his Resurrection) the element, or the *medium*, of his humanity that is in us.

It is appropriate, at the conclusion of this *analysis of the incarnation* (finitude, suffering, and death), to move toward the difficult but still possible topic of an *analysis of the Resurrection* (birth and incorruptibility). In that way we shall re-find, as perhaps some already have, with the Resurrected Son as the unique *infant* at the heart of the Father, the roads to the Kingdom, suitable for today and for always. Those roads, always continuing and always still open for us, lead us to (re)discover our own fleshly infancy. Bernanos writes in the preface to *Les Grands Cimitières sous la lune*, "Ah, I know well how vain such a return to the past is. Certainly, my life is indeed already full of the dead. But the deadest of the dead is the little boy I once was. Still, when the hour comes, it is he who will take his place at the head of my life; it is he who will gather up the years of my poor life, down to the last one. And, like a young commander rallying his disorderly troop of veterans, it is he who will be the first to enter the House of the Father."[7]

Epilogue: From One Triptych to Another

A triptych of books is completed, one that I have put together under the title *The Philosophical Triduum*; now another commences. I have already suggested in my preface to this Triduum that my "triptych on the Passion will be followed, or could be followed, by a triptych on the Recapitulation."[1] That is to say, it was not enough to examine or describe philosophically the three days of the Passion: Good Friday (*The Guide to Gethsemane*), Easter Sunday (*The Metamorphosis of Finitude*), and Holy Thursday (*The Wedding Feast of the Lamb*). It is still necessary, in approaching the factual events, or rather in working out the theory behind these events, in relation to the life of the Son and the Resurrection, to go deep into essences (even better, into ontologic and theoretical essences), insofar as we are concerned with the works of the Father and the power of the Holy Spirit. We need to consider the dawn and the end of time, and indeed the descent into the hell that supports (or underlies) them.

There is the temporal, but that is also *where* we find the eternal—not, as I have tried to show throughout this Triduum (see especially Part III of *Metamorphosis of Finitude*, Chapter 7: "The World Become Other"), that we need to construct an opposition of worlds or of the "ecstases of temporality."[2] But in the "life of the Father" there is formed a specific Being-there that is certainly linked to the ordeal of the Son through the power of the Holy Spirit and yet concerns him in his own right in relation to the ontological dimension of the world and of salvation. My planned triptych of Recapitulation, following on from this triptych on the Passion, will then newly examine certain "days"—this time not those within a temporal sequence, but days of the eternal. After the three historic days of Holy Thursday, Good Friday, and Easter Sunday (*Philosophical Triduum*) come the three symbolic days of Holy Saturday (the Great Sabbath), the First Day of Creation, and the Last Day of the End of Time (*Theological Recapitulation*). These symbolic days, which are directly performed in the eternal, are no less obvious because they do not first of all open their scene in the temporal (historic days). The descent into hell, protology [the study of first things], and eschatology still need, each in its own way, to be accorded the ontologic and theoretical existential that appertains to them. To look in them for (indeed to find in them) the prospect of salvation will not simply be a perspective that is temporal and historical (the Revelation), but also one that is eternal and symbolic (myths of creation and of the end of time).

The approach in this new triptych (that of the "Recapitulation") will however be no less philosophical, despite or perhaps by "grace" of the fact that its perspective is at the same time theological. In what concerns God—whether we are talking of days when we humans were not there (Creation) or days when we shall no longer be there (the Last Judgment)—nothing speaks or is spoken without passing through humankind, in that God was made man. We need, as we shall find, these new ontological and theoretical existentials to signify and describe the depths: the "World" for "Creation" (the First Day); "Evil" for "Sin" (Holy Saturday or the Day in Between); "Childhood" for the "Kingdom" (the Last Day). Here again, it is not enough, and never will be enough, that we translate the philosophical "into" the theological—in the double sense of the French verb *traduire*—that is, "to translate" in a linguistic conversion or "to bring someone in front of a court of justice." Theology itself possesses the means, by a kind of "return shock" (See my *Crossing the Rubicon*),[3] to transform the philosophical and put it into question, as the *Philosophical Triduum* has attempted to show. We can start by looking at sin (facing God) as the conversion of transgression (facing humankind); at Creation (divine) in the form of a transformation of the horizon of the (human) world; and at childhood (of the Kingdom) as a form of the unsurpassable, or what cannot be overcome (toward adult age).

The Son, a type of New Adam, "recapitulates" (*anakephalaiosis*) all the "world" (creation), of "transgression" (sin), and of "childhood" (the Kingdom), in the singularity of his own Person. But he only works such a synthesis in being "subjected" to the Father (1 Cor 15:28), in the "power" of the "Holy Spirit" (Acts 1:8). The three parts of the Trinity are thus entirely engaged not just in the days of the Passion (Holy Thursday, Good Friday, and Easter Sunday), but also in a "Recapitulation" (Holy Saturday, First

Day of Creation, Last Day of the End of Time). It is to this last order, an order dictated by "the things themselves," and indeed by God in the inspiration that he wished to breathe into us, that we need to commit ourselves. We can be sure that strength will be given us to know humbly how to bend ourselves to the task. The anonymous Ancient Homily for Holy Saturday tells us, *"Awake, O sleeper, and arise from the dead, and Christ shall give you light."*[4]

Granges d'Ans, February 18, 2015
(Ash Wednesday)

Notes

Translator's Note

1. See Christina M. Gschwandtner, in her essay "Emmanuel Falque: A God of Suffering and Resurrection," in *Postmodern Apologetics? Arguments for God in Contemporary Philosophy* (New York: Fordham University Press, 2013), 192–94, 315.

Preface to the English-Language Edition

1. The three books mentioned are republished in French in a single volume, now entitled *Triduum Philosophique: Le Passeur de Gethsémani; Métamorphose de la Finitude; Les Noces de l'Agneau* (Paris: Les Éditions du Cerf, 2015), where they have a preface and epilogue justifying the whole enterprise. The present volume offers a translation of *Le Passeur de Gethsémani*, along with part of the preface and the epilogue at its conclusion. [Trans.—A "Triduum" is three days of prayer and religious observance, for example, at Easter or Christmas.]

2. "Pope John's Opening Speech to the Council," October 11, 1962, Vatican II—Voice of the Church, accessed December 24, 2016, http://vatican2voice.org /91docs/opening_speech.htm.

3. Maurice Blondel, *The Letter on Apologetics*, trans. Alexander Dru and Illtyd Trethowan (London: Harvill, 1964), 129.

4. See Chap. 2, note 25.

5. Emmanuel Falque, *Crossing the Rubicon: The Borderlands of Philosophy and Theology*, trans. Reuben Shank (New York: Fordham University Press, 2016).

Opening: The Isenheim Altarpiece or "The Taking on Board of Suffering"

1. [Trans.—Falque distinguishes between two terms for suffering in French, *souffrir* and *pâtir*. He uses *souffrir* in the sense of feeling pain and *pâtir* when the suffering is something that does not come from oneself, but is taken on board. The latter (*pâtir*) is particularly appropriate for the suffering that Christ takes on board and *passes* through in Gethsemane.]

2. Emmanuel Levinas, *Time and the Other*, trans. Richard A. Cohen (Pittsburgh Pa.: Duquesne University Press, 1987), 69.

3. [Trans.—The use of the name "Grünewald" derives from a biography of the artist published in 1675 by Joachim von Sandrart. The Isenheim artist may have been known at the time as "Mathis Gothart Nithart," or "Neithart." Some specialists, however, prefer the suggestion that there was another painter who worked along with Grünewald called "Nithart."]

4. Agnès Lacau St. Guily, *Grünewald: Le retable d'Issenheim* (Paris: Mame, 1996), 48.

5. See on this point Emmanuel Falque, "Éthique du corps épandu [Ethics of the Spread-Out Body]," concerning end-of-life care, in *Revue d'éthique et de théologie morale* (RETM), no. 288 (March 2016): 53–82.

6. Blaise Pascal, *Pensées*, trans. A. J. Krailsheimer (London: Penguin, 1966), L165:B120, 82.

7. Martin Heidegger, *Being and Time*, trans. John Macquarrie and Edward Robinson (New York: Harper Perennial Modern Thought, 2008), §48:245. [Trans.—Quotations from *Being and Time* are given from the Macquarrie and Robinson translation throughout this book, except where the translation by Joan Stambaugh is closer to the French translation used by Falque. Unless otherwise stated, the quotations are from the Macquarrie and Robinson translation.]

8. [Trans.—Biblical quotations are cited from the New Revised Standard Version, except where the translation in the Jerusalem Bible (JB), the King James Bible (AV), or the Amplified Bible (AMP) is closer to the French translations used by Falque.]

9. Alphonse Daudet, *In the Land of Pain*, trans. Julian Barnes (New York: Vintage Classics, 2016), 65, 24–25.

10. Friedrich Nietzsche, *On the Genealogy of Morals*, trans. Walter Kaufmann and R. J. Hollingdale (New York: Vintage, 1969), §28, 162.

11. Heidegger, *Being and Time: A Translation of Sein und Zeit*, trans. Joan Stambaugh (Albany: State University of New York Press, 1996), note vi to §49:249, p. 408.

12. Charles Péguy, *Dialogue de l'histoire et de l'âme charnelle*, in *Oeuvres en prose complètes*, Pléiade ed. (Paris: Gallimard, 1992), 3:743.

13. I am following the interpretation given by Paul Baudiquey, in the film *Le retable d'Issenheim de Mathias Grünewald*, (DVD/Audiovisuel Musique Évangélisation, 2004), rather than that of St. Guily (*Grünewald*, 105), whose

book sees here baptism and a leap into a heavenly other world, not a depiction of the wretchedness and sickness to be found on earth.

14. Leo the Great, 15th Sermon on the Passion, in Milton Walsh, *Witness of the Saints: Patristic Readings in the Liturgy of the Hours* (San Francisco: Ignatius, 2012), §443.

15. Pierre Corneille, *Polyeucte* (1643), II:335, in *Harvard Classics*, trans. Thomas Constable (New York: P. F. Collier and Son, 1909–14).

Introduction: Shifting Understandings of Anxiety

1. See Pierre Thévenaz, *L'Homme et sa raison* (Neuchâtel: La Baconnière, 1956), 1:287–307.

2. Martin Heidegger, *Being and Time: A Translation of Sein und Zeit*, trans. Joan Stambaugh (Albany: State University of New York Press, 1996), note vi to §49:408.

3. Heidegger, *Being and Time*, trans. John Macquarrie and Edward Robinson (New York: Harper Perennial, 2008), §51:252.

4. Hans Urs von Balthasar, *The Glory of the Lord: A Theological Aesthetics*, vol. 2, *Studies in Theological Style: Clerical Styles*, trans. Andrew Louth, Francis McDonagh, and Brian McNeil (San Francisco: Ignatius, 1969), 79 (my emphasis).

5. Heidegger, *Being and Time*, §48:245.

6. Heidegger, *Being and Time*, trans. Stambaugh, note vi to §49:408.

1. From the Burden of Death to Flight before Death

1. See Albert Camus, *The Myth of Sisyphus and Other Essays*, trans. Justin O'Brien (New York: Vintage, 1991), 4. Camus records here a news item concerning "an apartment building manager who had killed himself. I was told he had lost his daughter five years before." This experience had "undermined him." Camus adds, "A more exact word cannot be imagined. Beginning to think is beginning to be undermined."

2. Georges Bernanos, *Les Grands Cimetières sous la lune* (Paris: Plon, 1938), iii–iv.

3. Epicurus, "Letter to Menoeceus": "Death, therefore, the most awful of evils, is nothing to us, seeing that, when we are, death is not come, and, when death is come, we are not. It is nothing, then, either to the living or to the dead"; in *Stoic and Epicurean (Epochs of Philosophy)*, trans. Robert Drew Hicks (Barcelona: Edicions Enoanda, 2016), 127–28.

4. Epictetus: "Death, for instance, is not terrible, else it would have appeared so to Socrates. But the terror consists in our notion of death that it is terrible"; *The Enchiridion* 5, trans. Elizabeth Carter, Internet Classics Archive, accessed August 7, 2016, http://classics.mit.edu/Epictetus/epicench.html.

5. [Trans.—Pelagianism: The belief that human beings are not touched by original sin and are capable of choosing between good and evil without the aid of God.]

6. Much reference to this pietistic attitude can be found in theological literature of the end of the nineteenth century and the start of the twentieth century. Thus, for example, the work by Abbot Francis Mugnier, *Souffrance et rédemption: Étude de théologie dogmatique, ascétique et mystique* (Paris: André Blot, 1925) 67–68: "[Apart from the disorder of sin] everything else in man must contribute to the work of salvation. It is not simply suffering that has its *providential role* here. . . . From there on, to accept suffering or to find out why it is there can be an excellent deed that will turn to the good of man, like the swallowing of a bitter medicine." This perspective of a salvation that is earned through suffering, deriving from *The Imitation of Christ*, can be related to the notion of the atonement for humanity by the Son faced with the wrath of his avenging Father. See in this connection the "dark compendium" drawn up by Bernard Sesboüé, *Jésus-Christ l'unique médiateur* (Paris: Desclée, 1988), 67–83.

7. [Trans.—The views attributed to Origen (early Christian theologian, c.184–c. 253) and responsible for his condemnation at the Synod and Council of Constantinople in 543 and 553. Here particularly *apokatastasis* (the idea that there will be an ultimate restoration of all things to their original state).]

8. See Jean-Luc Marion, "Evil in Person," in *Prolegomena to Charity*, trans. Stephen E. Lewis (New York: Fordham, 2002). I disagree with Gustave Martelet, who considers that we should deny the reality of hell to posit the absolute nature of divine Love (*L'Au-Delà retrouvé* [Paris: Desclée, 1995], 149–55). Apart from the well-known condemnation of *apokatastasis* (see note 7) pronounced against the doctrine of Origen at the Synod of Constantinople [see Gervais Dumeige, *La Foi catholique* (Paris: Éditions de l'Orante, 1975), 507, and Heinrich Denzinger, *Enchiridion symbolorum*, no. 411 (San Francisco: Ignatius, 2012)], it is also appropriate to note here that it is less a question of believing ourselves "unloved" in hell by God (Martelet, *L'Au-Delà retrouvé*, 14) than that God remains for each of us the possible horizon of our liberty, and, paradoxically, as we possess the ability to choose, it is this that renders God supremely loving. See the remarkable turnaround by Charles Péguy, who, having believed for a time that he must leave the church because "the dogma of an eternal hell seemed to him intolerable," returned to the church, defining the dogma as the possibility of choice or like a *hardening of the ready-made soul*, which excluded and refused a perpetual Bergsonian "making oneself" in salvation; see "Péguy, "The Metamorphoses of Hell," in *The Glory of the Lord: A Theological Aesthetics*, vol. 3, *Studies in Theological Style: Lay Styles*, by Hans Urs von Balthasar, trans. Andrew Louth, John Saward, Martin Simon, and Rowan Williams (San Francisco: Ignatius, 1986), 435–65.

9. Balthasar, *Dare We Hope "That All Men Be Saved"? With a Short Discourse on Hell*, trans. David Kipp and Lothan Krauth (San Francisco: Ignatius, 1988), chap. 4, "Hell for Others": "'Hell' here is something that falls to me personally—not hypothetically but by full rights—which, without any side glances at others, I have to withstand in utmost seriousness. . . . But woe is me if looking back, I see how others, who were not so lucky as I, are sinking beneath the

waves. . . . For at that moment everything is transformed: hell is no longer something that is ever mine but rather something that befalls 'the others,' while I, praise God, have escaped it."

10. On the theory of *apokatastasis*, see Origen, *De Principiis*, Book III, chap. 6:5–6, trans. Frederick Crombie, in *Ante-Nicene Fathers*, vol. 4 (Buffalo, N.Y.: Christian Literature, 1885); revised by Kevin Knight for New Advent, accessed August 8, 2016, http://www.newadvent.org/fathers/04123.htm; see also Balthasar, *Dare We Hope "That All Men Be Saved"?*, chap. 8.

2. The Face of Death or Anxiety over Finitude

1. I am borrowing this distinction from Gustave Martelet, "Dieu n'a pas crée la mort," in *Christus* 68 (October 1995): 456–67.

2. On the Niceno-Constantinopolitan creed, see Gervais Dumeige, *La Foi catholique: Textes doctrinaux du magistère de l'Église* (Paris: Éditions de l'Orante, 1961), no. 2, p. 6 (Nicée) and no. 8/1, p. 8 (Constantinople), and Heinrich Denzinger, *Enchiridion symbolorum* (San Francisco: Ignatius, 2012), nos. 125 and 150. "*Qui propter nos homines et propter nostram salutem descendit de caelis*" ["For us men and for our salvation, he came down from heaven"].

3. Martin Heidegger, *Being and Time*, trans. John Macquarrie and Edward Robinson (New York: Harper Perennial Modern Thought, 2008), §48:245.

4. Heidegger, *Being and Time: A Translation of Sein und Zeit*, trans. Joan Stambaugh (Albany: State University of New York Press, 1996), note vi to §49, 408.

5. There are many and celebrated studies of this topic. For an exegetical analysis, see Pierre Gibert, *Bible: Mythes et récits des commencements* (Paris: Éditions du Seuil, 1986), in particular, the table (126–28) demonstrating spiritedly the way in which the narrative of the Fall (Gen 3) is rooted in the incest between Amnon and Tamar at the court of King David [2 Sam 13]. For a philosophical reading, see Paul Ricoeur, *The Symbolism of Evil*, trans. Emerson Buchanan (Boston: Beacon Press, 1969), 232–52, on "The Penitential Motivation of the 'Adamic' Myth" and "The Structure of the Myth: The 'Instant' of the Fall."

6. [Trans.—For a fuller discussion of the translation of this verse in French, see §14.]

7. Gustave Martelet, *Libre réponse à un scandale: La faute originelle, la souffrance et la mort* (Paris: Éditions du Cerf, 1992), ix–x.

8. On this bold uncoupling of physical suffering (or biological death) from the thematic of original sin, see in particular the crucial work of Gustave Martelet (ibid.). Probably this is in fact the only way to give substance, in theology, to a human finitude that is so often seen as simply the deficient mode of the uncreated. All the same, this author's theme would benefit, as I see it, from being readjusted in three respects: (a) first, in separating the argument from an orientation that is, at least at the start, too uniformly epistemological and insufficiently metaphysical; (b) next, in specifying precisely what there is of finitude in its nonconfusion (as I see it) with the duality of the couple finite and

infinite; and (c), finally, in showing how the uncoupling of sin from biological death, far from denying the sense of sin, displays it and its true nature, spiritual this time, as the self-confinement of humankind by humankind in our own finitude. These are perspectives that I develop as far as possible in this book, to readjust and to deal metaphysically with certain of Martelet's basic perspectives. As far as the Darwinian hypothesis of transformation is concerned, we can acknowledge how this has been taken up, or at least recognized, by John Paul II in his *Message on Evolution*, delivered to the Pontifical Academy of Sciences on October 22, 1966, no. 4. "Today, more than a half-century after the appearance of that encyclical [*Humani Generis*], some new findings lead us toward the recognition of evolution as more than an hypothesis. . . . The convergence in the results of these independent studies—which was neither planned nor sought—constitutes in itself a significant argument in favor of the theory"; accessed August 9, 2016, https://www.ewtn.com/library/PAPALDOC/JP961022 .HTM. The well-known writer for *Le Monde*, Henri Tincq, after an editorial of October 25, 1996 had taken note of John Paul II's statement, could not resist, in a longer article of November 29, 1996, saying that "the Catholic Church has then definitely come over to Darwin's theses, but does not mean to align itself with the materialist and reductionist conclusions that are often drawn from them. However, it cannot be exempt from an inquiry into the coherence of a recognition of Darwin along with its dogma on original sin and redemption." I hope that the present book can participate in the very necessary task of an attempt at coherence without confining itself behind epistemological frontiers, but enlarging its field also to the metaphysical questions that are thus posed.

9. Martelet, *L'Au-Delà retrouvé* (Paris: Desclée, 1995), 50.

10. Despite the "profound unity and harmony" that Mgr. Duval asserts in his preface to the French bishops' *Catechism for Adults (Catéchisme des évêques de France)* and the more or less contemporary *Catechism of the Catholic Church* (1992), the "different format of the two works" marks a surprising difference of perspective in their way of looking at sin and its relation to biological death and physical suffering. This indicates that the theological debate remains open even at the heart of different *voices* or *pathways taken* in the ecclesiastical hierarchy. Certain formulae of the *Catechism of the Catholic Church* in fact bring into question, for the theologian as well as for the ordinary Christian, the status that is accorded in theological terms to suffering, sickness, or death. Thus, for example (from the *Catechism of the Catholic Church* [Libreria Editrice Vaticana, 1993]), on the subject of sin: "As a result of original sin, human nature is weakened in its powers, subject to *ignorance*, and suffering and the domination of death" (no. 418). Or again, in relation to sickness and the "Anointing of the Sick": "On the cross Christ took upon himself the whole weight of evil and took away the 'sin of the world' (John 1:29) of which *illness is one consequence*" (no. 1505). On the other hand, the French Bishops' *Catechism for Adults* is careful not to consider death or suffering unilaterally as a consequence of original sin. It only sees it, symbolically, as a sign: "The transgression of what is

forbidden, that the tree of the knowledge of good and evil had characterized, is at the origin of a broken world. Suffering is the *sign* of this" (no. 116). Moreover, the description of biological death in the book of Genesis ("You are dust, and to dust you shall return" [Gen 3:19]) is related to the finitude of the human condition and its limits rather than some fault that humankind would then have to carry as a burden. "In the representation that is given of our condition bearing the stamp of death through the narrative of the Fall, the human being is above all returned to the *constitutive limits of the creature*. He will know that he is not God" (no. 116). As far as sickness and the "Anointing of the Sick" are concerned (called here the "Sacrament of the Compassion of Christ and the Church"), nothing is said of any causal link between original sin and sickness or physical suffering. Only "the particular compassion of Christ for the sick," and thus the possible association of the sick "with the passion and agony of Christ as far as his last battle with death," is emphasized (nos. 445–49). The silence here is eloquent and opens the way to new theological breakthroughs that are able to take on board the question of human finitude as such in its relation to the problematic of original sin.

11. This limitation of objects perceived—whether ideal objects or ones given in sensation—to the single horizon *of* consciousness (or *of* the flesh) is in fact the basis of phenomenological intentionality. The paradigm of intentionality thus opens up a field that is in reality within the narrow but necessary "limits" of a single intention—so that it neutralizes definitively this time (by the act of the phenomenological reduction) any realist or dualist claims of the relationship between the subject and the world. See, for example, "When that is taken into account the formal-logical possibility of realities outside the world, the *one* spatiotemporal world, which is *fixed* by our *actual* experience, materially proves to be a countersense. If there are any worlds, any real physical things whatever, then the experienced motivations constituting them must be *able* to extend into my experience and into that of each Ego"; Edmund Husserl, *Ideas Pertaining to a Pure Phenomenology and to a Phenomenological Philosophy*, First Book, trans. Fred Kersten (Dordrecht: Kluwer Academic, 1983), 108–9.

12. Irenaeus, *Against Heresies* (Adversus haereses) IV:38:1, trans. Alexander Roberts, from *Ante-Nicene Fathers*, vol. 1, ed. Kevin Knight (Buffalo, N.Y.: Christian Literature, 1885); New Advent, ed. Peter Knight, accessed May 27, 2017, http://www.newadvent.org/fathers/0103438.htm.

13. Martelet, "Dieu n'a pas créé la mort," 458: "But thus to praise existence is not however to declare that what exists is so *good* that it is not going to become *better*, as if all things appeared from the outset in *the most excellent* mode that there is." This is a point of view that one can very simply set in opposition to that of a "classic" theology—deriving the imperfection of the created (marked then in its structure by a negative coefficient) from a "Fall" from the original state of perfection. See for example, Bernard Sesboüé, *Jésus-Christ l'unique médiateur* (Paris: Desclée, 1988), 318: "It seems that we could not escape from the biblical affirmation under which, through the sinful

intervention of the originary freedom of man, however impossible it might be to show it, something is broken in humankind, between mankind and nature, that is to say that our relationship with the world is no longer that which God placed at the origin in the order of a creation where all was good."

14. See Jean-Jacques Rousseau, *A Discourse upon the Origin and the Foundation of the Inequality among Mankind*, Internet Modern History Sourcebook, accessed August 9, 2016, http://sourcebooks.fordham.edu/mod/1782rousseau -inequal.asp.

15. Paul Ricoeur, *The Symbolism of Evil*, trans. Emerson Buchanan (Boston: Beacon Press, 1969), 233.

16. There is a celebrated Cartesian proof of the existence of God through the idea of the infinite: the infinite is something I conceive, but "I myself cannot be its cause" (*Meditations on First Philosophy*, Third Meditation, trans. John Cottingham [Cambridge: Cambridge University Press, 1996], 29). The no-less-celebrated contemporary return to this argument ["But the idea of infinity is exceptional in that Its *ideatum* surpasses its idea"; Emmanuel Levinas, *Totality and Infinity: An Essay on Exteriority*, trans. Alphonso Lingis (The Hague: Martinus Nijhoff, 1979), 49] in order to read there a representation of an Other, falls short, as I see it, of a true taking into account of *finitude*. Such treatments of the idea of the infinite that are at the heart of a concept of finitude—defined solely here as the "imperfection of my knowledge" (Descartes)—do certainly lead to the ideal of an absolute perfection as the horizon of all our thoughts, or indeed of all our acts (see Emmanuel Kant, *Critique of Pure Reason*, trans. Paul Guyer and Allen W. Wood [Cambridge: Cambridge University Press, 1998], V: "The Existence of God as a Postulate of Pure Reason"). In contradiction to such "postulates," we can say that the infinite in reality is not discovered first of all in *myself*—insofar as, on the one hand, its ideality according to Descartes means that it is not the site of an authentic "meeting," and on the other hand that I *only* experience my finitude in my own presence in the world (for which reason, as we shall see, it is important to separate finitude off from the couple finite-infinite). It is, on the contrary, only as far as Christ himself goes through and also himself suffers his own finitude through-and-through that the infinity of the Father is *given* to him fully in the act of Resurrection—and ultimately is given thereby even to us. Far from being a notion that is above all idealizing, the infinite of the Father is disclosed *only* in the breaking up of finitude of the Son and of what has been created in him, which reveals to us the figure of a God before whom at last—as opposed to the *causa sui* [caused of itself, uncaused]—it would be possible "for man to . . . fall to his knees in awe . . . play music and dance" (Heidegger, *Identity and Difference*, trans. Joan Stambaugh [Chicago: University of Chicago Press, 2002], 72).

17. St. Gregory of Nyssa, *On the Making of Man* XXII.4, trans. H. A. Wilson, in *Nicene and Post-Nicene Fathers*, Second Series, vol. 5 (Buffalo, N.Y.: Christian Literature, 1893), available on New Advent, ed. Kevin Knight, accessed August 9, 2016, http://www.new advent.org/fathers/2914.htm.

18. See Karl Rahner, *On the Theology of Death*, trans. Charles H. Henkey (New York: Herder and Herder, 1961), 37. Without going so far as to recognize in finitude itself an image of God in humankind, Rahner remains one of the first theologians who affirmed as necessary "the natural character" of death "also in Christianity." An "ontology of death" that would not immediately make the end of existence into the "exclusive result of that absurd error" is also developed, at least partially, in his *Foundations of Christian Faith*, trans William V. Dych (New York: Herder and Herder, 1982). However, in contrast to the perspective of *Theology of Death*, the *Foundations* seeks less to show how Christ lived through anxiety about his own death as a proof of his own finitude, rather sketching out in what measure the hope embodied in the Resurrection remains inscribed in the nature of humankind. As I see it, this openness toward the transcendental in humankind still neglects a true analysis of anxiety about death, either for mankind or Christ, that is not identically and immediately the result of anxiety over sin.

19. I try to show in this respect (Part III) how Christ himself, so to speak in phenomenological fashion, seeks less the *what* (*quid*), or the *why* (*cur*), of his own suffering (Gethsemane) than that of the suffering of others (the healing of the man born to be blind)—for which moreover he never finds or gives an answer—and the *how* (*quomodo*) of their lived experience, as it is considered sinful or offered and open to others.

20. [Trans.—See 1 Cor 1:25–27: "God's weakness is stronger than human strength. . . . God chose what is weak in the world to shame the strong."]

21. On the exegetical validity of this reading of the address in the Epistle to the Ephesians (Eph 1:3–14) showing how "redemption has its part to play in the plan of God *without however being its basis*," I would recommend the analysis of Chantal Reynier, "La bénédiction en Éphésiens, 1, 3–14: Élection, filiation, rédemption," *Nouvelle revue théologique*, no. 118 (1996): 182–99.

22. Hans Urs von Balthasar, *The Glory of the Lord: A Theological Aesthetics*, vol. 1, *Seeing the Form*, trans. Erasmo Leiva-Merikakis (San Francisco: Ignatius, 1982), 401.

23. Celebration of the Unveiling of the Restoration of Michelangelo's Frescos in the Sistine Chapel: Homily of His Holiness John Paul II, April 8, 1995, §5. On the theological sense of such a perspective and its roots in the Franciscan corpus (and in particular in Bonaventure's writings), see the outline by John J. Coughlin, in "La théologie franciscaine de la Chapelle Sixtine," in *Pierre d'Angle* (Review of the Monastic Fraternity of Apostolic Monks in the Parish of Saint-Jean-de-Malte), Aix-en-Provence, no. 3 (1997): 127–37.

24. Balthasar, *The Christian and Anxiety*, trans. Dennis D. Martin and Michael J. Miller (San Francisco: Ignatius, 2000), 86: "If it is true that anxiety . . . about death and anxiety about perhaps inescapable guilt—lies at the root of modern consciousness; if it is true that this anxiety is the basis of contemporary neuroses and that this anxiety is supposed to be overcome through a modern existentialist philosophy by entering into it and affirming it

and enduring it with determination to the very end, then to all of this Christianity can only say a radical No. *By no means does a Christian have permission for* or *access to this kind of anxiety*. If he nevertheless is a neurotic and an existentialist, then he suffers from a lack of Christian truth, and his faith is *sick or frail*" (my emphases).

25. [Trans.—For the basis of the idea of recapitulation [*anakephalaiosis*], see Eph 1:9–10: "According to [God's] good pleasure that he set forth in Christ, as a plan for the fullness of time, to gather up all things in him, things in heaven and things on earth." See also the *General Audience* of John Paul II, February 14, 2001, where he cites Irenaeus, *Against Heresies*, as a source for the theory that "all creation will be 'recapitulated' in Christ": "The Word became man. He recapitulated all things in himself, so that, just as the Word of God has primacy over heavenly, spiritual and invisible beings, so he does over visible and corporeal beings"; accessed November 4, 2016, at https://w2.vatican.va/content/john-paul-ii/en/audiences/2001/documents/hf_jp-ii_aud_20010214.html.]

26. Besides the North Portal of Chartres Cathedral and the "side-by-side" (rib-to-rib) of Adam and the Word incarnate, we can also find an artistic expression of this Trinitarian prefiguration of the finitude of the Son in Andrei Rublev's icon of the Trinity, according to the interpretation by Nicolaï Greschny (*L'Îcône de la Trinité d'André Roublev* [Albi: Éditions du Lion de Juda, 1986]). The Son is represented (dressed in green and blue) in the character sitting to the left of the Father—and not as usual in the central figure—the uncreated Word looks down at the cup in the center of the altar [table] as though he can already see the image of the sacrificial lamb (an image that was originally to be at the center and that new methods of pictorial research have revealed there). Before being sacrificed for sin, the lamb remains always—as I see it, and on this point I agree with the usual interpretation—a living being that must also therefore have a future death. The Son in his being in the Trinity would see then, in my interpretation, in the figure of the lamb traced on the center of the cup, not simply the site of a prefiguration of *redemption through death* for humankind (along with the sacrificial perspective that goes with it), but also that of a *communion of death* along with all humankind destined naturally to corruption.

27. Gustave Martelet does not seem able to escape from the couple "finite-infinite," apart from in his judicious definition of *finitude* as "the fact of not being able to exist unless supported [shouldered] by the world" (*L'Au-Delà retrouvé*, 142). In "Finitude de l'homme et incarnation du Christ," chapter 2 of his book, which perspective has greatly influenced me here, numerous formulae lead us toward a complete identification—unjustifiable at least from the point of view of existentialism and phenomenology—of finitude with finite. Thus, for example, "since God is *Infinite* and Perfect in himself, *finitude* and a certain imperfection are inherent in our humanity as in the universe" (51); or again, "God never wished that our *finitude*, open toward the *Infinite* itself, would carry in its flesh the mortal wound of its native infirmity" (53) (my emphasis). Such a reduction of finitude to the finite seems in reality to derive in the work in

question from a certain, probably Hegelian, reading of theology that, in my opinion, does not allow for the limiting of finitude, insofar as it is overwhelmed, indeed swallowed up in this case (*Aufhebung*), in the very heart of the Infinite. We find the same in many dialectical formulations that cannot in reality arrive at a description of finitude as such and independently of any consideration of the Infinite—as if the latter (the Infinite), absent at first glance from our horizon, must always take precedence over the former (finitude), although finitude is the only one of which we have experience. For example, "the *Infinite* becomes *finite* in order to introduce the *finite* into life even of the *Infinite*," or again, "God wanted to make the *non-God* so that the *non-God* itself could become *God*" (54). Far from condemning this author, in my comments ⌐ here I aim simply to point out that a shift of the problematic of the Hegelian field of the dialectic to the existentialist field and to the phenomenology of the descriptive would better serve his purpose, which is defining and theologically reexamining the concept of finitude that belongs historically to Sartre and ⌐ Heidegger rather than to Hegel.

28. Heidegger, *Being and Time*, §38:176.

29. Heidegger, *Kant and the Problem of Metaphysics*, trans. Richard Taft (Bloomington: Indiana University Press, 1997), 154.

30. Heidegger, *Being and Time*, §49:248.

31. Ibid., §38:179–80.

32. "Most writers on the emotions and on human conduct seem to be treating rather of matters outside nature than of natural phenomena following nature's general laws. They appear to conceive man to be situated in nature as a kingdom: for they believe that he disturbs rather than follows nature's order, that he has absolute control over his actions, and that he is determined solely by himself"; Benedict de Spinoza, *The Ethics*, part 3, *On the Origin and Nature of the Emotions*, trans. R. H. M. Elwes, Project Gutenberg EBook, accessed August 13, 2016, http://www.gutenberg.org/files/3800/3800-h/3800-h.htm.

33. It would probably be an error to accuse St. Augustine of all the problems and of being the one who introduced Christianity to such a disparagement of the flesh as well as of human corruptibility. See, for example, in a somewhat unilateral perspective, Jean-Claude Eslin, "Le grand tournant augustinien," *Esprit* 10 (1988): 119–24; Elaine Pagels, *Adam, Eve, and the Serpent: Politics in Early Christianity* (New York: Vintage, 1989); Peter Brown, *The Body and Society: Men, Women and Sexual Renunciation in Early Christianity* (New York: Columbia University Press, 1988). It should be enough, to correct such a point of view, simply to read St. Augustine himself: "I read [in some books of the Platonists translated from Greek into Latin] . . . the Word, God, is 'born not of the flesh, nor of blood, nor of the will of man nor of the will of the flesh, but of God.' But that 'the Word was made flesh and dwelt among us,' (John 1:13–14) I did not read there"; *Confessions* VII.ix.14, trans. Henry Chadwick (Oxford: Oxford University Press, 1991). See also on this point two classic and well-known studies: Jean Clémence, "Saint Augustin et le péché originel," *Nouvelle*

revue théologique 70 (1948):726–54, and Aimé Solignac, "La condition de l'homme pécheur d'après saint Augustin," *Nouvelle revue théologique* 88 (1956): 359–85. For an appropriate contemporary reaction to this unilaterally anti-Augustinian perspective, see in particular the formulation by Goulven Madec, "Saint Augustin est-il le malin génie de l'Europe?," *Petites études augustiniennes*, Institut d'études augustiniennes, Paris (1894), série anticipée, 142, chap. XIX. Aside from this debate, which certainly has been polemical, we can say that there remains disdain for corporality in works by St. Augustine, such as his *Commentary on the Literal Meaning of Genesis* (in contrast to his *Sermons* or his *Tractatus on the Gospel of John*). See in particular *On the Literal Meaning of Genesis* (bk. ix for the question of the flesh and bk. xi for his interpretation of the narrative of the Fall). Taking this in a more nuanced fashion, we could say that St. Augustine, rather than being incorrect, represents very effectively a turning point in the history of theology, out of which arises precisely this question of the status of the body, and it is where original sin takes on a new direction. See, for example, Balthasar, *The Glory of the Lord*, vol. 1, *Seeing the Form*, 401: "Only so can we also get away from the fateful move in these questions which has been customary since the time of the Fathers (in a reaction against Montanism), and particularly since Augustine, whereby everything having to do with the senses and the imagination in mystical experience is held to be questionable in the extreme." And for the question of the status of sin in relation to death, see Martelet, *Libre réponse à un scandale*, 42.

34. Martelet, *Libre Réponse à un scandale*, 41.

35. Fernando Pessoa, *The Book of Disquiet*, trans. Richard Zenith (London: Penguin, 2001), 158.

36. Heidegger, *Being and Time*, §49:246.

37. Ibid., §51:253. On the effects of the televised image as a "counter-world" or "anti-world" and the substitution of the viewer [*voyeur*] for the one who sees, as well as the reversal of the original and image—characteristics that one could well apply to the status of a cadaver that is always simply seen from afar, as it were, enclosed by a "screen"—see Jean-Luc Marion, *The Crossing of the Visible*, trans. James K. A. Smith (Stanford, Calif.: Stanford University Press, 2004), especially "The Blind at Shiloh," 46–65.

38. Heidegger, *Being and Time*, §51:252–53. My object in this book is not simply to repeat or to give a commentary upon these famous pages. I would simply send the interested reader to the commentary by Jean Greisch, in a book that is interesting in its own right: Greisch, *Ontologie et temporalité: Esquisse d'une interprétation intégrale de Sein und Zeit* (Paris: PUF, 1994), 277–78.

39. Heidegger, *Being and Time*, §51:253: "Someone or other 'dies,' be he neighbour or stranger [*Nächste oder Fernerstehende*]. People who are no acquaintances of ours are 'dying' daily and hourly. 'Death' is encountered as a well-known event occurring within-the-world."

40. Ibid., §47:240 (emphasis in original).

41. Ibid., §47:239.

42. [Trans.—In the Auschwitz concentration camp Maximilian Kolbe, a Franciscan friar arrested by the Gestapo in 1941, took the place of Franciszek Gajownicek, who had been condemned to death, but who pleaded that he had a wife and children. Kolbe was starved for two weeks, then given a lethal injection, and died in August 1941. He was later canonized and given the title of a "martyr of charity."]

43. Heidegger, *Being and Time*, §47:240 (emphasis in original).

44. On this question of the death of another and impossible substitution for the other, see the commentary by Jean Greisch, in *Ontologie et temporalité*, 268–72: "Death of the other: a false approach?" Without denying the crucial character of the death of the other or ignoring the question of substitution envisaged by Emmanuel Levinas (see *Totality and Infinity* [1969] and *Otherwise than Being or Beyond Essence* [1991]), I would follow Jean Greisch (272) in underlining how the ethico-metaphysical questions posed by Levinas often, if not always, depart from Heidegger's ontic-ontological distinction. I would note nonetheless that the one (ontic) presupposes the other (ontological) and that the ethical turn, even in the work of Levinas, sets great store on an analysis that is first of all existential.

45. Marcel, "Valeur et immortalité" (paper given in December 1943), in *Homo viator* (Paris: Aubier-Montaigne, 1944), 205.

46. Heidegger, *Being and Time*, §53:263: "Death is Dasein's *ownmost* possibility." For an exploration of the question of death as "mineness," see Greisch, *Ontologie et temporalité*, 279–83.

47. [Trans.—*The Seventh Seal (Det sjunde inseglet)*, Ingmar Bergman's film set in Sweden during the Black Death. In Bergman's film the narrator quotes Rev 8:1–6: "When the Lamb opened the seventh seal, there was silence in heaven for about half an hour. . . . And the seven angels who had the seven trumpets made ready to blow them."] The dialogue of the film begins:

Knight: Who are you? *Death*: I am Death. *Knight*: Have you come for me? *Death*: I have been walking by your side for a long time. *Knight*: I know. *Death*: Are you prepared? . . . *Knight*: Wait a moment. . . . You play chess, don't you? . . . *Death*: Yes, in fact I'm quite a good chess player. . . . *Knight*: The condition is that I may live as long as I hold out against you. If I win, you will release me. Is it agreed? (Internet Movie Script Database, accessed August 17, 2016, http://www.imsdb.com/scripts/Seventh-Seal,-The .html).

48. [Trans.—Albrecht Dürer, *Ritter, Tod und Teufel* (1513), engraving in Cabinet des estampes et des dessins, Strasbourg.]

3. The Temptation of Despair or Anxiety over Sin

1. Michel de Montaigne, *Essays*, trans Charles Cotton, ed. W. C. Hazlitt (1877), chap. xix: "That to study philosophy is to learn to die"; "Let us converse and be familiar with him, and have nothing so frequent in our thoughts as

death. Upon all occasions represent him to our imagination in his every shape; at the stumbling of a horse, at the falling of a tile, at the least prick with a pin let us presently consider, and say to ourselves, 'Well, and what if it had been death itself?' and, thereupon let us encourage and fortify ourselves"; Project Gutenberg, accessed August 18, 2016, http://www.gutenberg.org/files/3600/3600.txt.

2. Blaise Pascal, *Pensées*, trans. A. J. Krailsheimer (London: Penguin, 1966), L 434, B 199, p. 165: "Imagine a number of men in chains, all under sentence of death, some of whom are each day butchered in the sight of others; those remaining see their own condition in that of their fellows, and looking at each other with grief and despair await their turn. This is an image of the human condition." As in the famous passage on the two abysses of infinity (disproportion of man, L 199), Pascal makes real here "the scene of death" as a way of leading toward the necessity of conversion for his readers. What we might call here, strictly speaking, a "fear therapy" (see Vincent Carraud, *Pascal et la philosophie* [Paris: PUF, 1992], 403–22) uses death itself—experienced in a certain way, through the death of others, as "anticontemplation." I am in agreement with Carraud that the Christian, like the atheist, can and should feel this "fear," since God himself makes this his dwelling place. And, like Carraud on this point precisely, I do not agree with Heidegger's view of the "interpretation of 'life'" in Christianity as something made in order to depart the better from it: "In any event, it is impossible for us not to think that the world is silent, and thus frightening, *as much for the Christian as for the atheist*" (403, note 1); "All the same, we are opposed to those analyses that see in this fragment a repetition of traditional themes of contemplation . . . like that of Valéry who thinks that *fear cannot be Christian*" (404, note 1) (my emphasis).

3. Jean-Paul Sartre, "Existentialism Is a Humanism" (1946), trans. Philip Mariot: "For at bottom, what is alarming is the doctrine that I am about to explain to you is—is it not?—that it confronts man with a possibility of choice"; Marxists.org, accessed August 17, 2016, https://www.marxists.org/reference/archive/sartre/works/exist/sartre.htm.

4. Pascal, *Pensées*, L427, B 195, p. 427: "All I know is that I must soon die, but what I know least about is this very death which I cannot avoid." Heidegger retains this Pascalian paradox with regard to death, which is certain as an event, but unknown in its nature (Martin Heidegger, *Being and Time*, trans. John Macquarrie and Edward Robinson [New York: Harper Perennial Modern Thought, 2008], §53). The degree of certainty is moreover such for him that he does not hesitate to oppose a modern *sum moribundus* (I am in dying) against the *sum, existo* (I am, I exist) of Descartes. The first (my becoming dying) indicates in a definite and definitive way the fundamental certainty of my *Dasein*, while the second (the "*cogito*"—[I think]) seems to be an existential statement that concerns my own being (see Heidegger, *History of the Concept of Time: Prolegomena*, trans. Theodore Kisiel [Bloomington: Indiana University

Press, 2008]—cited and discussed by Jean Greisch, *Ontologie et temporalité: Esquisse d'une interprétation intégrale de Sein und Zeit*, 281–82.

5. The very Kierkegaardian note in my double formula of despair and anxiety is obvious, and it would be wrong to deny what I owe to that great tradition. I concur with the Danish philosopher that it is the temptation of despair rather just death or sickness and destitution that is the true "fatal sickness" (see Kierkegaard, *The Sickness Unto Death*, trans. Howard V. Hong and Edna H. Hong [Princeton N.J.: Princeton University Press, 1980], 17. [The French translation is published under the title *Traité du désespoir*, or "Treatise on Despair"]. It is this temptation that gives death, in the book of Genesis, a spiritual rather than simply a biological status. I also agree with Kierkegaard that anxiety over sin, or "sin's anxiety" (a formula used by Kierkegaard in *The Concept of Anxiety*, trans. Alastair Hannay [New York: Liveright, 2014], chap. 4), points first of all simply to our anxiety faced with the actuality of freedom. It is nonetheless true that nothing allows us to assent that anxiety over sin also signifies that this anxiety is a consequence of sin in the individual. Anxiety (over sin), far from being the *consequence* of a previous sin, in what is primarily a causal model, points, as we shall see, to sin itself as humankind's self-enclosure in a finitude that is not in itself sinful. The anxiety of sin *is* thus the sin, rather than it being sin that generates the anxiety. As for the suggestion that we should give some status to anxiety (about existence) over and above transgression, even if it is original and originary, this is probably what is most pertinent—and original—in Kierkegaard's discussion of anxiety (chaps. 1 and 5). At the same time, what I have called "anxiety over finitude" does not at all stem from the "mystery of innocence and ignorance," as Kierkegaard maintains. If humankind in fact is anxious "in the face of nothing," and this demands that we distinguish anxiety from fear, it remains nonetheless true that finitude in itself points to the prospect of our biological death independently of any transgression, rather than the simple psychological "melancholy" of the child in its innocence and ignorance, and before any consciousness of death. Anxiety in the face of the nothingness of death and the destruction of the self, an anxiety that can be thoroughly mature and well-considered, may on the other hand lead us, toward the feelings of childhood and innocence (see my Conclusion). Far from being something that precedes original sin, childhood, or the entrusting of oneself to another, follows sin simply with transformative acts of redemption and of resurrection. From maturity back to childhood, rather than from childhood to maturity: such is the route, in opposition to that of Kierkegaard this time, that I wish to follow in the present discussion.

6. [Trans.—Genesis uses two verb forms for "dying" here, an imperfect and the infinitive absolute. Most translators into English interpret this simply as intensifying ("You shall most surely die"). Robert Alter's translation comes closer to Falque's with "You are doomed to die"; see *Genesis*, translation and commentary by Robert Alter (New York: W. W. Norton, 1996). "You will die

of death" is given here as a direct translation of Falque's translation from the Hebrew into French, "*tu mourras de mort.*"]

7. The French version of *The Jerusalem Bible* gives "Tu deviendras passible de la mort" ["You will become liable [*passible*] to death"]. And this comes close to my interpretation of the double sense of our liability [*passibilité*]: that it is at once connected to sin in the manner that we live (spiritual death) and is like suffering in the fact of not knowing how to live (anxiety over death).

8. See the argument put forward by Gustave Martelet in *Libre réponse à un scandale: La faute originelle, la souffrance et la mort* (Paris: Éditions du Cerf, 1992), 37. And in particular, in support of this translation, see Stanislas Lyonnet, "Péché originel," in *Supplément au Dictionnaire de la Bible* (Paris: Letouzey, 1966), 7:537–38.

9. See Martelet, "Dieu n'a pas crée la mort," *Christus*, no. 68 (October 1995): 459.

10. Joseph Huby, *L'Épître aux Romains* (Paris: Beauchesne, 1957), 197, note 1; cited in Lyonnet, "Péché originel," 537–38, and Martelet, *Libre réponse à un scandale,* 33.

11. It is sometimes surprising to note how little Gustave Martelet insists upon this double role of picking up and revealing original sin, even as he is dissociating it from biological death. In defining sin here in its spiritual nature, as a self-enclosure of humankind in its own non-sinful finitude, I aim to dispel thoroughly those misunderstandings that have wrongly led to a possible identification of the fact that "one does not die biologically *simply* because of sin" with that of "purely and simply *no longer sinning.*" Although he does not fully develop it, I should like to note the incipient concern—which we might hope is more and more pressing—in Martelet's work: "Sin risks passing unheeded or being rejected if its serves to justify pain and death that is characteristic of human finitude" ("Dieu n'a pas créé la mort," 642).

12. St. Bonaventure, *Breviloquium: Opéra Omnia* (Florence: Quarrachi, 1891), III, chap xi (V.240). See also the *Commentaire des Sentences*, bk. II, d. 41, a. 2, q. 1 (II.947–50) on the definition of sin: "*Utrum omne peccatum actuale sit voluntarium,*" and bk. II, d. 43 (II.981–98) on mortal sin, or the sin against the Holy Spirit: "*De peccato in Spiritum sanctum.*"

13. St. Bonaventure, *Breviloquium*, III, chap. 8 (V.237): "Sin is a distancing of the will from the first principle [*recessum voluntatis a primo principio*]. Insofar as the will is made so that it can act for itself [*ab ipso*], according to itself [*secundum ipsum*] and by itself [*propter ipsum*], all sin is a misappropriation of the spirit [*inordinatio mentis*], that is to say of the will which, of its nature, is capable of virtue or vice."

14. "Thinking about our own death, that is to say the only event in the future that can be regarded as certain, can exercise a fascination over us such that in some way it totally invades our field of experience, extinguishes our joys, and paralyses our initiatives"; Gabriel Marcel, *La Fidélité créatrice (1939): Essai de philosophie concrète* (Paris: Gallimard, 1967), 258.

15. Ibid., 258.

16. Charles Péguy, *Dialogue de l'histoire et de l'âme charnelle*, in *Oeuvres en prose complètes*, Pléiade ed. (Paris: Gallimard, 1992), 3:727–28. Part of this important text by Péguy has been the object of a very rewarding study by Jean Bastaire, under the title *Gethsémani* (Paris: Desclée de Brouwer, 1995). On the subject of the "habituated soul" and the asperging of grace, see Péguy's *Note conjointe sur M. Descartes et la philosophie cartésienne*, in *Oeuvres en prose complètes*, 3:1311–33.

17. Sylvie Germain, *Les Èchos du silence* (Paris: Desclée de Brouwer, 1996), 36–37.

4. From the Affirmation of Meaninglessness to the Suspension of Meaning

1. Albert Camus, *The Myth of Sisyphus and Other Essays*, trans. Justin O'Brien (New York: Vintage, 1991), 10.

2. Ibid., 15.

3. Ibid., 1.

4. Ibid., 2.

5. For this distinction between "existentiell" [ontic-factual] and "existential" [ontologic-theoretical], see Martin Heidegger, *Being and Time*, trans. John Macquarrie and Edward Robinson (New York: Harper Perennial Modern Thought, 2008), Introduction, 12; ibid., "The Theme of the Analytic of Dasein," §9 42–46, and "The Existential Analytic and the Interpretation of Primitive Dasein," §11.

6. See the analysis of vanity in Jean-Luc Marion, *God Without Being: Hors-Texte*, trans. Thomas A. Carlson (Chicago: University of Chicago Press, 1991): "The Reverse of Vanity."

7. Marcel Neusch, *Aux sources de l'athéisme contemporain* (Paris: Centurion, 1993), 8: "It is a matter then of a new situation, where atheism gives way to unbelief, the explicit denial of God to agnosticism, the open battle to an indifferent neutrality"; see also Marcel Gauchet, *Le Désenchantment du monde: Une histoire politique de la religion* (Paris: Gallimard, 1981), 133–41.

8. Friedrich Nietzsche, *The Will to Power*, sect. 1, no. 22b (Spring–Fall, 1887), trans. Walter Kaufmann and R. J. Hollingdale (New York: Vintage Giant, 1968). See also On *the Genealogy of Morality*, trans. Carol Diethe (Cambridge: Cambridge University Press, 2006), Preface, §5:7: "Precisely here I saw the beginning of the end, standstill, mankind looking back wearily, turning its will *against* life, and the onset of the final sickness become gently, sadly manifest . . . *nihilism*" (my emphases).

II. Christ Faced with Anxiety over Death

1. See the translation proposed by Michel Laroche, in *Seconde naissance: De l'homme de l'angoisse à l'homme de la résurrection* (Paris: Nouvelle Cité, 1986), 20.

2. These references are more fully developed in Hans Urs von Balthasar's book *The Christian and Anxiety*, trans. Dennis D. Martin and Michael J. Miller

(San Francisco: Ignatius, 2000). See also a similar perspective on anxiety considered as "birth," and in particular relying upon the fathers of the church (above all Evagrius Ponticus and Symeon the New Theologian) in Laroche, *Seconde naissance*.

3. Søren Kierkegaard, "A Simple Psychology Orienting Deliberation on the Dogmatic Issue of Hereditary Sin," in *Kierkegaard's Writings*, vol. 8, *Concept of Anxiety*, trans. and ed. Reidar Thomte (Princeton N.J.: Princeton University Press, 1980), 155.

4. See Karl Barth, *Evangelical Theology: An Introduction*, trans. Grover Foley (Grand Rapids, Mich.: Eerdmans, 1979. Barth maintains that a person who believes knows and publicly confesses that he or she cannot come to believe just through reason or through the force of reason. In other words, faith will always be an *event* that is produced in the face of the incredulity that accompanies it and takes strength in the person."

5. Maurice Merleau-Ponty, *Sense and Non-Sense*, trans Hubert L. Dreyfus and Patricia Allen Dreyfus (Evanston, Ill.: Northwestern University Press, 1964), 67.

6. Martin Heidegger, *Being and Time*, trans. John Macquarrie and Edward Robinson (New York: Harper Perennial Modern Thought, 2008), §50.

7. While making reference to Kierkegaard, Eugen Drewermann explicitly recognizes the psychoanalytic aim of his analysis of anxiety (Drewermann, *La parole qui guérit* [Paris: Éditions du Cerf, 1991], 310–11): "Søren Kierkegaard has taught me to see the fundamental problem of human existence. I rely essentially upon psychoanalysis to identify concretely the forms that this anxiety can take—anxiety in the context of an existence where one has lost sight of God." In schematic terms, two routes are opened up, as I see it, on the basis of the Kierkegaardian analysis of anxiety (see Kierkegaard's *Concept of Anxiety*, chaps. 1 and 5). One—psychological and psychoanalytic—would go by way of Freud and asks questions about desire and loss: the other—metaphysical and phenomenological—would work through Heidegger and questions the sense of the "Being-there" of humankind (*Dasein*), even at the heart of anxiety. As far as these two routes are concerned, I would evidently choose to follow (and indeed to push further along) the second.

8. We should note that "the fear of decease" is not directly described as "psychological," either by Heidegger or Merleau-Ponty. If it is seen as existential, this goes beyond the ontic to the ontological and is not, strictly speaking, psychological. I follow this restriction methodologically here to emphasize—in posing it against anxiety—how much Christ's experience at Gethsemane is *metaphysical* rather than psychological.

9. [Trans.—*The Amplified Bible* (Grand Rapids, Mich.: Zondervan, 1995). JB has "And a sudden fear came over him, and great distress." NSRV has "And began to be distressed and agitated." The French translation used by Falque includes the word "*angoisse*" (anxiety) as a translation of *adêmonein*.]

10. H. G. Liddell and R. Scott, *Greek-English Lexicon* (Oxford: Oxford University Press, 1940): *Adêmoneô*—to be sorely troubled or dismayed; to be in anguish (21:b); *Thambeô*—to be astonished (783:b).

11. [Trans.—Heidegger's term *Erschrecken* is translated by Stambaugh as well as by Macquarrie and Robinson as "alarm." An alternative translation of "startled dismay" is used for Heidegger's *Contributions to Philosophy*, trans. Parvis Emad and Kenneth Maly (Bloomington: Indiana University Press, 1999), 11.]

12. The German translation of the New Testament (Stuttgart: Vela Katholisches Bibelwerk, 1965) translates what in English would be "fear" with *entsetzen* and "great distress" (or "anxiety") with *unruhig zu werden*: "*und er fin an, sich zu entsetzen and unruhig zu werden*" (Mark 14:33), without directly employing the Heideggerian terms for fear (*Furcht*), alarm (*Erschrecken*), or anxiety (*Angst*). These two terms show nonetheless on the one hand a recoil or step backward, faced with what is terrifying (*ent-setzen*), and on the other hand the absence of calm or tranquility in the one who is frightened (*un-Ruhe*); see Erich Weis and Heinrich Mattutat, *Handwörterbuch Französich-Deutsch (Nouveau Dictionnaire français-allemand)* (Paris: Bordas, 1968), articles on *Entsetzen* and *Unruhe*.

5. The Fear of Dying and Christ's "Alarm"

1. I am relying here on a somewhat loose interpretation of §30 in *Being and Time*. In reality, the disclosure of the precariousness of existence is only a characteristic of the third aspect of fear (the "why" of fear), while to have fear "with" or "for" the other is an addendum (§30). For a strict exegesis of the Heideggerian text—something that is not my aim here—see Jean Greisch, *Ontologie et temporalité: Esquisse d'une interprétation intégrale de Sein und Zeit* (Paris: PUF, 1994), 184–87.

2. [Trans.—Falque's term is *effroi*, used in the French version of the Jerusalem Bible (Mark 14:33). *Effroi* is usually translated in English as "terror" or "dread." Falque's key reference is to the passage in Mark, where NSRV gives "distressed and agitated," JB gives "sudden fear," and AMP gives "terror and amazement." Falque, however, relates *effroi* to the German term *Erschrecken* used by Heidegger in *Being and Time*, §30:142, where both English translations of Heidegger (Joan Stambaugh [Albany: State University of New York Press, 1996] and John Macquarrie and Edward Robinson [New York: Harper Perennial Modern Thought, 2008]) give "alarm" for the German term *Erschrecken*.]

3. Heidegger, *Being and Time*, §30:142.

4. See Greisch, *Ontologie et temporalité*, 187.

5. Before we decide to call this an "allegory of sacrifice" for someone who is proceeding purposefully toward death, we should note that in the Old Testament the symbol of the *cup* shows all the sufferings that are to come. Moreover, the addition of *baptism* to the image of the cup in the question Christ addresses to James and John ("Are you able to drink the cup that I drink, or be baptized

with the baptism that I am baptized with?" [Mark 10:38]) further reinforces the imminence of the threat of death and thus the potential recoil before it. According to the note in the French ecumenical translation of the New Testament, "to the image of the cup, Mark adds that of a baptism that denotes the sufferings that overwhelm human beings in general when they are put to the test, and more specifically, to the death of martyrdom" [*Nouveau Testament: Traduction ecuménique de la Bible* (TOB) (Paris: Éditions du Cerf, 1972), Mark 10:38, note b].

6. Pierre Corneille, *Polyeucte* II.vi.335, trans. Thomas Constable (New York: Harvard Classics, P. F. Collier and Son, 1909–14); cited by Charles Péguy, in *Dialogue de l'histoire et l'âme charnelle*, in *Oeuvres en prose complète*, Pléiade ed. (Paris: Gallimard, 1992), 3:734.

7. Although this book only has the aim—sufficiently demanding at least as far as I am concerned—to deal with the being in the world of humankind and of Christians as it is before suffering and death, we can be certain that the "existential" [i.e., ontological] commitment in the Resurrection as a hope or modality of my being has even more to tell us than its purely "existentiell" [i.e., ontic, factual] characteristics, or factual hope, of a being in life after life. [See chap. 4, §19 and chap. 4, note 5, for the distinction between "existential" and "existentiell."] The outlines of such a perspective can be found in Karl Rahner's view of the "transcendental prospect of resurrection as the horizon of the experience of the Resurrection by Jesus" (Karl Rahner, *Traité fondamental de la foi* [Paris: Centurion, 1983], 302–8). It is, however, nonetheless appropriate, as I see it, to radicalize this hypothesis in phenomenological terms, in bracketing off (*epochê*) definitively all hope of the Resurrection as *fact* to disengage the pure and simple *possibility* in the form of a hope of my being, lived in every moment (here below on earth). As for affirming in such a perspective that "first of all we are in the world," probably that is to deny, in opposition to Levinas this time, that "the true life is absent" [Emmanuel Levinas, *Totality and Infinity: An Essay on Eternity*, trans. Alphonso Lingis (Norwell, Mass.: Kluwer Academic, 1991), 33]. Christ's Resurrection breaks, in fact, as we shall see, Levinas's definition of metaphysics as "to die for the invisible" (35). The gulf that separates Judaism and Christianity needs to be respected in the statements even of philosophers [see Levinas, *Entre Nous: On Thinking of the Other*, trans. Michael B. Smith and Barbara Harshav (New York: Columbia University Press, 1998)]. I would point out, as a Christian this time, that the metaphysical experience of God, as far as the believer is concerned, consists above all of him "dying as *visible*," even if he will be transformed and irradiated by the glory of the Resurrection. Suffice it to say here that we need to be wary of the contemporary taking up of Levinas into Christian theology. We should be sure to be faithful to the ideas of the philosopher himself as well as to the specificity of the Christian mystery.

8. From the *Lives* of Jesus in the nineteenth century (D. F. Strauss, *The Life of Jesus Critically Examined* [1808]; Ernest Renan, *The Life of Jesus* [1863]), up to

contemporary narrative theology (Christian Duquoc, *Jésus, homme libre* [1975; Éditions du Cerf, 2003]; Gerd Theissen, *The Shadow of the Galilean: The Quest of the Historical Jesus*, trans. John Bowden [1987; Minneapolis: Fortress Press, 2007]), this aspect of the death of Jesus, which is, strictly speaking, historical and political, has been powerfully demonstrated. Without entering into what has been a stormy (and often sterile) debate, I rely on these works simply to affirm what is well-known about punishment on the cross for Jesus in his own time.

9. Philippe Ariès, "La mort inversée," *La Maison-Dieu*, no. 101 (1970): 63; discussed and cited by Bernard Sesboüé, in *La Résurrection et la Vie: Petite catéchèse sur les choses de la fin* (Paris: Desclée de Brouwer, 1990), 87.

10. Hans Urs von Balthasar, *The Glory of the Lord*, vol. 7, *Theology: The New Covenant*, trans. Brian McNeil (Edinburgh: T. and T. Clark, 1989), 537.

11. As far as this abandonment of the self and to the self (*Überlassenheit*) is concerned, it is relevant to note from the start that the soul (*psuchê*), saturated with sorrow unto death, denotes here not so much a part of the human composite—as in Greek anthropology—as the total being of the Son, in a classic return to the Semitic tradition. In this sense it is the totality of the Son in his Being-there (*Dasein*)—that is to say, in his incarnate agony—that is in some sense struck by death.

12. Heidegger, *Being and Time*, §48. My aim here, as elsewhere, is not to provide an exegesis of the Heideggerian text. That has already been very well done elsewhere (see Greisch, *Ontologie et temporalité*). I am happy here to take up again and freely interpret the modalities of the end described by Heidegger. And I do that to look over them again through the figure of the incarnate Word.

13. Charles Péguy, *Dialogue de l'histoire et de l'âme chrétienne*, in *Oeuvres en prose complètes*, Pléiade ed. (Paris: Gallimard, 1992), 3:743.

14. We should note here that Heidegger's text only suggests these modalities of the end (disappearance, interruption, and completion). What I am doing here, in a deliberately interpretative fashion, is in some respects pushing the Heideggerian text to its limits.

15. If the apocryphal gospels in general say more about the birth of Jesus than the death (see the Protoevangelium of James and the Infancy Gospel of Thomas), we find nonetheless in the Gospel of Peter, the most ancient of the Christian apocrypha (c. 150–200), traces of a narrative of the death of Jesus that does not maintain or aim for the silence or sobriety of the gospels included in the recently established canon: "Now it was noonday, and darkness prevailed over all Judea: and they were troubled and in agony lest the sun should have set, for that yet he lived. . . . And many went about with lamps, supposing that it was night: and some fell. . . . And then they plucked the nails from the hands of the Lord and laid him on the earth: and the whole earth was shaken and there came a great fear on all" [the Gospel of Peter, from the *Apocryphal New*

Testament, trans. M. R. James (Oxford: Clarendon, 1924), 5:15–6:21], accessed May 10, 2016, http://www.gnosis.org/library/gospete.htm.

16. *The Council of Trent: Sixth Session*, chap. 7, trans. J. Waterworth (London: Dolman, 1848), Hanover Historical Texts Project, accessed October 23, 2016, http://history.hanover.edu/texts/trent/ct06.html.

17. *Gaudium et Spes: Pastoral Constitution on the Church in the Modern World* (promulgated December 7, 1965), accessed October 23, 2016, http://www .vatican.va/archive/hist_councils/ii_vatican_council/documents/vat-ii_const _19651207_gaudium-et-spes_en.html. On the relation between the deifying and reparative attitudes of the Council of Trent and Vatican II, see Bernard Sesboüé, *Jésus-Christ, l'unique médiateur* (Paris: Desclée, 1988), 125–53, 257–377.

18. [Trans.—Docetism: the doctrine that Christ only seems to have a body and to die, and is in reality wholly divine.]

19. See Karl Rahner, *Schriften zur Theologie XII* (Zurich: Benzinger, 1975), 238, cited and translated in *Karl Rahner: Theologian for the Twenty-First Century*, ed. Pádraic Conway and Fáinche Ryan (Bern: Peter Lang, 2010).

20. Balthasar, *La Foi du Christ* (Paris: Éditions du Cerf, 1994), 38, 30.

21. See the classic studies: Jacques Guillet, *Jésus devant sa vie at sa mort* (Paris: Aubier, 1973); Heinz Schürmann, *Comment Jésus a-t-il vécu sa mort? Exégese et théologie* (Paris: Éditions du Cerf, 1977); Xavier Léon-Dufour, *Face à la mort: Jésus et Paul* (Paris: Éditions du Seuil, 1979).

22. Péguy, "Dialogue de l'histoire," Pléiade ed., 3:743.

23. This perspective is developed by Monique Rosaz and Édouard Pousset, in "Passion-résurrection selon l'évangile de saint Marc," a supplement to *Vie chrétienne*, no. 276 (1984). Although it is relevant to the textual analysis of the gospel, the "performative" approach based on the structural analysis of the text cannot give us the final word on the meaning of the death of Christ in its particular originality.

24. Hans Jonas, *Le Principe responsabilité* (Paris: Éditions du Cerf, 1990), 74. And see ibid., 72–93, on the general sense of a "hermeneutic of fear."

25. Greisch, "L'amour du monde et le principe de responsabilité," *Autrement*, Serie morale no. 14 (January 1994): 76, note 9: "It is clear that this description [referring to the affect of fear in Heidegger's *Being and Time*, §31] is from the perspective of a subject beset by danger. Such is not exactly the case for the heuristic of fear (see Jonas, *Le Principe responsabilité*). We might say that as far as danger is concerned, one has to know how to go and look for it, something that supposes imagination and an effort of intellection."

26. [Trans.—See Heidegger, *Being and Time*, §65:329: "*Temporality is the primordial 'outside-of-itself' in and for itself.* We therefore call the phenomenon of the future, the character of having been, and the Present, the '*ecstases*' of temporality" (emphasis in original). A footnote by Macquarrie and Robinson tells us that the root-meaning of "ecstasis" is "standing outside" and points out that Heidegger also connects the word with "existence."]

6. God's Vigil

1. Martin Heidegger, *Being and Time*, trans. John Macquarrie and Edward Robinson (New York: Harper Perennial Modern Thought, 2008), §65:329–31.

2. Heidegger, "Introduction to the Phenomenology of Religion," lectures from the Winter Semester 1920–21, in *The Phenomenology of Religious Life*, trans. Matthias Fritsch and Jennifer Anna Gosetti-Ferencei (Bloomington: Indiana University Press, 2004), 3–42. There is an excellent account and analysis of this by Claude Romano (to which I am much indebted), in "Le possible et l'événement (I)," *Philosophie*, no. 40 (December 1993): 68–95. For a complete dossier devoted to Heidegger, see *Transversalités: Revue de l'Institut catholique de Paris*, no. 60 (October–December 1996): 67–112. On the eschatological question and Heidegger's interpretation of the Epistle to the Thessalonians, see Jean Greisch, "La facticité chrétienne: Heidegger, lecteur de saint Paul," *Transversalités: Revue de l'Institut catholique de Paris*, no. 60 (October–December 1996): 85–101 (in particular 97–99).

3. Heidegger, *Being and Time*, §65:329: "*Temporality is the primordial 'outside-of-itself' in and for itself.* We therefore call the phenomenon of the future, the character of having been, and the Present, the '*ecstases*' of temporality" (emphasis in original).

4. Claude Romano, "Le possible et l'événement (I)," 71.

5. Ibid., 72. Romano is discussing Heidegger's "Introduction to the Phenomenology of Religion."

6. Ibid., 72.

7. "What gives the temporality of factitial experience in the Christian life its authentic structure, is not the waiting for an event, but the awakening of the Christian before the imminence of what-is-possible-at-any-moment"; ibid., 74.

8. "Prolepsis": technical term used by Wolfhart Pannenberg, *Esquisse d'une christologie* (Paris: Éditions du Cerf, 1971), 55: "The unity of Jesus with God is not ever based on a claim implied in his pre-Paschal behavior, but solely in his resurrection from among the dead."

9. I take up here Heidegger's analysis of the *ecstases* of time [*Being and Time*, §65: "Temporality as the Ontological Meaning of Care"] to apply it to Christ and the Christian life. A very vigorous and precise commentary on this passage is given in Françoise Dastur, *Heidegger and the Question of Time*, trans. François Raffoul and David Pettigrew (Atlantic Highlands, N.J.: Humanities Press, 1998).

10. Jean-Luc Marion, *The Idol and Distance: Five Studies* (New York: Fordham University Press, 2001), 213–14.

11. Heidegger, *Gesamtausgabe*, XX:109–10: "Philosophical research is and remains an atheism"; cited by Romano, "Le possible et l'événement (I)," 75, note 17.

12. Romano, "Le possible et l'événement (I)," 75.

13. Heidegger, *Being and Time: A Translation of Sein und Zeit*, trans. Joan Stambaugh (Albany: State University of New York Press, 1996), §49:249, note 6, p. 408 (see introduction).

7. The Narrow Road of Anxiety

1. See Martin Heidegger, "The Basic State-of-Mind as a Distinctive Way in Which Dasein Is Disclosed," in *Being and Time*, trans. John Macquarrie and Edward Robinson (New York: Harper Perennial Modern Thought, 2008), §40. As when I examined §30, "Fear as a Mode of State-of-Mind," I do not attempt here to take up the characteristics of anxiety developed by Heidegger one by one, with its aspect of being "in the face of something," or *"anxiety about* something," or what "anxiety is anxious about." And once again, I am not trying here to develop a pure exegesis of Heidegger's text and only take up those characteristics of anxiety that will be retained later as part of a theological analysis of the anxiety of Christ. This is also why I refer, without seriously differentiating between them, to the existential analysis of anxiety in *Being and Time* and Heidegger's lecture of 1929 (practically contemporary with *Being and Time*), "What Is Metaphysics?" For a strict exegesis of §40 of *Being and Time*, I would refer the reader to Jean Greisch, *Ontologie et temporalité: Esquisse d'une interprétation intégrale de Sein und Zeit* (Paris: PUF, 1994), 230–236.

2. Heidegger, *Being and Time*, §40:231–32.

3. Ibid., §40:231.

4. Ibid., §40:186–87.

5. Heidegger, "What Is Metaphysics?," trans. David Farrell Krell, in *Pathmarks*, ed. William McNeill (Cambridge: Cambridge University Press, 1998).

6. [Trans.—For Heidegger's distinction between "existentiell" and "existential," see Chapter 4, note 5.]

7. Heidegger, "What Is Metaphysics?," in *Pathmarks*, 88.

8. Jean-Luc Marion, *Reduction and Givenness: Investigations of Husserl, Heidegger and Phenomenology*, trans. Thomas A. Carlson (Evanston, Ill.: Northwestern University Press, 1998), 73.

9. Heidegger, *Being and Time*, §40:188: "Anxiety disindividualizes Dasein and thus discloses it as *'solus ipse.'*"

10. Ibid., §40:188. Emmanuel Martineau translated *vereinzelt* as "isolated," a term that is more appropriately kept for the *"solus ipse"* of the anxious *Dasein*; see Greisch, *Ontologie et temporalité*, 233–34.

11. Heidegger, *Being and Time*, note iv to division 1, chap. 6, p. 492.

12. Dietrich Wiederkehr, *Esquisse d'une christologie systématique* (Paris: Éditions du Cerf, 1975), 210–11: "La mort et la résurrection de Jésus comme dialogue existentiel."

13. See Edmund Husserl, *Ideas Pertaining to a Pure Phenomenology and to a Phenomenological Philosophy*, vol. 2, *Studies in the Phenomenological Constitution*, trans. Richard Rojcewicz and André Schuwer (Dordrecht: Kluwer Academic, 1989), §36:152.

14. See Hans Urs von Balthasar, *Mysterium Paschale*, trans. Aidan Nichols (San Francisco: Ignatius, 1990): "On the Mount of Olives, Christ's anguish was

a co-suffering with sinners" (chap. 3, §3b). We can find the idea of solidarity in death in Karl Rahner, *On the Theology of Death*, trans. C. H. Henkey and M. J. O'Hara (London: Burns and Oates, 1962). Rahner maintains that death is the culminating point of appropriation and redemption in Christ's redemptive act. Before simply opposing solidarity and substitution to one another, however, it is appropriate first of all to recognize that there is an ultimate point of convergence. This allows us to avoid falling into the bitter argument that neglects the reality of how much these diverging points of view stem from a common base.

15. For a very relevant account of such a theology and its significant link with the *Cur Deus Homo* of St. Anselm, see Balthasar, "Crucifixus etiam pro nobis, le mystère de la substitution," *Communio* 5, no. 1 (1980): 52–62.

16. Charles Péguy, *Dialogue de l'histoire et de l'âme chrétienne*, in *Oeuvres en prose complètes*, Pléiade ed. (Paris: Gallimard, 1992), 3:750.

17. "What is called a reason for living is also an excellent reason for dying": Albert Camus, *The Myth of Sisyphus and Other Essays*, trans. Justin O'Brien (New York: Vintage International, 1991), 4.

18. Balthasar, *Mysterium Paschale*, chap. 3, §3b. Balthasar cites Robert Pullus (1080–c.1147) on *timor gehennalis*.

19. Ibid., chap. 3, §3b.

20. Notwithstanding the first and most obvious meaning of the verb *teleô* as accomplishment or completion of a *telos* or action, it is the case that this verb in Greek (and in the passive) can also show—in a more ordinary but no less correct way—the coming to its term of a particular course, as in the coming to the end of a race, or "coming to the end of the road," or "come to one's end" completely exhausted or doomed; see H. G. Liddell and R. Scott, *A Greek-English Lexicon* (Oxford: Oxford University Press, 1940), article *teleô*, 1772a, citing Aeschylus, *The Choephori*. This is an interpretation that we shall need to reconsider later, at least in relation to the death of the Son, which is precisely something that will never be "finished"—and what renders it exemplary and without sin, i.e., his constant relation to the Father.

21. See Hans Jonas, "The Concept of God after Auschwitz: A Jewish Voice," *Journal of Religion* 67, no. 1 (January 1987): 1–13. Jonas suggests that the drama of Auschwitz could not truly arrive, theologically speaking, at the Christian's concept of God, solely because Christians always expect true salvation in another world, making of this world here "always an object of suspicion . . . because of original sin" (3) Although such mistrust may be historically appropriate at the level of Western theology, we should note carefully that it is in obscuring matters through too much reference to sin that Christians lose in some degree the sense of a finitude that is not necessarily a fall from grace. To reconsider Gethsemane in the light of this kind of finitude that is strongly affirmed in modern thought brings us back, along with Hans Urs von Balthasar, to fight against what he calls, quite rightly, the fatal option of the Platonizing Fathers when they take sides against all that is in the senses, ascending toward

God for the unique experience of God in the immediacy of naked faith; see Balthasar, *The Glory of the Lord: A Theological Aesthetics*, vol. 1, *Seeing the Form*, trans. Erasmo Leiva-Merikakis (San Francisco: Ignatius, 1982), In this context, see also Emmanuel Falque, "Hans Urs von Balthasar lecteur d'Irénée ou 'la chair retrouvée,'" in *Nouvelle revue théologique*, no. 5 (September–October 1993): 683–98.

22. [Trans.—See the *Mishneh Torah*, or *Yad ha-Hazakah* ("strong hand"), the systematic code of Jewish law written by Moses Maimonides (1135–1204).]

23. [Trans.—Theodicy: Justification of God, or attempts to answer why God permits evil in the world.]

24. Etty Hillesum, *An Interrupted Life: The Diaries, 1941–1943*, trans. Arnold J. Pomerans (New York: Henry Holt, 1996), 178.

25. For a contemporary return to the theory of the *tzimtzum* or the withdrawal and the auto-limitation of God in the act of creation developed by Isaac Luria (1534–72), see, for example, from a Jewish perspective, Jonas, *The Concept of God after Auschwitz*. From a Christian perspective, see Sylvie Germain, *Les Echos de silence* (Paris: Desclée de Brouwer, 1996), 60–63. There is a fine account of this doctrine and its influences in Gershom Scholem, *Major Trends in Jewish Mysticism* (1941; repr. New York: Schocken, 1955), "Isaac Luria and His School," 244–86.

26. See Gregory of Nyssa, *Contra Eunomia (Against Eunomius)*, trans. H. C. Ogle and H. A. Wilson, bk. 2, 11: "Accordingly, when we hear the name '*Almighty*' [*Pantokrator*], our conception is this, that God sustains in being all intelligible things as well as all things of a material nature"; New Advent (2009), ed. Kevin Knight, accessed September 3, 2016, http://www.newadvent .org/fathers/290102.htm; St. Augustine, *Confessions*, trans. J. G. Pilkington, bk. XI, chapter 13:15: "You, God Almighty [*omnipotentem*], and All-creating [*omnicreantem*], and All-sustaining [*omnitenentem*]"; New Advent (2009), ed. Kevin Knight, accessed September 3, 2016, http://www.newadvent.org/ fathers/110111.htm. See on this point the essay by Olivier Boulnois, "Puissance divine," in *Dictionnaire critique de théologie* (Paris: PUF, 1998), 959–60.

27. Catherine Chalier, editor of the French edition of *The Concept of God after Auschwitz* (Hans Jonas) points out "the concept of all powerfulness does not exist as such in the Bible. When we find in French translation 'I am the all-powerful [tout-puissant] God' (Gen 35:11, for example), the Hebrew text uses *El-Chaddaï*, literally He who says 'enough,' who poses limits"; Jonas, *Le Concept de Dieu après Auschwitz: Une voix juive* (Paris: Rivages-Poches, 1994), 42, note 4.

28. Jonas, *Le Concept de Dieu*, 3.

29. Ibid., 8.

30. Hugh of Saint-Cher, from the *Commentaire des Sentences* of Hugues de Saint-Cher, bk. 1:42, 1, in the translation (modified here) by Boulnois in *La Puissance et son ombre: De Pierre Lombard à Luther* (Paris: Aubier, 1994), 138, cited by Jean-Luc Solère, "Le concept de Dieu avant Hans Jonas: Histoire,

création et tout-pouissance," *Mélanges de science religieuse* (Lille), no. 1 (January–March 1996): 7–38. On this difficult question of the status of the powerlessness of God and its implications in Christianity, as in a certain Kabbalistic Gnosis, this article forcefully shows how such questions have also been posed in the theological tradition, in which they have even managed to find solutions and orientations for more research. We can find in the essay a Christian response to the text by Hans Jonas that has been referred to here at length. Nonetheless, I would not fully endorse the conclusion of the author, which I find somewhat extreme, of the radical incompatibility of the "powerlessness of God" and of "creationist monotheism" (38). I think we need to understand the meaning of such powerlessness and recognize that it retains a true theological status, insofar as it accepts precisely a marking out, in terms of its originality and its specificity, even of the power of God.

31. See the perspective of a pure and simple powerlessness of God at Gethsemane and on Golgotha developed, for example, by Eugen Drewermann, *La Parole et l'Angoisse* (Paris: Desclée de Brouwer, 1995), 387.

32. Jonas, *Le Concept de Dieu*, 9.

33. William of Auxerre [Guillaume d'Auxerre], *Summa aurea*, vol. 9, chapter 4, cited and translated by Jean-Luc Solère in "Le concept de Dieu avant Hans Jonas," 29.

34. Heidegger, What Is Metaphysics?," in *Pathmarks*, 88.

35. Ibid.

36. On the meaning of kenosis as the giving up of glory and not of divine filiation, as well as for the limits of post-Hegelian perspectives on kenosis (particularly that of Gottfried Thomasius), see Balthasar, *Mysterium Paschale*, chap. 1, §4, "The Kenosis and the New Image of God."

37. Marion, *God without Being*, trans. Thomas A Carlson, 2nd ed. (Chicago: University of Chicago Press, 2012), 122.

38. Balthasar, *Mysterium Paschale*, chap. 3, §3a.

39. Monique Rosaz and Édouard Pousset, "Passion-résurrection selon l'évangile de saint Marc," supplement to *Vie chrétienne*, no. 276 (1986): 37: "Jesus covers the distance from the first focus [the sleeping disciples] to the second [the Father invoked in prayer] and there, alone, he prays. Then he goes from one to the other, several times, until in the end *it* ends."

40. Ibid., 38.

41. Jürgen Moltmann, *The Crucified God*, trans. R. A. Wilson and John Bowden (Minneapolis: Fortress, 1993): "What happened on the cross was an event between God and God. It was a deep division in God himself, in so far as God abandoned God and contradicted himself" (244).

42. Ibid., 56.

43. "I am alone with all that human fate / I undertook through Thee to mitigate, / Thou who art not. Oh, shame too consummate"; Rainer Marie Rilke, "The Olive Garden," in *Possibility of Being*, trans. J. B. Leishman (New York: New Directions, 1977), 28.

44. See the French ecumenical translation of the Bible, *Traduction œcuménique de la Bible* (2010), note to Mark 14:35.

45. Péguy, *Dialogue de l'histoire et de l'âme charnelle*, in *Oeuvres en prose complètes*, Pléiade ed. (Paris: Gallimard, 1992), 3:751.

46. Heidegger, *Being and Time*, §40:188.

47. A similar perspective criticizing the view of Jürgen Moltmann has, at least in part, already been outlined by Balthasar, in "Fragments sur la croix trinitaire," *Communio* 2, no. 3 (May 1977): 29–30: "But let us say from now on, if the 'Christian' response (if one can speak in these terms) sends us back to the divine Trinity, it is not then in the sense that the Father (conceived as God-Lord) would abandon his Son to suffering, without pity, like a human larva that one treads underfoot (Ps 22:7). . . . It is, on the contrary, the one and only *Trinitarian plan* that is accomplished for our salvation, in a perfect equality of freedom, of love, of giving, in the same Holy Spirit." A confirmation of this convincing critique can be found in Balthasar's *Mysterium Paschale*: "Isolation vis-à-vis the God who distances himself, but has not yet disappeared, and on whom Jesus calls with pleading tenderness, 'dear Father,' *Abba*" (chap. 3, §3a).

48. Drewermann, *La Parole et l'Angoisse*, 387.

49. Gustave Martelet, "Dieu n'a pas créé la mort," *Christus*, no. 168 (October 1995): 461.

50. Drewermann, *La Parole et l'Angoisse*, 387.

8. Death and Its Possibilities

1. Martin Heidegger, *Being and Time*, trans. John Macquarrie and Edward Robinson (New York: Harper Perennial Modern Thought, 2008), §48:245.

2. Heidegger, *History of the Concept of Time: Prolegomena*, trans. Theodore Kisiel (Bloomington: Indiana University Press, 1992), 317.

3. In the perspective of death—rather than in the imminence of decease—the "It is accomplished" of John's Gospel (19:30 JB) would not any longer signify here some kind of "It is finished" (see §35). This is because on the one hand a consciousness of the end opens up onto the possibility of life, and on the other hand, as far as such possibilities are concerned (as we shall see later), the statement remains always anchored in a relation with the Father that will not be (this time) ever at an end.

4. [Trans.—"Ek-sistence" is Heidegger's term for standing in the truth of Being, taking an open stance, something "that is proper only to the human being." "Ek-sistence so understood is not only the ground of the possibility of reason, *ratio*, but is also that in which the essence of the human being preserves the source that determines him"; Heidegger, *Letter on Humanism* (1946), in *Pathmarks*, trans. Frank A. Capuzzi (Cambridge: Cambridge University Press, 1998), 247.]

5. Heidegger, *Being and Time*, §48:242.

6. Ibid., §49:246.

7. Ibid., §48:241–46 (particularly 245). I am drawing loosely here on the paragraph from *Being and Time*. For a more thorough exegesis, see Jean Greisch, *Ontologie et temporalité: Esquisse d'une interprétation de Sein un Zeit* (Paris: PUF, 1994), 272–73.

8. Heidegger, *Being and Time*, §50:250.

9. Ibid., §50:250.

10. Emmanuel Levinas, *Time and the Other* (Pittsburgh, Pa.: Duquesne University Press, 1987), 74.

11. Heidegger, *Being and Time*, §47:240 (emphasis in original).

12. Ibid., §53:263.

13. Ibid., §53:266.

14. Ibid., §50:250.

15. Heidegger, *Being and Time*, §53:263–64. Heidegger adds to the characteristics of death as "ownmost" possibility, "absolute" and "not to be outstripped," the characteristics of "certitude" and "indefiniteness." I shall not elaborate on these here, except to add that one recalls Pascal's paradox of death (see Chapter 3, §13, note 2 of this volume: Blaise Pascal, *Pensées*, trans A. J. Krailsheimer [London: Penguin, 1966], L 434, B 199, 165: "Imagine a number of men in chains, all under sentence of death, some of whom are each day butchered in the sight of others; those remaining see their own condition in that of their fellows, and looking at each other with grief and despair await their turn. This is an image of the human condition"). The other ["indefiniteness"] was dealt with in the analysis of anxiety (always indefinite unlike fear). On these different characteristics of "death," see also the detailed commentary by Jean Greisch in his *Ontologie et temporalité*, 218–82.

16. After having looked at the hypothesis, in the form of a preliminary interpretation, of "It is accomplished" (John 19:30 JB) as "That is the end" (see §35), I see here the ultimate reason that authorizes us not just to invalidate the hypothesis, but also to go beyond it. It is not simply that the prospect of death (more than the act of decease) opens up possibilities in life, but the wakefulness of the Son amounts this time to never breaking (and thus never interrupting) his relation to his own Father.

17. [Trans.—"*Ek-sistence*": see note 4.]

18. [Trans.—"*Ekstasis*": to be or stand outside oneself. Used by Heidegger in this sense for being outside oneself in relation to time; Heidegger, *Being and Time*, §65:329.]

19. Ibid., §50:250.

20. Ibid., §47:238.

21. Ibid., §47:239.

22. Roger Munier, *Le Moins du monde* (Paris: Gallimard, 1982), 44.

23. Heidegger, *Being and Time*, §53:262 (emphasis in original).

24. Michel de Montaigne, "That to Philosophise Is to Learne How to Die" (1580), *Literary and Philosophical Essays* (Cambridge, Mass.: Harvard Classics,

P. F. Collier and Son, 1909–14). Accessed on Bartleby.com, October 25, 2016, http:www.bartelby.com/32/103.html.

25. Heidegger, *Being and Time*, §53:261–62. See also in this context Greisch, *Ontologie et temporalité*, 280, which decrypts the *ars moriendi* of the Middle Ages under what Heidegger calls the "rumination" over the thought of death.

26. Ibid., §39:179.

27. Ibid.

28. Ignatius of Loyola, *The Spiritual Exercises and Selected Works*, ed. George E. Gaus (New York: Paulist Press, 1991), 165 (186) (my emphasis).

29. [Trans.—Cf. Jacques Derrida, on the subject of Maurice Blanchot's *L'arrêt de mort* (*Death Sentence*): "This 'more,' this more-than-life [*sur-vie*], marks . . . a temporal extension of life in the form of a reprieve. Before dying, in these, 'few minutes, she lived more than a lifetime [*plus qu'une vie*]'"; Derrida, "Living On: Border Lines," in *Deconstruction and Criticism*, trans. James Hulbert (New York: Seabury, 1979), 124.]

30. Heidegger, *Being and Time*, §52:263 (emphasis in original).

31. Charles Péguy, *Dialogue de l'histoire: Oeuvres en prose completes,* Pléiade ed. (Paris: Gallimard, 1992), 3:751.

32. This formula is cited and commented upon in Bernard Sesboüé, *Jésus dans la tradition de l'Église* (Paris: Desclée, 1990), 161. For the second council of Constantinople (533), see Gervais Dumeige, *La Foi catholique* (Paris: Éditions de l'Orante, 1975), no. 326, p. 197: "He who was crucified in the flesh, our Lord Jesus Christ, in true God, Lord of glory and one of the holy Trinity"; see also Heinrich Denzinger, *Enchiridion Symbolorum* (San Francisco: Ignatius, 2012), nos. 125, 250.

33. Jürgen Moltmann, *The Crucified God*, trans. R. A. Wilson and John Bowden (Minneapolis: Fortress, 1993), 243. I refer to this distinction made by Moltmann between the suffering of the Father and the suffering of the Son as "traditional" not in the sense that the Christian tradition would always have endorsed such a thesis (the constant philosophical imperative concerning divine impassibility would be enough to demonstrate the contrary). I simply want to suggest here that the roots of this distinction can *also* be found in the tradition, while we must allow to Moltmann, as to Hans Urs von Balthasar, the credit of having given them a formulation that is explicitly Trinitarian.

34. Origen, *Homilies on Ezekiel*, trans. Thomas P. Scheck (Mahwah, N.J.: Newman Press, 2010), 6:3:3.

35. See Moltmann, *Crucified God*, 200–274.

36. Heidegger, *Being and Time*, §60:297.

37. Ibid., §60:297.

38. See Ernest Renan, *The Life of Jesus*, trans. C. E. Wilbour (New York: Carleton, 1866); Jacques Duquesne, *Jesus: An Unconventional Biography,* trans. Catherine Spencer (Barnhart, Mo.: Liquori, 1997).

39. The mention of "body" (*sôma*) in Heb 10:5 is all the more significant because the author of the Epistle to the Hebrews, in substituting the Greek term for "body" for the term "ear" used in the citation of the *Septuagint* (Ps

40:6), seems, according to the note in the TOB, to have in mind precisely an "allusion to the incarnation."

40. "[Christ] was destined by His Father as a sacrifice, and carried the cross whereon he suffered"; Tertullian, *Against Marcion*, bk. 3, 18, trans. Peter Holmes, in *Ante-Nicene Fathers* (1885), vol. 3, ed. Alexander Roberts and James Donaldson (Buffalo, N.Y.: Christian Literature, 1885). On New Advent site, ed. Kevin Knight, accessed September 5, 2016, http://www.newadvent.org/fathers/0312.htm.

41. Ibid., bk. 3, 11.

42. Tertullian, *On the Flesh of Christ*, 6, trans. Peter Holmes, in *Ante-Nicene Fathers* (1885), vol. 3, On New Advent site, ed. Kevin Knight, accessed September 5, 2016, http://www.newadvent.org/fathers/0315.htm.

43. Heidegger, *Being and Time*, §53:264.

44. Emmanuel Levinas, *Time and the Other*, 70.

45. This debate, at once close to and distant from Christianity in *Being and Time*, could be the subject on its own of a lengthy study. In this respect it is worth looking at Marlène Zarader's work, even if it is concerned with Judaism rather than Christianity (see Zarader, *The Unthought Debt: Heidegger and the Hebraic Heritage*, trans Bettina Bergo [Stanford, Calif.: Stanford University Press, 2006]). Despite many possible convergences, Heidegger indicts more or less explicitly the "anthropology of Christian theology" as it "stands in the way of the basic question of Dasein's Being" (*Being and Time*, §10:48) or obstructs in a burdensome way the philosophical perspective, for example, with its "contention that there are eternal truths" (*Being and Time*, §44:229).

46. On this move, see the *active* passage—in the double sense of rushing forward and overshooting the mark—from chapter 1 to chapter 2 of the second section of Heidegger, *Being and Time* (in particular, §52–54), going from "Being-towards-the-end" to "Authentic Existentiell Possibility."

47. Ibid., §50:250.

III. The Body-to-Body of Suffering and Death

1. Martin Heidegger, *Being and Time: A Translation of Sein und Zeit*, trans. Joan Stambaugh (Albany: State University of New York Press, 1996), note vi to §49:408.

2. For the neologism "encharnement," see Charles Péguy, *Le Porche du mystère de la deuxième vertu*, in *Oeuvres poétiques complètes*, Pléiade ed. (Paris: Gallimard, 1957), 1:586: "His incarnation, which is really his assumption of the flesh [*encharnement*]."

3. See Heidegger, *Being and Time*, §16:73–75.

4. Didier Franck, *Heidegger et le problème de l'espace* (Paris: Éditions de Minuit, 1986): "The term *Vorhand* . . . doesn't it presuppose that *Dasein* is equipped with hands, incarnate?" (30), and "On this further condition that Being-in-the-world, the *Dasein*, could have hands and be incarnate without contravening its mode of being . . . that these hands and flesh could appear in the world" (62).

9. From Self-Relinquishment to the Entry into the Flesh

1. See Friedrich Nietzsche, *The Gay Science*, trans. Josefine Nauckhoff (Cambridge: Cambridge University Press, 2001): "Anyone who wants to know from the adventures of his own experience, how it feels to be the discoverer or conqueror of an ideal, or to be an artist, an old-style divine lover—any such person needs one thing above all—*the great health*" (bk. 5, 382, 246) (emphasis in original).

2. Edmund Husserl, *Cartesian Meditations*, trans. Dorion Cairns (The Hague: Martinus Nijhoff, 1960), Fourth Meditation, §38, "Active and Passive Genesis," 78.

3. Plato, *The Republic*, trans. Benjamin Jowett, bk. 6, 511b, accessed October 26, 2016, http://classics.mit.edu/Plato/republic.7.vi.html.

4. See John 13:2 JB: "It was before the festival of the Passover, and Jesus knew that the hour had come for him to pass from this world to the Father." On the "hazardous" word in the interpretation of the passing of Christ as *passivity* and not simply as *passage*, see the brief comment, "in passing," by Édouard Pousset and Monique Rosaz (*Le Principe et la fin: Lectures en Saint Jean*, supplement to *Vie chrétienne*, no. 358 (1991): 42: "To pass in a *passivity*. This word must be hazardous" (my emphasis). Such an interpretation is nonetheless justified when we work from the Greek, where the verb *meta-bainô* in "to pass [*metabê*] from their world to the Father" indicates not simply a change of place, but also the act of changing or of *being transformed* by that which passes; see H. G. Liddell and R. Scott, *A Greek-English Lexicon* (Oxford: Oxford University Press, 1940): *Metabainô*, p. 1109, col. 6. We find the same sense in French of *metabainô* in the term *métabolisme* [English: metabolism] meaning, according to the *Dictionnaire Robert*, "an array of physico-chemical changes of a living being at the heart of a mechanism of exchange of nutrition, assimilation and discharge." While the transitive usage of the verb by St. John here seems to indicate first, and most simply, a passage like a jump from one river bank to another, nothing stands in the way of this other interpretation: a complementary one of "to pass" (*metabê*) as the ordeal or the *passivity* of the one who passes (a "Passeur" [see Introduction, note 4]) at the heart of this passage.

5. Emmanuel Levinas, *Entre Nous: On Thinking-of-the-Other*, trans. Michael B. Smith and Barbara Harshav (New York: Columbia University Press, 1998), §92: "Useless Suffering."

6. Husserl, "Foundational Investigations of the Phenomenological Origin of the Spatiality of Nature: The Originary Ark, the Earth, Does Not Move"; quoted in *Husserl at the Limits of Phenomenology*, by Maurice Merleau-Ponty, trans. Leonard Lawlor and Bettina Bergo (Evanston, Ill.: Northwestern University Press, 2002), 130 (my emphasis).

7. Heidegger, "Building, Dwelling, Thinking," from *Poetry, Language, Thought*, trans. Albert Hofstadter (New York: Harper Colophon, Perennial Classics, 2001), 145.

8. Ibid., 149.

9. *Fifty Spiritual Homilies of St. Macarius of Egypt* (c. 300–391), trans. A. J. Mason (London: SPCK, 1921), 49:4, accessed September 9, 2016, on e-Catholic 2000, http://www.ecatholic2000.com/macarius/untitled-52.shtml#_Toc385610664.

10. In connection with the theological interest in the term "dwelling" in the Heideggerian sense, see, from a liturgical and philosophical point of view, Jean-Yves Lacoste, *Expérience et absolu* (Paris: PUF, 1994), 42–45, para. 13. And from the sacramental viewpoint, Louis-Marie Chauvet, *Symbole et sacrement* (Paris: Éditions du Cerf, 1987), 404–8.

11. See respectively Husserl, *Cartesian Meditations*, §4, "pre-predicative evidence" (I return to this later), and §10 on the "pure—and, so to speak, still dumb—psychological experience." As for the meaning and necessity of the pre-predicative discourse as constitutive of the "life-world," see Husserl's *The Crisis of the European Sciences and Transcendental Phenomenology*, trans. David Carr (Evanston, Ill.: Northwestern University Press, 1970), §9 (h): "the life-world as the forgotten meaning-fundament of nature science" (48–53). On the purely kerygmatic dimension of faith as an act of language and place of decision here and now (*hic et nunc*), see Rudolf Bultmann, *Jésus: Mythologie et démythologisation* (Paris: Éditions de Seuil, 1968), preface by Paul Ricoeur, 178–80. As for the limits of such a perspective—which it is not surprising to find was a source of hermeneutic theology for Paul Ricoeur (see his preface to Bultmann), I would note the suggestive comments by Hans Urs von Balthasar, *The Glory of the Lord*, vol. 7, *Theology: The New Covenant*, trans. Brian McNeil (Edinburgh: T. and T. Clark, 1989), "Word-Flesh," 115–61. See also my discussion in §56.

12. Levinas, *Time and the Other*, trans. Richard A. Cohen (Pittsburgh, Pa.: Duquesne University Press, 1987), 74.

13. This is a formula taken up by Jean-Luc Marion in *Being Given: Toward a Phenomenology of Givenness*, trans. Jeffrey L. Kosky (Stanford, Calif.: Stanford University Press, 2002), and used by Marion in relation to what he calls the "saturated phenomenon."

14. Heidegger, *Being and Time*, §53:266: "*Anticipation reveals to Dasein its lostness in the they-self, and brings it face to face with the possibility of being itself, primarily unsupported by concernful solicitude, but of being itself, rather, in an impassioned **freedom towards** death—a freedom which has been released from the Illusions of the 'they,' and which is factical, certain of itself, and anxious*" (boldface in original).

15. Levinas, *Time and the Other*, 75.

16. See, for example, Levinas, *Basic Philosophical Writings*, ed. Adriaan T. Peperzak, Simon Critchley, and Robert Bernasconi (Bloomington: Indiana University Press, 1996), 54: "The 'absolutely other' is not reflected in the consciousness. It resists it to the extent that even its resistance is not convertible into a content of consciousness. Visitation consists in overwhelming the very egoism of the I which supports this conversion. A face confounds the

intentionality that aims at it." For a critique of the too-directly Christianizing readings of the philosophy of Levinas, see Marion, *Prolegomena to Charity*, trans. Stephen Lewis (New York: Fordham University Press, 2002), "The Intentionality of Love," and Marion, *Cartesian Questions: Method and Metaphysics* (Chicago: Chicago University Press, 1999), "Does the Ego Alter the Other?"

17. Gustave Martelet, "Dieu n'a pas crée la mort," *Christus*, no 68 (October 1995): 464. I put the phrase "the worst of" in brackets to indicate how, as I see it, and in accord with the author at this point, Christ comes not simply to liberate humankind from the "worst" (our sins), but also to embrace the simply human ("l'homme tout court") in the flesh (our finitude).

18. Husserl, *The Basic Problems of Phenomenology*, trans. Ingo Farin and James G. Hart (Dordrecht: Springer, 2006), §28: 59. See also Husserl's *Cartesian Meditations*, "Immanent Transcendence and Primordial World," §47:103–4.

19. Didier Franck, *Flesh and Body: On the Phenomenology of Husserl*, trans. Joseph Rivera and Scott Davidson (London: Bloomsbury, 2014), 97 (emphasis in original); see also Husserl, *Cartesian Meditations*, §49:107: "The *intrinsically first other* (the first "non-Ego") *is the other Ego*" (emphasis in original).

20. St. Augustine, *Confessions*, trans. Henry Chadwick (Oxford: Oxford University Press, 1992), III.vi.11.

21. Husserl, *Cartesian Meditations*, 157: "'*Noli foras ire,*' says Augustine, '*in te redi, in interiore homine habitat veritas.*'"

22. This is of course the route followed, albeit with a more implicit reference to Husserl by Michel Henry, *C'est moi la Vérité* (Paris: Éditions de Seuil, 1996), 142–67, "l'homme en tant que Fils dans le Fils"; see especially 158–64.

23. See Paul Ricoeur, *Oneself as Another*, trans. Kathleen Blamey (Chicago: Chicago University Press, 1992). Most relevant here is the "tenth study," "What Ontology in View?" (297), where—very unusually—the author seems to leave the hermeneutics of language and develop the necessity of an ontology of the flesh (see also 319–29, "One's Own Body, or the Flesh"). As for the interpretation of "oneself as an other" as alteration and alterity of the self through Husserl and Levinas, see Ricoeur's account of "The Otherness of Other People," 329–41.

24. Marion, "Réponses à quelques questions," *À propos de "Réduction et donation," Revue de métaphysique et de morale* (January–March 1991): 75.

25. See Henry, *I Am the Truth: Toward a Philosophy of Christianity*, trans. Susan Emmanuel (Stanford Calif.: University of Stanford Press, 2003), 25. [Trans.—Emmanuel prefers the translation "self-affection" (e.g., 210) for the French "auto-affection," though Anglophone commentators have in general preferred "auto-affection." "Affect" is used here in the psychological sense to mean emotion or desire influencing behavior.]

26. As far as the theological legacy of Michel Henry in *I Am the Truth* is concerned, we might note that he could be said to neglect both "the route of the flesh" and that of the "world"—at least within the global framework of a "philosophy of Christianity"; see Xavier Tilliette, "Note de lecture," *Études*, no. 6 (June 1996): 841–43.

27. This perspective of a definition of the man-God (the Christ) "as Son of God" and of humankind as "Son in the Son" is brilliantly developed at length in Michel Henry's *I Am the Truth*, chaps. 6–7.

28. Levinas, *Difficult Freedom: Essays in Judaism*, trans. Seán Hand (Baltimore: Johns Hopkins University Press, 1990), "What Is the Messiah?," 85–91.

29. See Marion, "The Intentionality of Love: In Homage to Emmanuel Lévinas," in *Prolegomena to Charity*, trans. Stephen Lewis (New York: Fordham University Press, 2002), 83–86.

30. On the specifically Christian sense of the incarnation of the other in the singularized figure of the brother, see Balthasar, *The Glory of the Lord*, vol. 7, *Theology*.

31. Balthasar, *The Glory of the Lord*, vol. 1, *Seeing the Form*, trans. Erasmo Leiva-Merikakis (San Francisco: Ignatius, 2009), 234.

32. [Trans.—For Heidegger's distinction between "existentiell" and "existential," see Chapter 4, §19, note 5.]

33. Levinas, *Totality and Infinity: An Essay on Exteriority*, trans. Alphonso Lingis (Dordrecht: Kluwer Academic, 1991), 194.

34. See Balthasar, *The Glory of the Lord*, vol. 1, *Seeing the Form*, 117–18. On the central aspect of this concept in Balthasar's theology, see the excellent account in Henriette Danet, *Gloire et croix de Jésus-Christ* (Paris: Desclée, 1987), 312–14.

35. [Trans.—Docetism: The (heretical) doctrine according to which Jesus only seemed or appeared to be human and to have suffered, that his body was an illusion or celestial substance.]

36. Heidegger, *Being and Time*, §40:190.

37. Ibid., §40:186.

38. Heidegger, "What Is Metaphysics?," trans. David Farrell Krell, in *Pathmarks*, ed. William McNeill (Cambridge: Cambridge University Press, 1998), 89.

39. Ibid., 89.

40. Husserl, *Cartesian Meditations*, §16:38–39.

41. [Trans.—The French translation used by Falque gives "*parole*"—"speech"— rather than "Word" here.]

42. Balthasar, *The Glory of the Lord*, 7:152, n.8: "It is clear that with this statement we mark off the boundary between ourselves and a theology (like that of Bultmann) for which the existence of Jesus is an irrelevant fact that disappears behind the kerygmatic speech-event of the early church; we distance ourselves equally from a theology for which the relevance of the historical Jesus lies only in the 'speech-event' which occurs in the speech to others, or in his faith as this makes itself known in words (Ebeling, Fuchs), or in his self-expression in parabolic discourse (E. Jüngel)."

43. St. Mark the Ascetic, "Letter to Nicolas the Solitary," in *Philokalia* VI.155, accessed October 28, 2016, http://www.holybooks.com/wp-content/uploads/Philokalia.pdf.

10. Suffering Occluded

1. Paul Ricoeur, *Oneself as Another*, trans. Kathleen Blamey (Chicago: Chicago University Press, 1992), 327–28.

2. I am synthesizing here the three fundamental currents described by Marcel Neusch in *Le Mal* (Paris: Centurion, 1970), 82–89: "The Traps of Christian Masochism."

3. This is implicit in Hans Urs von Balthasar's *Love Alone is Credible*, trans. D. C. Schindler (San Francisco: Ignatius, 2004), chapter 3, "The Third Way of Love," and chapter 9, "Love as Form."

4. John Paul II, Apostolic Letter, 1984, *Salvifici Doloris* III:12: "Suffering must serve *for conversion*, that is, *for the rebuilding of goodness* in the subject, who can recognize the divine memory in the call to repentance" (emphasis in original); accessed September 18, 2016, http://w2.vatican.va/content/john-paul -ii/en/apost_letters/1984/documents/hf_jp-ii_apl_11021984_salvifici-doloris .html. A formula of this kind can probably be used in discussing certain experiences of mystics (Francis of Assisi, Thérèse of Lisieux) but should never be set up as a *norm* for all suffering (see §69, "Useless Suffering").

5. Ricoeur, *Oneself as Another*, 328.

6. Christian Bobin, *Une petite robe de fête* (Paris: Gallimard, 1991), 62.

7. Heidegger, *Being and Time*, §2:7: "This entity which each of us is himself and which includes inquiring as one of the possibilities of its Being, we denote by the term 'Dasein,'" and Heidegger, *What is Called Thinking*, trans. Glenn Gray (New York: Harper and Row, 1976), part I, page 5: "Interest, *interesse*, means to be among and in the midst of things, or to be at the center of a thing and to stay with it. But today's interest accepts as valid only what is interesting."

8. Heidegger, *Being and Time*, §2:27.

9. Edmund Husserl, *Ideas Pertaining to a Pure Phenomenology*, trans. Fred Kersten (The Hague: Martinus Nijhoff, 1983), §132:316 (emphasis in original).

10. John Paul II, *Salvifici Doloris* III:13.

11. André Comte-Sponville, *Une éducation philosophique* (Paris: PUF, 1995), 323.

11. Suffering Incarnate

1. For the necessity of a phenomenological discourse that is above all purely descriptive, we go back to the essentials of phenomenology as they were established by Maurice Merleau-Ponty in the preface to *Phenomenology of Perception*, trans. Colin Smith (London: Routledge and Kegan Paul, 1962), viii: "It is a question of describing, not of explaining or analysing. Husserl's first directive to phenomenology, in its early stages, to be a 'descriptive psychology,' or to return to the 'things themselves,' is from the start a rejection of science."

2. Marc Richir, *Le Corps: Essai sur l'interiorité* (Paris: Hatier, 1993), 13.

3. Aristotle, *De Anima (On the Soul)*, trans. J. A. Smith, bk. II:12(A), Internet Classics Archive, accessed September 19, 2016, http://classics.mit.edu /Aristotle/soul.html.

4. Ibid., bk. II:11.

5. Despite certain differences (in particular in the denial of a simple union of contradictory body and spirit), this idea—above all Aristotelian—of the flesh as element, or constituent medium of the human, will be very largely taken up again and developed by Maurice Merleau-Ponty: "What we are calling flesh, the interiorly worked-over mass, has no name in any philosophy. As for the formative medium of the object with the subject, it is not the atom of being, the hard in itself that resides in a unique place and moment. . . . We must not think the flesh starting from substances, from body and spirit—for then it would be the *union of contradictories*—but we must think it, as we said, as an element, as the concrete emblem of a general manner of being"; Merleau-Ponty, *The Visible and the Invisible*, trans. Alphonso Lingis (Evanston, Ill.: Northwestern University Press, 1968), 147 (my emphasis).

6. There are numerous references to the experience of the toucher-touching in the work of Maurice Merleau-Ponty, and they probably constitute a point of origin of his philosophy; see, for example, Merleau-Ponty, *Phenomenology of Perception*, "The Experience of the Body and Classical Psychology," 92–99; *Signs*, trans. Richard McCleary (Evanston, Ill.: Northwestern University Press, 1968), "The Philosopher and His Shadow," 159–81; *The Visible and the Invisible*, trans. Alphonso Longis (Evanston, Ill.: Northwestern University Press, 1968), "The Intertwining— The Chiasm," 130–54; and *The Prose of the World*, trans, John O'Neill (Evanston, Ill.: Northwestern University Press, 1973), "Dialogue and the Perception of the Other," 131–46. All these have their origin in a single but exemplary text by Edmund Husserl, *Ideas Pertaining to a Pure Phenomenology and to a Phenomenological Philosophy: Second Book*, trans. Richard Rojcewicz and André Schumer, in *Collected Works* (Dordrecht: Kluwer Academic, 1989), §36, "Constitution of the Body as a Bearer of Localized Sensations (Sensings)," 3:152–54.

7. Emmanuel Levinas, *Time and the Other*, trans. Richard A. Cohen (Pittsburgh, Pa.: Duquesne University Press, 1987), 89.

8. Ibid., 89.

9. Merleau-Ponty, *Visible and the Invisible*, 135.

10. Ibid., 141; see 114 for the flesh of "tactile texture." As for the hypothesis of a possible incorporation of Christ through cloth or (as I see it) by a touch in the manner of a caress, see Édouard Pousset and Monique Rosaz, "La principe et la fin: Lectures de saint Jean," Supplement to *Vie chrétienne*, no. 358 (1991): 42–43, 51–54.

11. Levinas, *Time and the Other*, 89.

12. On the sense of contingence as contact, see Didier Franck, *Chair et corps: Essai sur la phénoménologie de Husserl* (Paris: Éditions de Minuit, 1981), 168.

13. [Trans.—Circumincession: The relations of the three persons of the Trinity.]

14. Michel Henry, *I Am the Truth: Towards a Philosophy of Christianity*, trans. Susan Emmanuel (Stanford, Calif.: Stanford University Press, 2003), 67–68.

15. See Merleau-Ponty, *Prose of the World*, 131–46.

16. Husserl, *The Crisis of the European Sciences and Transcendental Phenomenology*, trans David Carr (Evanston, Ill.: Northwestern University Press, 1970), 108; Cartesian *Meditations*, trans. Dorion Cairns (The Hague: Martinus Nijhoff, 1960), §43–44. On the usage of these terms and difficulties in their translation, see Natalie Depraz, *Transcendence et Incarnation: Le statut de l'intersubjectivité comme alterité à soi chez Husserl* (Paris: Vrin, 1995), 344–45.

17. For the idea of constituting a "common world" or an intersubjective nature through the meeting of flesh, see Husserl's *Cartesian Meditations: Fifth Meditation*, §55: "Establishment of the community of monads. The First Form of Objectivity: Intersubjective Nature."

18. Moltmann, *The Crucified God*, trans. R. A. Wilson and John Bowden (Minneapolis: Fortress, 1993), 243.

19. Bonaventure, *De reductione artium ad theologiam* 26 (5:325b), *Works* III.31, accessed September 24, 2016, http://www.intratext.com/IXT/LAT0918/.

20. Gabriel Marcel, *Being and Having*, trans. Katharine Farrer (Westminster: Dacre, 1949), "Note of March 31st, 1931," 85, accessed September 23, 2016, http://www.dhspriory.org/kenny/PhilTexts/Marcel/BeingAndHaving.pdf.

21. One finds today many instances of this idea in modern and contemporary philosophy (Nietzsche, Gabriel Marcel, Levinas, Merleau-Ponty, Sartre). The roots of the concept are undoubtedly found in the work of Maine de Biran (1766–1824). And see, in particular, Henry, *Philosophy and Phenomenology of the Body*, trans. Girard Etzkorn (The Hague: Martinus Nijhoff, 1975), 196: "We should replace the affirmation 'I have a body' with the more original one 'I am my body.'"

22. Marc Richir, *Le Corps*, 13.

23. Martin Heidegger, *What Is Called Thinking*, trans. J. Glenn Gray (New York: HarperCollins, 1976), 14. For an analysis of the inadequacy of the object, see the two paradigmatic paragraphs in *Being and Time*, §15 (the example of hammering), and §16 (when a tool or equipment is found missing and the modes of conspicuousness, obtuseness, and obstinacy of my Being-there that this provokes). As for the example of the cabinet maker—where we might point out the irony in the parallel between the carpenter's apprentice of Nazareth (Jesus) and the son of the master cooper and sexton of St. Martin's Church at Messkirch (Heidegger)—we find a trace of this in *What Is Called Thinking*. On all this question of the relationship between *Dasein* that is concerned with the world and the sense of the lack of a tool or equipment, see Franck, *Heidegger et le problème de l'espace* (Paris: Éditions de Minuit, 1986), 40–56.

24. See Merleau-Ponty, *Phenomenology of Perception*, 112–77: "The Spatiality of One's Own Body and Motility."

25. Levinas, *Totality and Infinity: An Essay on Exteriority*, trans. Alphonso Lingis (Dordrecht: Kluwer Academic, 1991), 129–30.

26. Levinas, *Time and the Other*, 69.

27. Ibid., 69.

28. See St. Augustine's commentary on the Epistle to the Philippians, quoted in François Dolbeau, *Augustin d'Hippone: vingt-six sermons au peuple d'Afrique* (Paris: Études augustiniennes, 1996), 93, cited and commented upon in Goulven Madec, "*Caro Christiana*, Saint Augustin et la corporalité," *Transversalités, Revue de l'Institut catholique de Paris*, no. 63 (July–September 1997): 151.

29. Charles Péguy, *Dialogue de l'histoire et de l'âme charnelle*, in *Oeuvres en prose complètes*, Pléiade ed. (Paris: Gallimard, 1992), 3:743–44.

30. Heidegger, "Plato's Doctrine of Truth," trans. John Barlow, in *Philosophy in the Twentieth Century: An Anthology*, ed. William Barrett and Henry Aiken (New York: Random House, 1962), 3:270.

12. The Revealing Sword

1. Maurice Blondel, *Action* (1893), trans. Oliva Blanchette (Notre Dame, Ind.: University of Notre Dame Press, 2004), 305.

2. Ibid.

3. [Trans.—The French word used here by Falque is "*sanglot*," which is usually translated as "sob." It should be noted, however, that French definitions of the word "*sanglot*" strongly emphasize the physical aspect of sobbing and connect sobs with spasmodic and noisy contractions of the diaphragm at a time of strong emotion. "*Sanglot*" has a stronger physical nuance than "sob" in English and is widely used in phrases that could be translated as "having a voice choked with emotion."]

4. See Louis Lavelle, *Le mal et la souffrance* (Paris: PUF, 1941), 86: "As for pain, I undergo it; but as for suffering, I take possession of it, I do not try so much to reject it as to enter into it. I know it and make it mine. When I say 'I suffer,' it is always an act that I perform."

5. Emmanuel Levinas, *Time and the Other*, trans. Richard A. Cohen (Pittsburgh, Pa.: Duquesne University Press, 1987), 69: "While in moral pain one can preserve an attitude of dignity and compunction, and consequently already be free; physical suffering in all its degrees entails the impossibility of detaching oneself from the instant of existence. It is the very irremissibility of being."

6. Gabriel Marcel, *Being and Having*, trans. Katharine Farrer (Westminster: Dacre, 1949), "Note of March 31st, 1931," 85, accessed September 23, 2016, http://www.dhspriory.org/kenny/PhilTexts/Marcel/BeingAndHaving.pdf (my emphasis).

7. Levinas, *Time and the Other*, 72 (my emphasis).

8. Charles Péguy, *Dialogue de l'histoire et de l'âme charnelle*, in *Oeuvres en prose complètes*, Pléiade ed. (Paris: Gallimard, 1992), 3:749.

9. Blondel, *Action*, 350.

10. Ibid., 351.

11. "That He should bear the flesh, or the cross?"; Tertullian, *On the Flesh of Christ*, chap. 5, trans. Peter Holmes, *Ante-Nicene Fathers*, vol. 3; New Advent, ed. Peter Knight, accessed September 26, 2016, http://www.newadvent.org/fathers/0315.htm.

12. Étienne Gilson, *The Spirit of Mediaeval Philosophy* (Notre Dame, Ind.: University of Notre Dame Press, 1990), 461.

13. See Gilson, *God and Philosophy* (New Haven: Yale University Press, 2002), and Martin Heidegger, *Being and Time*, trans. John Macquarrie and Edward Robinson (New York: Harper Perennial Modern Thought, 2008), §5:17.

14. Péguy, *Victor-Marie, comte Hugo* (1910), in *Oeuvres en prose complètes*, Pléiade ed., 3:236. The various interpretations of Exodus 3:14 ('èhyèh 'asher 'èhyèh) [I AM WHO I AM (NSRV)] abound, and there is no question here of reviewing them or deciding between a God "without" Being (Jean-Luc Marion) and one "with" Being (Dominique Dubarle). I note simply that this "conflict of interpretations" has its original source in what Étienne Gilson saw fit to call the "Metaphysic of Exodus" linked to the hypothesis of a "Christian philosophy" (Gilson, *Spirit of Mediaeval Philosophy*, 133). Martin Heidegger was to vehemently criticize such a philosophy without, as I see it, growing tired of also remaining within the horizon of being—even if in a radically different sense (see his *Introduction to Metaphysics*, trans. Gregory Fried and Richard Polt (New Haven: Yale University Press, 2000).

15. Péguy, *Dialogue de l'histoire*, 748.

16. Blaise Pascal, *Pensées*, trans. A. J. Krailsheimer (London: Penguin, 1966), §919:313.

17. Jean-Yves Lacoste, *Experience and the Absolute: Disputed Questions on the Humanity of Man*, trans. Mark Raftery Skehan (New York: Fordham University Press, 2004), 171.

18. Levinas, *Difficult Freedom: Essays in Judaism*, trans. Seán Hand (Baltimore: Johns Hopkins University Press, 1990), 90.

19. Jürgen Moltmann, *The God Crucified*, trans. R. A. Wilson and John Bowden (Minneapolis: Fortress, 1993), 56.

20. [Trans.—"Substitution" refers here to the theological doctrine of "substitutionary atonement," which holds that Christ dies on the cross instead of, or as a substitute for, others. The "penal" version of the substitution theory (to which Falque is opposed) maintains that God sent Jesus to repay the debt to God's justice incurred through sin. It suggests that Christ died to bear the punishment we deserve.]

21. Friedrich Nietzsche, *The Gay Science*, trans. Josefine Nauckhoff (Cambridge: Cambridge University Press, 2001).

22. Heidegger, *Being and Time*, §48:245.

23. For the "impossible substitution" and his virulent critique of the Christian employment of this idea, see Levinas, *Otherwise Than Being, or Beyond Essence*, trans. Alphonso Lingis (Dordrecht: Kluwer Academic, 1982), chap. 4, 113–17. It is to say the least surprising, given his criticism, often implicit, in relation to the theological topic of "substitution," that Levinas's phenomenology has been so frequently taken up, rather too directly, in Christianity.

24. See Jean-Luc Marion, *Prolegomena to Charity*, trans. Stephen Lewis (New York: Fordham University Press, 2002), 19, and Philippe Némo, *Job ou L'Excès du mal* (Paris: Grasset, 1978), 145.

25. Levinas, "Un Dieu homme?"—Paper delivered at the Week for Catholic Intellectuals (Paris, April 1968); see also Levinas, *Entre Nous: Thinking-of-the-Other*, trans. Michael B. Smith and Barbara Harshav (London: Continuum, 2006).

26. St. Thérèse Couderc, Letter of June 26, 1864, in Ghislaine Côté, *Le Cénacle: Fondement Christologiques et Spiritualité* (Paris: Beauchesne, 1991), 121.

27. On the sense of the doubling of such a donation (the gift of a gift) operating through a quadruple scheme of reciprocity, the donor, the receiver, and the gift itself, there is an enlightening discussion [starting off from Jacques Derrida's *Given Time: Counterfeit Money*, trans. Peggy Kamuf (Chicago: University of Chicago Press, 1992)] between Derrida and Jean-Luc Marion, developed in "Un concept phénoménologique du don," *Archivo di filosofia, filosofia della rivelazione*, nos. 1–3 (1994): 75–94, and then given further rich development in Marion, *Being Given: Toward a Phenomenology of Givenness*, trans. Jeffrey L. Kosky (Stanford, Calif.: Stanford University Press, 2002), bk. II, 71–118. The existential of birth is more originary than that of death (although, as we have seen throughout this book, death was so important for Heidegger) because it is always and directly received from another, see Claude Romano, "Le possible et l'évènement," *Philosophie* 1, no. 40 (December 1993): 92: "One is born to oneself without ever being able to take upon oneself one's own birth; it is I who am born, certainly, but I cannot proffer even this affirmation myself in the first person, because above all, others have taken responsibility for it and announced it in my name."

28. Blondel, *Action*, 351.

29. [Trans.—According to Maurice Blondel, "Suffering cuts through life like a revealing sword"; *Action*, 351.]

30. [Trans.—Marthe Robin (1902–81), founder of the Foyers de Charité, bedridden from the age of twenty-one, suffered stigmata. Jacques Fesch (1930–57) murdered a police officer, converted to Catholicism in prison, and accepted his punishment by guillotine, writing, "In five hours, I will see Jesus."]

31. John Paul II, *Salvifici doloris* III.12, VI.26, accessed October 4, 2016, http://w2.vatican.va/content/john-paul-ii/en/apost_letters/1984/documents/hf_jp-ii_apl_11021984_salvifici-doloris.html.

32. Levinas, *Entre Nous*, 79.

33. For the method of the step backward [*Shritt zurück*] and of phenomenological investigation as a "long path," see Heidegger, *Identity and Difference*, trans. Joan Stambaugh (Chicago: University of Chicago Press, 2002), 49–51.

34. Levinas, *Time and the Other*, 72.

35. See Hans Urs von Balthasar, *Unless You Become Like This Child*, trans. Erasmo Leiva-Merikakis (San Francisco: Ignatius, 1991), 7.

Conclusion: The *In-Fans* [without-Speech] or the Silent Flesh

1. Edmund Husserl, cited in Didier Franck, *Flesh and Body: On the Phenomenology of Husserl*, trans. Joseph Rivera and Scott Davidson (London: Bloomsbury, 2014), 81.

2. Emmanuel Levinas, *Time and the Other*, trans. Richard A. Cohen (Pittsburgh, Pa.: Duquesne University Press, 1987), 72 (my emphasis).

3. There is a psychoanalytic usage of this term *infans* as the stage before the child has acquired the use of speech, when the child is "in its primordial form . . . before language restores to it, in the universal, its function as subject," in Jacques Lacan, *Écrits: A Selection*, trans. Alan Sheridan (New York: Norton, 1972), 2; see also Lacan, "The Mirror Stage as Formative of the Function of the *I* as Revealed in Psychoanalytic Experience," 16th International Congress of Psychoanalysis, Zurich (July 17, 1949). See also Lacan, "The Mirror Stage," in *Psychanalyse*, ed. Alain de Mijolla (Paris: PUF, 1966): "Body fragmented because not yet established by speech" (90). I would suggest on the other hand—relying here on an originary and phenomenological description of the flesh—that the *in-fans*, far from having a lack or absence of speech that has to be filled in, manages to establish a world that is precisely and silently what is given by the flesh, or "as an infant" (Husserl; see this chapter, note 1).

4. Husserl, *Cartesian Meditations*, trans. Dorion Cairns (The Hague: Martinus Nijhoff, 1960), §16:38–39.

5. Bonaventure, *Breviloquium* V.6, in *The Works of Bonaventure*, trans. José de Vink (Paterson N.J.: St. Anthony Guild, 1963).

6. See Husserl, *Cartesian Meditations*, §50:108–11: "The mediate intentionality of perceiving someone else, as 'appresentation' (analogical apperception)," and "apperceptive transfer from my animate organism."

7. Georges Bernanos, *Les Grands Cimitières sous la lune* (1937), quoted in Balthasar, *Bernanos: An Ecclesial Existence*, trans. Erasmo Leiva-Merikakis (San Francisco: Ignatius, 1996), 4:1.

Epilogue: From One Triptych to Another

1. [Trans.—See Chap. 2, note 25.]

2. [Trans.—See Chap. 5, note 26.]

3. Emmanuel Falque, *Crossing the Rubicon: The Borderlands of Philosophy and Theology*, trans. Reuben Shank (New York: Fordham University Press, 2016).

4. "The Lord's Descent into Hell," Pontifical University Saint Thomas Aquinas, accessed October 8, 2016, http://www.vatican.va/spirit/documents/spirit_20010414_omelia-sabato-santo_en.html.

Index

Aeschylus, xxiii, 139n20
Alter, Robert, 129n6
Anselm (Saint), 139n15
Ariès, Philippe, 135n9
Aristotle, 88–89, 151n5
Athanasius, 71
Augustine (Saint), 18, 46, 77–78, 95,
    125–26n33, 140n26

Balthasar, Hans Urs von, xiv, 2, 15–16,
    24, 38, 49, 54, 79–80, 83, 85, 106,
    118–19nn8–10, 123nn22,24,
    126n33, 131n2, 138n14, 139–40n21,
    141n36, 142n47, 144n33, 147n11,
    149nn34,42
Barth, Karl, 30, 132n4
Bastaire, Jean 131n16
Baudiquey, Paul, 116n13
Bergman, Ingmar, 21, 127n47
Bernanos, Georges, 8, 109
Blanchot, Maurice, 144n29
Blondel, Maurice, xv, 97, 99, 104,
    115n3
Bobin, Christian, 85
Bonaventure (Saint), 24, 93–94, 108,
    123n23, 130n12–13
Boulnois, Olivier, 140nn26,30

Brown, Peter, 125n33
Bultmann, Rudolf, 75, 147n11, 149n42

Camus, Albert, 1, 3, 22, 24, 26–28, 46,
    48, 117n1, 139n17
Carraud, Vincent, 128n2
Chalier, Catherine, 140n27
Claudel, Paul, 2
Clémence, Jean, 125n33
Clement of Alexandria, 71
Comte-Sponville, André, 87
Corneille, Pierre, xxxi, 34
Couderc, Thérèse (Saint), 103
Coughlin, John, 123n23
Crampon, Augustin, 23

Danet, Henriette, 149n14
Dante, Alighieri, xiii
Darwin, Charles, 120n8
Dastur, Françoise, 137n9
Daudet, Alphonse, xxiii–xxiv
Denzinger, Heinrich, 118n8, 119n2,
    144n32
Depraz, Natalie, 152n16
Derrida, Jacques, 144n29, 155n27
Descartes, René, 13, 122n16, 128n4
Dilthey, Wilhelm, 82

Drewermann, Eugen, 30, 55, 132n7, 141n31
Dubarle, Dominique, 154n14
Dumeige, Gervais, 118n8, 119n2, 144n32
Duquesne, Jacques, 65
Duquoc, Christian, 135n8
Dürer, Albrecht, 21
Duval, Joseph, 120–21n10

Ebeling, Gerhard, 75, 149n42
Epictetus, 8, 22, 117n4
Epicurus, 8, 22, 117n3
Eslin, Jean-Claude, 125n33
Evagrius Ponticus, 132n2

Fesch, Jacques, 105, 155n30
Francis of Assisi (Saint), 105, 150n4
Franck, Didier, 70, 77, 145n4, 151n12, 152n23, 156n1
Freud, Sigmund, 132n7
Fuchs, Josef, 149n42

Gadamer, Hans-Georg, 82
Gandhi, Mahatma, 39
Gauchet, Marcel, 131n7
Germain, Sylvie, 25, 140n25
Gibert, Pierre, 119n5
Gilson, Étienne, 100, 154n14
Gregory of Nyassa (Saint), 13, 140n26
Greisch, Jean, 126n38, 127n44, 129n4, 133nn1,25, 137n2, 138n1, 143nn7,15, 144n25
Greschny, Nicolaï, 124n26
Grünewald, Matthias, xviii–xxx, 116n3
Gschwandtner, Christina M., xiv, 115n1
Guillet, Jacques, 136n21

Hegel, Georg W. F., 1, 76, 125n27
Heidegger, Martin, xiv, xxii, xxv, 1–3, 10–11, 16–20, 24–25, 27–28, 30–31, 39–47, 52–54, 57–59, 61–62, 64–67, 69–70, 74–76, 80–82, 84–86, 94–96, 100, 102, 106, 122n16, 125n27, 126n38, 127n44, 128nn2,4 131n5, 132nn7–8, 133nn1–2,11, 135nn12,14, 136nn25–26, 137nn2–3,5,9, 138nn1,9, 139n15, 142n4, 143nn15,18, 144n25,

145nn45–46, 147n14, 152n23, 154n14, 155n27
Henry, Michel, 78–79, 91, 148nn22, 25–26, 152n21, 155n33
Hillesom, Etty, 49, 52
Huby, Joseph, 24
Hugh of Saint-Cher, 50,
Husserl, Edmund, 3, 73–75, 77–78, 87, 89, 92, 107–8, 121n11, 138n13, 147n11, 148nn22–23, 149n40, 150n1, 151n6, 152n17, 156nn3–4

Ignatius of Loyola (Saint), 62, 93
Irenaeus (Saint), 2, 12, 71, 124n25

John of the Cross (Saint), 62, 105
John Paul II, 87, 120n8, 123n23, 124n25, 150n4, 155n31
John XXIII, 115n2
Jonas, Hans, 39, 50–51, 136n25, 139n21, 140nn25,27, 140–41n30
Jüngel, Eberhard, 149n42

Kant, Emmanuel, 17, 122n16
Kierkegaard, Søren, xiv, 1, 29–30, 46, 129n5, 132n7
Kolbe, Maximilian, 20, 127n42

Lacan, Jacques, 156n3
Lacau St. Guily, Agnès, 116n4, 116–17n13
Lacoste, Jean-Yves, 101
Laroche, Michel, 131nn1–2
Lavelle, Louis, 153n4
Leo I (the Great), xxx
Leon-Dufour, Xavier, 136n21
Levinas, Emmanuel, xvii, 3, 58, 74–77, 79–80, 90, 95, 99, 102, 105, 122n16, 127n44, 134n7, 145n44, 147n16, 148n23, 152n21, 153n5, 154nn18,23, 155nn25,34, 156n2
Luria, Isaac, 49, 140n25
Luther, Martin, xviii, 46
Lyonnet, Stanislas, 130n8

Macarius (Saint), 74
Madec, Goulven, 126n33, 153n28
Maimonides, Moses, 140n22
Maine de Biran, 152n21

Marcel, Gabriel, 21, 25, 94, 98, 130n14, 152n21
Marion, Jean-Luc, 43, 45, 53, 78–79, 118n8, 126n37, 131n6, 147n13, 148n16, 154n14, 155nn24,27
Mark the Ascetic (Saint), 83
Martelet, Gustave, 11, 18, 21, 55, 77, 118n8, 119n1, 119–20n7, 121n13, 124–25n27, 126n33, 130nn8–11, 148n17
Martineau, Emmanuel, 138n10
Merleau-Ponty, Maurice, 30, 89, 91, 132n8, 150n1, 151nn5–6, 152nn21,24
Michelangelo, 15
Moltmann, Jürgen, 54, 63, 93, 101–2, 141n41, 142n47, 144n33
Montaigne, Michel de, 22, 61, 127–8n1
Mugnier, Abbot Francis, 118n6
Munier, Roger, 61

Némo, Philippe, 155n24
Neusch, Marcel, 84, 131n7
Nietzsche, Friedrich, xxiv, 28, 37, 66, 73, 131n8, 146n1, 152n21, 154n21
Novalis, 106

Origen, 8, 9, 63, 93, 118nn7–8, 119n10

Pagels, Elaine, 125n33
Pannenberg, Wolfhart, 137n8
Pascal, Blaise, xxii, 22, 101, 128nn2,4, 143n15
Paul (Saint), xvi, 41, 52–53, 60, 78
Péguy, Charles, xxv, 22, 25, 34, 36, 38–39, 48, 55, 63, 70, 96, 99–101, 104, 118n8, 131n16, 145n2
Pelagius, 11
Pessoa, Fernando, 19
Plato, 73
Pousset, Édouard, 54, 136n23, 141n39, 146n4, 151n10

Rahner, Karl, 13, 38, 123n18, 134n7, 139n14
Renan, Ernest, 65, 134n8

Reynier, Chantal, 123n21
Richir, Marc, 88, 94
Ricoeur, Paul, 13, 75, 78, 82, 84–85, 119n5, 147n11, 148n23
Rilke, Rainer Marie, 54, 141n43
Robin, Marthe, 105, 155n30
Romano, Claude, 41–42, 44, 137nn2,5,7, 155n27
Rosaz, Monique, 54, 136n23, 141n39, 146n4, 151n10
Rousseau, Jean-Jacques, 12
Rublev, Andrei, 124n26

Sartre, Jean-Paul, 1, 3, 22, 24, 27–28, 46, 76, 125n27, 128n3, 152n21
Saussure, Ferdinand de, 82
Scholem, Gershom, 140n25
Schürmann, Heinz, 136n21
Segond, Louis, 23
Sesboüé, Bernard, 118n6, 121–22n13, 135n9, 136n17, 144n32
Socrates, 8, 22, 29, 39, 85
Solère, Jean-Luc, 140n30, 141n33
Solignac, Aimé, 126n33
Spinoza, Benedict de, 125n32
Strauss, David, 134n8
Symeon the New Theologian, 132n2

Tertullian, 65, 100, 145n40
Theissen, Gerd, 135n8
Theresa of Avila (Saint), 62
Thérèse of Lisieux (Saint), 105, 150n4
Thévenaz, Pierre, 117n1
Thomasius, Gottfried, 141n36
Tilliette, Xavier, 148n26
Tincq, Henri, 120n8

Valéry, Paul, 128n2
Virgil, xiii

Wiederkehr, Dietrich, 46
William of Auxerre, 51

Zarader, Marlène, 145n45

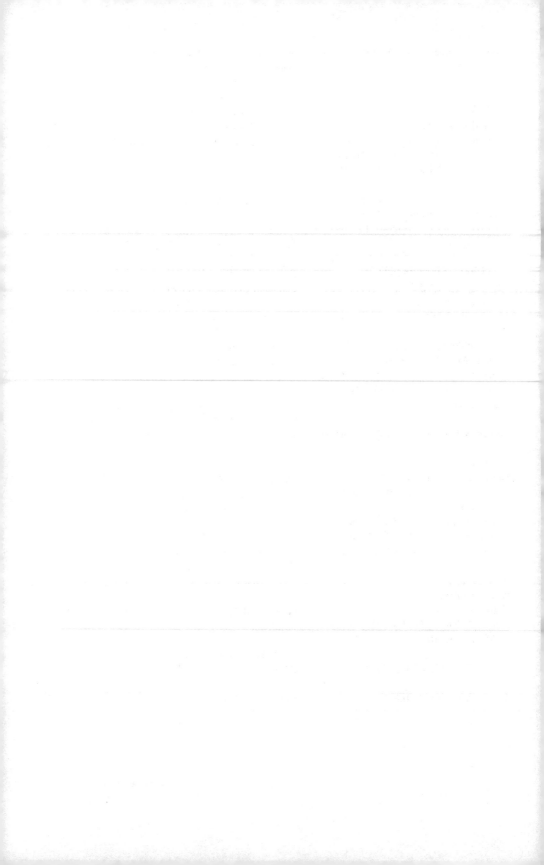

Perspectives in Continental Philosophy

John D. Caputo, series editor

Recent titles:

Emmanuel Falque, *The Guide to Gethsemane: Anxiety, Suffering, and Death*. Translated by George Hughes.

Emmanuel Alloa, *Resistance of the Sensible World: An Introduction to Merleau-Ponty*. Translated by Jane Marie Todd. Foreword by Renaud Barbaras.

Françoise Dastur, *Questions of Phenomenology: Language, Alterity, Temporality, Finitude*. Translated by Robert Vallier.

Jean-Luc Marion, *Believing in Order to See: On the Rationality of Revelation and the Irrationality of Some Believers*. Translated by Christina M. Gschwandtner.

Adam Y. Wells, ed., *Phenomenologies of Scripture*.

An Yountae, *The Decolonial Abyss: Mysticism and Cosmopolitics from the Ruins*.

Jean Wahl, *Transcendence and the Concrete: Selected Writings*. Edited and with an Introduction by Alan D. Schrift and Ian Alexander Moore.

Colby Dickinson, *Words Fail: Theology, Poetry, and the Challenge of Representation*.

Emmanuel Falque, *The Wedding Feast of the Lamb: Eros, the Body, and the Eucharist*. Translated by George Hughes.

Emmanuel Falque, *Crossing the Rubicon: The Borderlands of Philosophy and Theology*. Translated by Reuben Shank. Introduction by Matthew Farley.

Colby Dickinson and Stéphane Symons (eds.), *Walter Benjamin and Theology*.

Don Ihde, *Husserl's Missing Technologies*.

William S. Allen, *Aesthetics of Negativity: Blanchot, Adorno, and Autonomy*.

Jeremy Biles and Kent L. Brintnall, eds., *Georges Bataille and the Study of Religion*.

Tarek R. Dika and W. Chris Hackett, *Quiet Powers of the Possible: Interviews in Contemporary French Phenomenology*. Foreword by Richard Kearney.

Richard Kearney and Brian Treanor, eds., *Carnal Hermeneutics*.

A complete list of titles is available at http://fordhampress.com.

Lightning Source UK Ltd.
Milton Keynes UK
UKHW04f1212081018
330112UK00002B/204/P